Entrepreneurship in Spain

The figure of the entrepreneur has become a relevant factor that explains the process of growth and economic development. Rising unemployment rates have generated among institutional and private agents a significant interest in promoting entrepreneurship as a formula to eradicate this social scourge of unemployment. Active policies that favor business culture and initiative are being promoted in all areas.

In the university world, academic research has multiplied the work on entrepreneurship, a term that includes a triple meaning: the figure of the entrepreneur, the business function, and the creation of companies. This versatile meaning must be based on a consistent theory about the company and the entrepreneur. This book presents specific cases of companies and entrepreneurs that have had their role throughout the history of Spain. The intention is to show the techniques and learning acquired by those agents, which have allowed a considerable advance in the knowledge of the structure and business development.

This book brings together the research carried out by its authors with primary sources and makes it accessible to a wide audience—Spanish and Latin American—and will be of value to researchers, academics, and students with an interest in Spanish entrepreneurship, business, and management history.

Juan Manuel Matés-Barco is Professor of Economic History at the University of Jaen, Spain.

Leonardo Caruana de las Cagigas is Professor at the University of Granada, Spain.

Routledge Studies in Entrepreneurship

This series extends the meaning and scope of entrepreneurship by capturing new research and enquiry on economic, social, cultural and personal value creation. Entrepreneurship as value creation represents the endeavours of innovative people and organisations in creative environments that open up opportunities for developing new products, new services, new firms and new forms of policy making in different environments seeking sustainable economic growth and social development. In setting this objective the series includes books which cover a diverse range of conceptual, empirical and scholarly topics that both inform the field and push the boundaries of entrepreneurship.

New Frontiers in the Internationalization of Businesses
Empirical Evidence from Indigenous Businesses in Canada
Fernando Angulo-Ruiz

Contextualizing Entrepreneurship Theory
Ted Baker and Friederike Welter

Entrepreneurial Marketing and International New Ventures
Antecedents, Elements and Outcomes
Edited by Izabela Kowalik

Entrepreneurship, Dyslexia, and Education
Research, Principles and Practice
Edited by Dr Barbara Pavey, Dr Neil Alexander-Passe, and Dr Margaret Meehan

Entrepreneurship in Spain
A History
Edited by Juan Manuel Matés-Barco and Leonardo Caruana de las Cagigas

Women and Global Entrepreneurship
Contextualising Everyday Experiences
Edited by Maura McAdam and James A. Cunningham

For more information about this series please visit: https://www.routledge.com/Routledge-Studies-in-Entrepreneurship/book-series/RSE

Entrepreneurship in Spain
A History

Edited by
Juan Manuel Matés-Barco and
Leonardo Caruana de las Cagigas

NEW YORK AND LONDON

First published 2021
by Routledge
52 Vanderbilt Avenue, New York, NY 10017

and by Routledge
2 Park Square, Milton Park, Abingdon, Oxon, OX14 4RN

Routledge is an imprint of the Taylor & Francis Group, an informa business

© 2021 selection and editorial matter, Juan Manuel Matés-Barco and Leonardo Caruana de las Cagigas; individual chapters, the contributors

The right of Juan Manuel Matés-Barco and Leonardo Caruana de las Cagigas to be identified as the authors of the editorial material, and of the authors for their individual chapters, has been asserted in accordance with sections 77 and 78 of the Copyright, Designs and Patents Act 1988.

All rights reserved. No part of this book may be reprinted or reproduced or utilised in any form or by any electronic, mechanical, or other means, now known or hereafter invented, including photocopying and recording, or in any information storage or retrieval system, without permission in writing from the publishers.

Trademark notice: Product or corporate names may be trademarks or registered trademarks, and are used only for identification and explanation without intent to infringe.

Library of Congress Cataloging-in-Publication Data
Names: Matés Barco, Juan Manuel, editor. | Caruana, Leonard, editor.
Title: Entrepreneurship in Spain : a history / edited by Juan Manuel Matés-Barco and Leonardo Caruana de las Cagigas.
Description: New York, NY : Routledge, 2021. |
Series: Routledge studies inentrepreneurship |
Includes bibliographical references and index.
Identifiers: LCCN 2020036186 (print) | LCCN 2020036187 (ebook) |
ISBN 9780367649227 (hardback) | ISBN 9781003126973 (ebook)
Subjects: LCSH: Business enterprises–Spain–History. |
Entrepreneurship–Spain–History.
Classification: LCC HD2887 .E58 2021 (print) | LCC HD2887 (ebook) |
DDC338/.040946–dc23
LC record available at https://lccn.loc.gov/2020036186
LC ebook record available at https://lccn.loc.gov/2020036187

ISBN: 978-0-367-64922-7 (hbk)
ISBN: 978-1-003-12697-3 (ebk)

Typeset in Sabon
by Newgen Publishing UK

To our dear Gregorio Núñez Romero-Balmas, Professor at the University of Granada.

For his continuous teachings, his permanent help, and his deep friendship.

Much of the work in this book has come from his ideas and guidance.

Thank you for everything.

Contents

List of Illustrations xi
Acknowledgements xii

Introduction 1
JUAN MANUEL MATÉS-BARCO AND
LEONARDO CARUANA DE LAS CAGIGAS

1 Entrepreneurship and the History of the Company 9
MARIANO CASTRO-VALDIVIA
Introduction 9
Which Example of Entrepreneur Should Be Disseminated? 9
What Do Case Studies Contribute? 13
Do Case Studies Support Entrepreneurship? 15
Do Case Studies Promote Entrepreneurial Culture? 16
*Which Values or Sets of Values Can Be Determined from
   Case Studies? 18*
Conclusions 19
References 19

2 Entrepreneurship, Strategy and Networks: The
Development of Commercial and Financial Companies in
Early Modern Castile 22
DAVID CARVAJAL
*The Commercial and Financial World at the End of the
   Fifteenth and Start of the Sixteenth Centuries 22*
The Company in Castile: A Multiform Institution 23
*The Keys to Castilian Entrepreneurial Success at the End of
   the Middle Ages and the Beginning of the Modern Age 28*
Conclusions 37
References 38

viii Contents

3 Windmills, Not Giants. Competition and Monopoly on the
   Reinosa Route   41
   RAFAEL BARQUÍN GIL
   Introduction 41
   The Flour Traffic between Castile and Santander in
      the Mid-Nineteenth Century 43
   Brokerage Revenues on the Reinosa Route 47
   Wheat Prices in Castile 49
   The Flour Traffic from Santander 50
   Conclusions 51
   References 53

4 *Lacave & Echecopar*: Strategies and Businesses in the
   Second Half of the Nineteenth Century   55
   MARÍA VÁZQUEZ-FARIÑAS
   Introduction 55
   The Origins of Lacave & Echecopar 57
   The Commercial Expansion of Lacave & Echecopar
      (1852–1862) 59
   The Last Years of Lacave & Echecopar (1862–1870) 63
   Conclusions 66
   Sources and References 68

5 The *Sociedad Azucarera Antequerana*, a Successful
   Company in Late Nineteenth-Century Spain   71
   MERCEDES FERNÁNDEZ-PARADAS AND
   FRANCISO JOSÉ GARCÍA ARIZA
   Introduction 71
   Antequera, a Different Sort of Municipality 71
   The Founders 73
   The Other Managers 76
   The Construction of the Sugar Factory 77
   A Growing Company 78
   Conclusions 79
   References 80

6 Small, Medium and Large Companies in the Supply of
   Water in Spain (1840–1940)   82
   JUAN MANUEL MATÉS-BARCO
   Introduction 82
   Public Utilities in Spain 84
   The Large Companies 85
   Small and Medium-Sized Companies 88
   Risk and Uncertainty in the Water Business 93
   Conclusions 95
   Sources and references 96

7 Credit Companies, Merchant-Bankers and Large National
  Banks. The Case of Andalusia (1800–1936)   99
  MARÍA JOSÉ VARGAS-MACHUCA
  Introduction 99
  Private Banking in the Nineteenth Century: Banks of Issue,
    Credit Companies and Merchant-Bankers 100
  Credit Companies in Andalusia (Nineteenth Century) 102
  Banks of Issue in Andalusia 103
  Private Bankers in Andalusia in the Nineteenth Century 105
  The Private Banking (1900–1936): Local Bankers and
    Large National Banks 106
  The Territorial Expansion of the National Banking in
    Andalusia in the First Third of the Twentieth Century 107
  Local Bankers' Behaviour until 1936 109
  Conclusions 112
  References 113

8 The Private Period of Spanish Railways 1848–1941:
  A Liberal Project to Modernise Spain   115
  MIGUEL MUÑOZ RUBIO AND
  PEDRO PABLO ORTÚÑEZ GOICOLEA
  The Early Steps of the Spanish Railway System: The National
    Way and the Foreign Way 115
  The Test of the Financial Crisis for the Companies 117
  The Modernising Impact of the Railway 118
  Spanish Railway Companies at the Beginning of their Decline:
    Circa 1900–1913 121
  The Change of Model: From the System of Concessions to
    Intervention, 1914–1931 123
  The End of the Concession System: 1931–1941 127
  Final Considerations 128
  References 128

9 The Spanish Travel Agency Business in the Early Years of
  the Franco Regime   130
  CARLOS LARRINAGA
  Introduction 130
  The Decree of 19 February 1942 Regarding Travel
    Agencies 132
  Travel Agencies in Spain After the Second World War 134
  The 1950s: New Business Possibilities 138
  References 142

10 The International Expansion of the Spanish Insurance
    Company MAPFRE   144
    LEONARDO CARUANA DE LAS CAGIGAS
    Introduction 144
    Planning the International Expansion 144
    International Expansion of MAPFRE REINSURANCE 147
    Expansion in the Direct Insurance Market 149
    Conclusion 154
    Sources and references 154

11 Spanish Entrepreneurs and the Two Transitions
    (1975–1986)   156
    JORGE LAFUENTE DEL CANO
    Introduction 156
    Domestic and International Transitions 157
    The Entrepreneurs and the Domestic Transition 158
    The Entrepreneurs and the International Transition 162
    Conclusions 166
    References 168

12 From the Sector to the Automobile Cluster of *Castilla y
    León*. Its Study through the History of Lingotes Especiales   170
    PABLO ALONSO-VILLA AND PEDRO PABLO ORTÚÑEZ GOICOLEA
    Introduction 170
    *The Agglomeration of Economic Activities in Economic
        Theory: A Brief Summary* 171
    From the Sector to the Regional Automobile Cluster 173
    *The Companies in the Sector: The Case of Lingotes
        Especiales* 178
    Final Notes 181
    References 182

List of Contributors   185
Index   189

Figures and Tables

Figure

3.1   Trading Income on the Reinosa Route (Percentage)   48

Tables

2.1   Castilian Companies According to Initial Investment, Products
    & Services and Markets (1489–1538)   26
3.1   Wheat Prices on the Reinosa Route. Reales/Fanega   49
3.2   Correlation Coefficients (r) between Flour Exports by
    Destination and the Price of Flour in Santander, 1848–1882   51
4.1   Wine Exports by *Lacave & Echecopar*, 1850–1857   62
4.2   Wine Exports by *Lacave & Echecopar*, 1858–1870   64
6.1   Large Water Supply Companies (1933)   87
6.2   Medium-Sized Water Supply Companies (1933)   89
6.3   Small Water Supply Companies (1933)   91
7.1   Number of Bankers in Andalusia (1922)   110
7.2   Bankers and Banking Houses with Activity in Andalusia
    (1922–1936)   111
10.1   Distribution of MAPFRE Employees in America in 1999   152

Acknowledgements

It is essential to sincerely thank the anonymous and external evaluators for the suggestions and guidance they provided to improve the contents of this book. The warm response offered by the *Taylor & Francis* group for the publication of this project through the *Routledge* publishing house must be acknowledged. Nor can we forget the help provided by Brianna Ascher as editor of the *Business & Management Research* collection. Her attention and assistance have been invaluable. Likewise, the debt owed to María Vázquez-Fariñas and Mariano Castro-Valdivia for their continuous, ongoing, and selfless collaboration cannot be overstated. Thank you very much to all of them.

Introduction

Entrepreneurship in Spain: A History

The entrepreneur is an essential element or actor in the economic fabric. They allow the economy to grow and society to progress. Entrepreneurship and the flourishing of business initiatives pave the way for growth and the creation of jobs and facilitate the generation of wealth. In this way, people can achieve higher levels of well-being.

It is no coincidence that there is a close correlation between the economic progress of nations and the presence of entrepreneurs. The classic example is that of the Anglo-Saxon countries, in which there is a long tradition of respect for hard work as well as a strong defence of market freedom. These countries were pioneers of the Industrial Revolution and have achieved the highest levels of income. But in reality, the same can be said of many other nations: France, Germany, Japan, the Netherlands and the Scandinavian countries, among others, as well as, in general, the countries of the Organisation for Economic Cooperation and Development, including Spain.

Working as an entrepreneur is not easy. Not all projects, initiatives, or ideas come to fruition. There is the fear of failure, of bankruptcy. The investment in capital and people is not always successful. Many companies are forced to close down because the products and services they offer, being new, are treated with indifference by consumers. Among the most important faculties of the entrepreneur is the ability to make decisions and manage new projects as well as to constantly strive for innovation and the development of increasingly efficient operations. It is necessary for entrepreneurs to continually reinvent themselves in a globalised society. In this increasingly open and competitive world, the entrepreneur must generate innovations that satisfy a demanding market that insists on greater performance, better services, more quality, and lower prices.

There is no shortage of good ideas, but managing to crystallise them in a profitable company that satisfies the interests of today's society is another matter entirely. Social responsibility, good practices, decent wages, respect for the environment, adaptation to the legal framework, legal certainty, etc. must all be taken into account. Therein lies the challenge, but at the same time the attraction of the figure of the entrepreneur – a rare bird – and the driving force behind Schumpeter's "creative destruction".

In Spain there are a great number of capable, excellent entrepreneurs, some of whom even have significant global companies, but it is clear that it is necessary to raise the bar in order to achieve an improvement in the standard of living – in employment rates and in the development of society in general. The complexity of entrepreneurship is considerable and can sometimes be determined by the family environment. But there is also a savoir-faire that is acquired at school and university and that is trained and perfected at work. In the end, learning by doing is the true essence of the entrepreneur.

The economic and social environment, the family atmosphere, education, the institutional sphere... these are elements that contribute to the emergence of companies and entrepreneurs. This is largely the objective of this collective book – to avoid the *Buddenbrooks effect* with respect to Spanish companies and promote an entrepreneurial culture that allows for greater economic and social development. For this reason, it is necessary to look back in order to learn from past entrepreneurs, to review those firms that endured and try to understand the reasons behind the failures.

The History of the Company has had a hard time making its way into the academic arena. There seem to be two factors that have hindered its progress. On the one hand, there is the legacy left by the historiography after the Second World War and, on the other hand, the negative prejudice that is found in a significant number of researchers when it comes to addressing issues related to this discipline, especially those stemming from historical materialism. The economic difficulties of many companies in the years of the "political transition" (1975–1986) and the consequent rise in the unemployment rate worsened the poor image of the figure of the entrepreneur, largely inherited from the period of General Franco's dictatorship. The "lack of company culture" or the "lack of industrial culture" should also be noted. A country like Spain, where an economy marked by excessive dirigisme has predominated, is inclined to downplay the role of the company and disregard the social function of the entrepreneur.

Despite the difficulties, the History of the Company has had a great impact on the teaching and university environment, both as an academic discipline and as a tool for research on topics related to this subject. In Spain, since the early 1990s, seminars, conference meetings, and debates in scientific forums have been held. This accredited academic activity has spawned a large number of works on company histories, biographies of entrepreneurs, and sectorial or regional studies. The economic historians who have dealt with such content are now numerous and have established a clear path for research. Despite a slow start, the progress made in this discipline in recent decades has led to research questions being addressed that are increasingly far from the classical core, such as the economic structure of companies, the degree of vertical integration, the importance of human capital, etc.

In this process of slowly incorporating new research on companies, the mistrust of entrepreneurs towards researchers, for a wide variety of reasons, cannot be ignored either. This suspicion means that studies are carried out using only those documents that the companies themselves publish for official or advertising reasons, as is the case with the Reports of the Shareholders' Meetings, summaries of income statements, works carried out, projects, etc. As a result, publications of a journalistic nature emerge – with little rigour – concerned with current business leaders, but which lack a documentary and critical base that allows for the development of in-depth studies. One even finds histories of companies produced for anniversaries, which often have little scientific value. On many occasions, entrepreneurs themselves take the initiative to have studies carried out on their companies that improve their image and that can be used as a form of advertising. Nevertheless, this does not prevent academic work being undertaken with a high degree of scientific rigour despite being supported by the entrepreneurs themselves, both in public and private companies, in sectors such as water, gas, railways, textiles, insurance, etc. Recently, the analysis of the business structure in regional areas has emerged as a promising new field.

In Spain, the progress made in recent decades in the History of the Company is evident, not only in lesson plans, programmes of studies, manuals or specific research on the subject, but also in the leading role played by the figure of the entrepreneur and the company at a social, political, and economic level. To a large extent, the fall of the communist regime in the Soviet Union and Eastern Europe left the market economy as the only alternative system and highlighted the importance of the entrepreneur and private enterprise.

Historiography has largely noted the limited amount of entrepreneurship in Spain. The reasons behind this are complex, but the debate about the existence of entrepreneurial spirit has been ongoing for a long time. During the 19th and 20th centuries, writers such as Pío Baroja, Ramiro Maeztu and Miguel de Unamuno or politicians such as Santiago Alba and Joaquín Costa, exponents of the movement known as "regenerationism", pointed to the absence of entrepreneurial spirit, the lack of a group of dynamic businessmen, or the indifference to economic profit as one of the problems of Spain's backwardness. This approach was taken up, without any criticism, by subsequent generations of intellectuals and politicians. With the passage of time it has been accepted by public opinion. Other authors have explained it as flowing from the aristocratic indolence towards work, the low level of education or the mercantilist tradition and the marked protectionist bias of the Spanish economy, which have led to an aversion to business risk.

In the 1990s, an extensive debate took place in the academic world. Firstly, aristocratic prejudices against work or – erroneously – Catholic mistrust of capitalism were once again touted as the primary causes of this entrepreneurial weakness. To all this was added the deficient educational level of the Spanish population. Secondly, emphasis was placed on the institutional obstacles to entrepreneurship, based on the conservatism of entrepreneurs. This situation generated a significant backwardness and produced a low level of innovation in the Spanish economy. Despite this, some studies have noted that Spanish entrepreneurs in the 19th and 20th centuries were not very different from those in other European countries, nor were there major disparities in their social and family backgrounds or in the type of training received, and not even in their attitude towards risk or innovation.

The purpose of this book has not been to "compile a series of cases of companies and entrepreneurs" but rather to provide some knowledge about "real experiences" that will enable university students and professionals to learn and thus make better decisions in the business world. At first, the "case study" was basically descriptive, but over time researchers have developed a greater knowledge of business processes.

The selected cases describe a broad panorama and are the result of numerous research projects undertaken by their authors. The companies, entrepreneurs, and sectors studied reveal the variety of enterprises and the multiple activities that have taken place in this southern European country. The search for cases has not been random. Regions have been analysed – Andalusia and Castile and León, for example – where traditional historiography had detected less business activity. The selection has sought to present companies and entrepreneurs from some lesser known areas, both from a regional and a sectoral point of view. However, some chapters deal with more general sectors such as water supply, railway transport, tourism, Spanish multinationals, and the evolution that occurred during the political transition from the Franco dictatorship to the current democracy.

The first chapter analyses the figure of the entrepreneur and the historiographical progress in the History of the Company. In essence, Mariano Castro-Valdivia examines the vision and role given to the company and the entrepreneur throughout the contemporary period. The intention is to present models and undertake an approach to the theoretical postulates that have been developed in disciplines such as Economic History or the History of the Company.

In the second chapter, Professor David Carvajal de la Vega carries out a study of companies and entrepreneurs in the pre-industrial stage: business companies in Castile during the sixteenth century. In the middle of that century, Castilian commercial and financial companies managed to establish themselves as one of the most prosperous business networks in Europe. Their presence in the main European cities and fairs (Antwerp, Bruges, Lyon, Florence, etc.) is an example of the capacity reached by Castilian merchants outside their borders. Similarly, in the Iberian Peninsula, commercial businesses grew during the first half of the sixteenth century, promoting economic integration and commercial networks. The objective of this text is to understand the foundations of the commercial and financial enterprise in Castile, the reasons that led this institution – in little more than half a century – to spawn powerful organisations, as well as the strategies developed by the merchants and financiers, or dynamic entrepreneurs, to prosper in a regional and international environment where competition never stopped growing.

Next, paraphrasing Don Quixote's famous phrase, "Not giants, but windmills", Professor Rafael Barquín addresses the topic of competition and monopoly in the purchase and sale of wheat on the Reinosa route during a good part of the nineteenth century. The thesis argued in this work notes that the set of activities developed between the production of wheat in the North of Castile and the sale of its flour in Europe, Cuba, and Catalonia, did not have an oligopolistic nature in any of its phases. In general terms, they were open markets with a significant peculiarity; wheat and flour imports from abroad were prohibited for many years. The calculation of intermediary income, the analysis of wheat prices in Castile, and the analysis of flour exports from Santander are three of the many arguments that support this thesis. The work also speculates on the possible origin of the opposite belief.

For her part, Professor María Vázquez, in her study of the entrepreneurs Lacave and Echecopar and the wineries of the same name analyses the strategies and businesses in which they operated in the second half of the nineteenth century. Traditionally, the wine business has been one of the main economic activities undertaken in the province of Cádiz. Although this Cádiz company was founded in the first third of the century, it gained particular importance after 1850, a period of growth and prosperity. However, towards the end of the century, the arrival of a crisis in the Andalusian wine sector would lead to serious hardship for the region's wineries. Through an analysis of business records, documentation from notarial protocols, and publications of the time, the chapter explores how this company undertook its business activity, what its main businesses and strategies were, and how it faced that crisis at the close of the nineteenth century.

Continuing with the study of another Andalusian company, the research of Professors Mercedes Fernández-Paradas and Francisco José García Ariza on the *Sociedad Azucarera Antequerana* (Antequera Sugar Company) at the end of the nineteenth century is presented. This firm enjoyed great prominence with respect to the production of sugar and illustrates the uniqueness of Antequera, an important municipality in the province of Málaga where the company was located. In addition, the chapter analyses the group of men who shaped the company, as well as other managers who played a significant role in establishing the sugar mill during the 1890s. The work also examines its evolution and other aspects such as the production of sugar and the income and profits of the company.

Professor Juan Manuel Matés-Barco studies the water supply sector from the perspective of small, medium, and large companies in the late 19th and early 20th centuries. All of them stimulated the development of this public utility, although their differences were closely related to the size of the cities they supplied. Likewise, the business strategy adopted by these companies to dominate the market and the risk management function existing in this type of business is analysed. The trajectory of these companies shows a flourishing sector that contributed to the modernisation of Spanish cities. Their establishment was determined by the very nature of the activity – considered a public service – which is based on the natural monopoly and the formula of the administrative concession.

Returning to the region of Andalusia, Professor María José Vargas-Machuca examines the credit societies, merchant-banks, and large national banks in this region of southern Spain. During the nineteenth century, banking activity in its private aspect was developed by two types of agents. On the one hand, bankers, merchant-banks, and banking houses were established individually or, on some occasions, as collective or limited partnerships. On the other hand, other entities were set up in the form of a corporation, such as banks and credit companies. In Andalusia, banking legislation in the mid-century led to the creation of four banks of issue and five self-funded credit societies, but with an ephemeral life as a result of the crisis of 1866 and the Echegaray Decree of 1874. The region has since been left without any indigenous banks. The financial needs of the population were covered by private bankers and by the large national banks that began to operate in this territory in the early years of the twentieth century.

The study of small businesses in the history of Spain is still not very developed. However, these types of firms, most of them having a family structure, have a long tradition and a singular importance in the Spanish economy, the same today as in the past. An initial assessment shows that these companies can be remarkably effective thanks to a range of qualities that are unique to them: simplicity, resilience, and an ability to adapt to and take advantage of different opportunities. As an example, Professor Gregorio Núñez presents the so-called "Escoriaza group", a cluster of companies and business initiatives that operated in different regions of Spanish over three generations of the same family. The history of the Escoriaza family and its leader, Nicolás Escoriaza Fabro, is representative of a group of small companies that emerged from a marginal position but that knew how to grow and sustain themselves for many decades.

Professors Pedro Pablo Ortúñez and Miguel Muñoz have carried out extensive research on the private phase of the railway in Spain between 1848 and 1941. Throughout their chapter they analyse the transformations that the transport sector underwent for technological and institutional reasons, especially in the second half of the nineteenth century. The difficulties that existed in the institutional sphere and in transport policy were completely intertwined and it is impossible to understand them separately. The Spanish liberal state at the end of the 19th and the first decades of the twentieth century was systematically weighed down by the scarcity of public resources and, despite the efforts made, the seriousness of the Spanish debt was one of the causes of the weak economic growth and the delay in the modernisation of Spain.

Professor Carlos Larrinaga examines the Spanish travel agency business in the early years of the Franco dictatorship. Although Spain became a major tourism power during the 1960s, the groundwork was laid earlier, initially during the first third of the twentieth century and then, after the Spanish Civil War (1936–1939), in the early years of Francoism (1940–1960). In those years the Spanish tourism sector was rebuilt with the goal of attracting new flows of travellers, which had dried up during the war years. In fact, travel agencies were a major part of the reorganisation of the tourism industry in the early decades of Franco.

As an example of the internationalisation of a Spanish company, Leonardo Caruana studies the keys to the overseas expansion of the insurance company MAPFRE. Their strategy has been one of growth, using reinsurance as a means to learn the real state of the companies that were later acquired. The leap in quality was substantial and the firm became one of the leaders in the Latin American market, not to mention its presence in the United States, China, Italy, Turkey, etc., to the point that by 2006 half of its business was done abroad. The expansion was based on its high levels of efficiency, with the advantage of having know-how and intangibles acquired in Spain, especially in the automobile insurance sector. This branch was the spearhead for its expansion into many countries and almost all areas of the insurance business.

In a more general and recent field, Jorge Lafuente examines the role played by Spanish entrepreneurs during the political and economic transition between 1975 and 1986. Spain underwent a profound process of transformation after the death of General Franco in 1975. With the end of the dictatorship and the arrival of democracy and the expansion of freedoms, new actors began to take on prominent roles in the country's debates and in public life. Entrepreneurs and their representative organisations emerged as necessary interlocutors. Domestic, foreign, and economic policies were intertwined at a time that was particularly serious and sensitive for companies and business leaders.

Finally, Pablo Alonso and Pedro Pablo Ortúñez present a paper on the automotive sector in the region of Castilla y León, through the study of the company Lingotes Especiales. The automotive sector began to develop in the mid-twentieth century in Spain. Since then it has expanded with the arrival of new foreign companies manufacturing parts and equipment and with the appearance of other firms funded from local capital. Currently, this region, together with Catalonia, is the national leader in the production and export of vehicles and their components. Behind this tremendous growth, based on competitiveness, are a series of advantages that have generated significant benefits for companies. These externalities have led to the spontaneous emergence of an automotive cluster that has become the driving force behind the regional industry, surpassing the sector itself in importance.

These cases – and this book as a whole – are intended to be a reference work for courses on the History of the Company, but also a study and consultation text for professionals and readers in general. These works are the result of rigorous and detailed studies and capture the business activity existing in Spain. In essence, these have been the main motivating factors behind the preparation of this work.

Finally, it is essential to sincerely thank the anonymous and external evaluators for the suggestions and guidance they provided to improve the contents of this book. The warm response offered by the *Taylor & Francis* group for the publication of this project through the *Routledge* publishing house must be acknowledged. Nor can we forget the help provided by Brianna Ascher as editor of the *Business & Management Research* collection. Her attention and assistance have been invaluable. Likewise, the debt owed to

María Vázquez-Fariñas and Mariano Castro-Valdivia for their continuous, ongoing and selfless collaboration cannot be overstated. Thank you very much to all of them.

Juan Manuel Matés-Barco
University of Jaén
Leonardo Caruana
University of Granada

1 Entrepreneurship and the History of the Company

Mariano Castro-Valdivia

Introduction

The businessman has become one of the factors that explains economic development and the growth process. Likewise, a significant interest in promoting entrepreneurship as a way to eradicate the social scourge of growing rates of unemployment has been generated among institutional and private agents. The promotion of active policies, which favour entrepreneurial initiative and culture, is being encouraged in all areas: political, educational, social, economic, and so on.

In the academic world, research has caused studies on entrepreneurship to multiply. Entrepreneurship has a triple meaning: the figure of the entrepreneur, entrepreneurial function, and creation of companies. This multi-purpose meaning needs to be supported by a consistent theory on the company and the entrepreneur (De la Torre & García-Zuñiga, 2013).

Research, through case studies in particular, provides answers to several questions related to entrepreneurship and the History of the Company while also generating debate. This chapter will look at what case studies contribute, which example of entrepreneurship should be disseminated, whether case studies support entrepreneurship, whether case studies foster entrepreneurial culture, and which values or sets of values can be determined from case studies. After exploring these questions, the chapter concludes with some brief conclusions and a list of the bibliographical references used.

Which Example of Entrepreneur Should Be Disseminated?

It is difficult to determine the direction in which the entrepreneurial factor acts: was it entrepreneurs who promoted development, or was it development which stimulated their appearance? The influence was most likely circular (González González 1995).

Case studies on firms and entrepreneurs provide insight into the different types of entrepreneurs that have emerged over the course of history and are therefore very useful. However, it is also necessary to understand how the concept of the entrepreneur evolved in order to define which business model should be promoted.

Richard Cantillon (1680–1734), of Irish origin, was the first to establish the theory that the entrepreneur is linked to the concept of uncertainty; that is, to assume that the risk of an activity is what determines whether an economic agent is an entrepreneur or not. The entrepreneur is the economic agent who, by assuming risk, allows society's needs to be covered through the market. For Cantillon, an entrepreneur was not the same as a capital provider as the profit of the entrepreneur is derived from the difference between what was foreseen and what happened, and the level of risk they assumed determined profit levels. The capital provider or capitalist, however, provides capital at an agreed interest rate with guarantees in the event of non-payment, which implies a different profile to the entrepreneur who assumes market risk.

The French economist Jean-Baptiste Say (1767–1832) furthered Cantillon's approach by breaking away from the ideas put forward by classic English economists referenced in Adam Smith's *Wealth of Nations*, who did not distinguish between capitalist profit and corporate profit. In Say's view, the return on capital is not corporate profit, since it is the profit obtained by assuming the risk of a commercial activity. He defended this position from the fourth edition of his *Traité*, published in 1819, onwards. Say's approach brought about yet another idea of the theory of the entrepreneur. He posits that the entrepreneur is the main agent of production, the one who combines productive factors, and that they should be introduced as a new actor to the traditional trilogy of interveners in the productive process (landowners, workers, and capitalists), so much so that without entrepreneurs, new industry would not exist (Castro-Valdivia 2015a, 2015b).

The classic economist had barely developed this line of thinking when the company and entrepreneurs came to have an almost irreverent position. It is worth mentioning, however, that the term entrepreneur was popularised by John Stuart Mill (1806–1873). Mill, an English economist, was the only one of Adam Smith's followers who understood the specific role of entrepreneurship. However, although he introduced risk and uncertainty into the equation of entrepreneurial profit, he was not able to completely abandon the Smithian position and continued to believe that the functions of the capitalist and the entrepreneur go hand in hand.

Neoclassical economists did not pay much attention to entrepreneurship either, but Alfred Marshall (1842–1924) highlighted the role of the entrepreneur in economic activity. Both he and John Bates Clark (1847–1938) tried to introduce the figure into their models of economic growth. The English economist Marshall stated that the entrepreneur is an essential agent of development. He considered their ability to organise business to be a specific factor of production. However, in keeping with the classic British economists, he did not distinguish between the role of the entrepreneur and the capitalist, as Say had indicated. He considered the remuneration of the entrepreneur to be a fusion of the remuneration of a qualified administrator, who manages the company, and that of a capitalist. In his analysis, he did not reference the effects of risk and uncertainty on business profits, as stated by Cantillon and Say, although he did not discount the possibility that these factors might affect profits, which he described as extraordinary. He also argued that the desire to accumulate wealth is not a bad pursuit – on the contrary, he saw it as a symbol of business success, as an incentive to become an entrepreneur, which fosters competitiveness. The American economist Clark continued Marshall's postulates, but he did distinguish between business profits. The profits that came from the work of the administration of the company, which he considered to be a type of salary, and which for him were ordinary profits were, for him, different to extraordinary profit, which he deemed determinant on risk and uncertainty.

Joseph Alois Schumpeter (1883–1950) went a step further, noting the innovation factor of the entrepreneur and their relationship with the degree of development of an economy. The Austrian thinker placed the entrepreneur at the centre of economic activity. In his model, the economy defaults to a situation of equilibrium, so that the world is neither uncertain nor profitable and, therefore, in the long term there is no development, which implies the stagnation of society. However, periodically, innovations emerge which cause imbalance in the economy and produce development. Therefore, in order to improve humanity's well-being we need to innovate, and the agent of innovation, for Schumpeter, is the entrepreneur. In short, the author associated entrepreneurial activity and innovation with the mechanisms of economic growth. This addresses the issue of the nature of the entrepreneur's profit, although Schumpeter did not offer any contrastable explanations. Furthermore, his model does not contain the issue of risk or the option of failure, implying the union between business activity and innovation always generates success.

For his part, Frank H. Knight (1885–1972) highlighted the realms of risk and uncertainty in which the entrepreneur moves. The American economist, after publishing his doctoral thesis in 1921 —*Risk, Uncertainty and Profit*— explained that the entrepreneur is the only factor of production, since the rest of the factors—land, work, and capital— are only the means of production. On the other hand, he pointed out that the main function of the entrepreneur is to assume the risk of an activity and that their profit will depend on it. As he indicated in his thesis, his business model is indebted to the work of the German economists Johann Heinrich von Thünen (1783–1850) and Hans von Mangoldt (1824–1868) and the American Frederick Barnard Hawley (1843–1929). In his model, Knight systematically organises and expands on the positions of these authors, who collated the seminal ideas of Cantillon and Say. In particular, he defines risk as an objective uncertainty, which can be estimated and therefore measured, i.e., it has a cost and can be insured. He introduces the idea of subjective uncertainty to explain the role of the entrepreneur. He points out that subjective uncertainty is the result of our limited rationality, which is conditioned by the expectations of the entrepreneur and the lack of certainty that the entrepreneur expects, i.e. not having perfect information about the future, and that it is what separates a manager from an entrepreneur. However, uncertainty, as well as an individual's own capabilities, accompany human beings throughout their lives. This leads to a specialisation of people, so that the individuals with the greatest capacity to manage uncertainty will be the entrepreneurs of society. For Knight, entrepreneurial skills are innate, although they can be improved upon through education and experience, and for precisely this reason they are not susceptible to commercialisation. The entrepreneur's remuneration, therefore, cannot be taken as a type of salary but rather as profit.

Later, Keynesian and neoclassical economists in the years following the Second World War dismissed protagonism in the company and the entrepreneur. Finally, the Austrian school with Israel Kirzner at its helm began to outline the value of the entrepreneurial function and, almost immediately, studies began to emerge which breathed new life into the contributions of Schumpeter and Knight. Other authors such as Casson or Shane have enhanced this by reaffirming the role of the entrepreneur in economic theory, combining Schumpeter's doctrine with aspects of Kirzner. Casson, for example, points out that entrepreneurial function is based on making decisions in conditions of incomplete information, while for Shane, entrepreneurship not only relies on the presence of enterprising individuals, but rather responds to the confluence of it together with the existence of initiative business opportunities. Studies on this issue have highlighted some elements to be taken into account such as geographical setting, political and institutional regime, financial system, and economic context, as well as the educational, scientific, and cultural model.

At times, company theory and the technical change brought about by evolutionary economics has played an important role for a large number of business history researchers. To a large extent, the ascendancy of evolutionary theory can be seen, as well as the weight of Schumpeter's contributions, which have led to the work of Rosenberg and Basalla. Some characteristics of this theory can be seen through the work of Richard Nelson and Sidney Winter. For these authors, the strategy of a company is marked by its "natural trajectory" and constitutes a characteristic and persistent feature of it. This is acquired through experience and is passed on hereditarily, although it is evident that in decision-making processes there can be elements of uncertainty.

On the other hand, some authors have developed a History of the Company which take their hypotheses from transaction cost theory. This is notable in the studies of Alfred Chandler and Oliver Williamson. Their study and application of the theory has proved controversial in its interpretation. For some, transaction cost theory, derived from Coase's work, has considerable nuances when adapting it to the current climate and, although it contributes to the analysis of business organisation, there are limitations which other theories could rectify. Williamson's work responds more to a theory of the company or industrial economy than to the History of the Company itself. While Chandler develops an eminently historical method, which makes no attempt to select contrasting data to validate general theories. However, for others, the history of the American company has been seen as a process of growth which culminated in the great multi-division and multinational corporation. For this reason, the theory, which focuses on the determinants of company size, allows for interesting relationships with the history of American companies. This is why Chandler's work is one of the most emblematic examples of its type, especially his work *The Visible Hand*. The history of American business is characterised by its being limited solely to the United States in the time after American independence. This sometimes invalidates the development of these proposals in other times or other territories. In any case, studies on companies and entrepreneurs in the United States have been very widely disseminated, perhaps more so than those carried out in Europe (Castro-Valdivia et al. 2019).

Spanish business history has sometimes been blamed for excessive empiricism and scarce theoretical analysis. It is therefore necessary to analyse the reality which drives the company, the historical context in which it was born and developed, and the aspects which mark its size and organisational form, as well as the particularities which determine the degree of vertical integration of an activity, internal organisation, or characteristics of contracts. The History of the Company allows us to contrast reality with the analysis to which theory has been alluding, never forgetting that the power of the businessperson is limited on many occasions, that they cannot be given an excessive role, and that their actions are generally determined, to a large extent, by the social and economic conditions of their environment. Here lies the importance of the History of the Company developed in the United States, which frames, in the context of economic history, the performance of the entrepreneur, never denying the existence of a personal factor but not exaggerating it either.

Therefore, in a context where technical-economic progress is indispensable to the growth of welfare, the entrepreneur is a reference to achieve the objective. In any case, the History of the Company should not be restricted to the confirmation of economic theories, or to trying to accentuate one theory over another, but rather to show that previous approaches determine which questions can be answered in any given research.

What Do Case Studies Contribute?

Evidently, when talking about the history of a company or the biography of an entrepreneur, one does not refer to the hagiographies of times gone by, although examples of this nature do still survive (Ballestero 2014). In academia, apart from the commitment to basic standards in all historical research, it is also necessary to maintain critical thinking which is incompatible with complacency. The dreaded "Stockholm syndrome" can be overcome through the deft management of sources and the rigorous search for information. In this context, case studies on companies and entrepreneurs prove to be useful tools to shed light specifically on the History of the Company as well as on economic history in general. In order to achieve this, the preservation of historiographical work is advisable. The alternative would be counterproductive (Fernández-Paradas & Matés-Barco 2016).

Knowledge of these case studies paints a picture of the entrepreneur as an economic agent and presents the company as the nucleus of productive activities. For this reason, it is important to frame the geographical setting in which the entrepreneurs and companies develop. In Andalusia, a region in southern Spain, the analysis of companies and entrepreneurs has aroused little interest among specialists. It is not in vain that Andalusian entrepreneurs have been given responsibility for the frustrated modernisation of the region. The owners of agricultural land and businesses in the late nineteenth and early twentieth centuries have been described as abstainers, speculators, and rentiers. Industrial entrepreneurs have even been accused of quickly abandoning prospects in a highly dynamic sector to become part of the group of rentiers and farm owners. This gave rise to the broad generalisation of Andalusia and Andalusians lacking entrepreneurial spirit, of being unable to assume the risks inherent in a capitalist system. Through a certain level of reductionism, this generalisation has come to define "the Andalusian" as the Andalusian of the Guadalquivir, when, in truth, the historical reality has been more complex. The response to the historical productivity differential of the Andalusian economy has been shown to be neither due to anthropology nor genetics, but rather due to factors such as the allocation of physical resources, human capital, and existing institutional framework (Parejo 2011, p. 12–13).

These three aspects, which vary according to the region or autonomous community being analysed, are fundamental to the understanding, not only of the workings of the productive structure, but also to how entrepreneurs adapt to it. In other words, the biographies can help us understand how these entrepreneurs overcame and even took advantage of the difficulties presented to them – in short, how they adapted to changing circumstances. In the life of a business over three, four, or even five decades, physical resources are, of course, important, but so are any changes in the rules of the game and the allocation or lack thereof of human capital. An entrepreneur must always seek to adapt to these phenomena in order to maintain and expand their business and not go bankrupt. This is a constant throughout history, however this chapter is essentially concerned with the entrepreneurs of the contemporary age. Knowledge of these biographies allows the reader an adequate vision of the changes which have occurred over time and the need to adapt to changing circumstances, a transformation which is not only carried out individually but also collectively. This is something that is highlighted by the transition from the First Industrial Revolution to the Second.

This transition meant access to managerial capitalism and the ascendancy of the multi-division company. This in turn involved the need to raise more capital, the separation of ownership from management, the introduction of new forms of energy, new labour relations, and the creation of new industries. Such changes also included a shift from partnership or limited partnership to the ascendancy of the corporation. There was simultaneously an evolution from individualistic capitalism to corporatist capitalism to the extent that agricultural, industrial, and commercial entrepreneurs influenced by corporatism set in motion their own pressure mechanisms. Through chambers of commerce and even political parties, they organised to ensure the government hear their demands above those of other organised parties. At a social level, in the face of labour movement organisation through unions and class parties, entrepreneurs managed to create the first employers' associations (Arana 1988; Calvo Caballero 2003). The businessperson, therefore, stopped acting alone, as they had done in the first industrial revolution, in order to carry out collective action. This is evidently a sign of adaptation to new circumstances.

Knowledge of these entrepreneur's biographies in the long term provides a great opportunity to learn not only of their individual life trajectories, but also of their adaptation to the changes which occurred in the aforementioned planes. Bibliographies provide knowledge and experience to both current and future businesspeople, on how to act in the face of similar problems, strategies to follow in certain scenarios, and lessons on how to avoid bad decision-making.

Do Case Studies Support Entrepreneurship?

During the First Industrial Revolution, entrepreneurs were not educated at universities or polytechnics. Many of them came from commercial activities, industry, and, to a lesser extent, trades and guilds or agriculture. They were entrepreneurs with an innovative spirit who saw the opportunity to create new goods from inanimate energy sources and new materials such as cotton which was destined not only for local or regional markets, but also national or even international markets. First through the canals, and then through railways and steam navigation, these entrepreneurs embarked on an unprecedented adventure, armed with little academic instruction but extensive practical knowledge. Their schools had been businesses or workshops, not classrooms. This situation started to change from the mid-nineteenth century onwards and, above all, with the dawn of the Second Industrial Revolution. From the mid-nineteenth century, the great engineering schools of mining, roads, and later forestry and industry trained not only qualified technicians for the administration of a liberal state under construction but also entrepreneurs. Many of the technicians educated in these higher education institutions became entrepreneurs, as well as managers of numerous companies (Garaizar 2008).

From the Second Industrial Revolution onwards, the relevance of human capital increased (Núñez 1992; Núñez & Tortella 1993). The introduction of new techniques and innovative production processes implemented at the end of the nineteenth century required personnel which were more highly qualified. The entrepreneur was no exception. It was normal that, at the turn of the century, an increasing number of businesspeople had a certain degree of education or training that was, at least, higher than that of the businesspeople of the First Industrial Revolution, although this was not always the case. As late as the end of the twentieth century, 43.9% of Andalusian entrepreneurs either had no studies or only primary education, 31.5% had completed secondary education or vocational training, and only 23.6% had entered higher education (Parejo 2011, p. 21). One of the most backward regions of the European Union may prove an exception, but behind this data, the existence of an entrepreneurial spirit in people with hardly any studies is notable. It may be that this was possible in sectors such as construction and mass tourism or those with little added value. Today such circumstances would be less likely.

In a globalised world and in the midst of a technological revolution led by Information and Communication Technology (ICT), most businesses require increasingly more highly qualified human capital. The acquisition of training is, therefore, also a way of adapting to change. It is not enough to have a good idea. You have to be able to implement it, and that is where education plays a key role. Once again, it is not necessary to resort to the theory of human capital. No one today doubts the benefit of education, so we should imagine an entrepreneur who is increasingly more educated. In the prologue to the book *One Hundred Andalusian Entrepreneurs*, former minister Manuel Pimentel points out the suitability of recommending it to students in Andalusian Business Schools and Faculties of Economic and Business Sciences, to provide them with clear references and possible examples to follow (Pimentel 2011, p. 10). It is true that knowledge of these case studies could be a useful tool in the promotion of entrepreneurship. Above all, they serve as examples of overcoming difficulties and adapting to change. It has never been easy to start a company and succeed, so knowledge of what has gone before can be an incentive, especially the success stories, which are usually the ones most studied.

In any case, this leads to a question which is difficult to answer: Are entrepreneurs born or are they made? Surely some are born, so do not need this knowledge, while others are made, and for them, this type of biography can be very useful.

Do Case Studies Promote Entrepreneurial Culture?

In the Anglo-Saxon historiographic tradition, the figure of the entrepreneur never lost its Schumpeterian character which was focused on innovation. In fact, in the United States, where Joseph A. Schumpeter spent a good part of his life, a tradition of business studies was consolidated, both historically and professionally. One example of this is the Harvard Business School, which began publishing the *Bulletin of the Business Historical Society* in 1926. This was subsequently renamed the *Business History Review* in 1954 and is now published by Cambridge University Press for the Harvard Business School. This was not the only initiative – other prestigious American universities created similar schools and academic journals of notable importance, such as *Explorations in Entrepreneurial History*. This was published by the Harvard University Research Centre of Entrepreneurial History between 1949 and 1958. From 1963–1965 a second series began, published by Earlham College, which was later continued by the University of Wisconsin. In 1969 the journal was renamed *Explorations in Economic History*. It is now a journal published by Elsevier. In Great Britain, great interest in this type of study followed, as demonstrated by the founding of *Business History* magazine at the University of Liverpool in 1958. It is now published by Routledge, Taylor and Francis Group (Tortella 2000, p. 13).

The company and the entrepreneur are analysed as economic agents capable of facing the challenges of competitiveness on a global scale. Changes in the political regimes which practiced centrally planned economies, the complexity and speed of the changes caused by new technology, as well as the public sector setbacks which have been experienced in some countries have been some of the issues which have prompted this change in perception (Matés-Barco & Castro-Valdivia 2017).

Growing interest in studying business and the role played by the entrepreneur could be due to several reasons. Firstly, there is the weight of the historiographic tradition in the late nineteenth and early twentieth centuries in which a large group of English and American historians –Toynbee, Hobson, Webb, Veblen, etc.– described the entrepreneur as a symbol of exploitation, selfishness, and excessive profit. At the same time, in Germany another group of historians applied an inductive methodology to analyse different social segments and, specifically, to the emergence and evolution of local companies and the changes experienced in business organisations. It is worth mentioning Gustav Schmoller, Karl Bucher, or Werner Sombart who promoted studies on particular companies and the development of "entrepreneurship" as a means to explain capitalist expansion.

Secondly, the trend of studying the History of the Company is largely due to the enormous field of exploration which this subject provides within the scope of Economic History (Castro-Valdivia, 2019). In recent decades, the importance of company archives has been highlighted, and there are still many to be studied. At the same time, emphasis has been placed on the need to use a methodology which combines economic theory with the detailed description of specific cases and their study through sources. Therefore, it is important to combine theoretical analysis with empirical data to obtain a reflection which allows us to understand a company's evolution.

On the other hand, studies on the industrial revolution in its different phases have shown the importance of the figure of the entrepreneur in the process of economic development. Publications on specific companies, sectors, and biographies of entrepreneurs have been frequent.

Interest in the study of past entrepreneurs is an instrument for the promotion of entrepreneurial culture. Knowledge of history is an excellent tool which helps confront the challenges of the present or the immediate future. In this sense, when reading the biographies of Spanish businesspeople contained in different dictionaries available today, it is notable that those who did not receive secondary or higher education made a point of educating their children more intensely both in terms of quantity and quality. This is clearly detectable in family sagas (Tortella 2000, p. 16–17). The self-made entrepreneurs, from the workshops and factories, with little training, ensured the next generation became educated entrepreneurs. The fact that several Basque steelmakers sent their children to study at the Liège School of Mining is an obvious example of this (Anduaga 2010). Of course, they were well aware of the need for the most advanced and exhaustive training possible, so, as far as they could, they did not hesitate to send their offspring to prestigious centres. These were centres where innovation and knowledge were the order of the day. In some cases, this not only served to develop their own businesses and companies, but also served to improve the educational centres in their respective countries of origin (Camprubí 2017).

Reading and careful analysis of entrepreneurs' biographies does help to promote entrepreneurial culture from this vantage point. In fact, the behaviour, risk taking, innovations in production processes and management styles, adaptation to state of the art technology and adaptation to the institutional changes which have occurred during the course of their professional lives can serve as examples and references for today's entrepreneurs. Above all, we should take into account that the development of entrepreneurial culture has become the main challenge for organisations nowadays (Schatsky & Schwartz 2015). One definition of business culture is "the set of rules, values, and ways of thinking which characterise behaviour, placement of staff at all levels of the company, management style, allocation of resources, corporation organisation, as well as company image" (Leyva Granados 2008, p. 30). In colloquial terms, one could say that corporate culture is the DNA of a company, hence its relevance (Robbins 2010). The study of companies through their owners or managers, especially those who have survived for decades, is a very useful way to understand the DNA of the company and would serve as a useful example.

Which Values or Sets of Values Can Be Determined from Case Studies?

From a practical point of view, reading case studies also helps us to analyse the values which could prove useful to the businesspeople and entrepreneurs of the future (Matés-Barco 2019). In the case of Spain, a distinct theme is the strength of the family, which has played a decisive role in the business sagas. This is evident not only in collective societies, but also in a few public limited companies, in which certain families played or continue to play a predominant role. The case of the Botín family at Santander bank is a paradigmatic example, which does not stand alone. Another value which can be extracted from reading these biographies is the complex relationship Spanish business has had with innovation. In general, Spanish entrepreneurs have innovated little and in many cases have devoted themselves to adapting innovations implemented in other countries (López & Valdaliso 1997, Ortiz-Villajos 1999.). Every business involves risk, however small. Here it is true that many entrepreneurs chose to obtain state concessions, which were considered more remunerative, rather than innovating. It is therefore worth analysing the institutional framework of the time, to discover the factors which helped or hindered entrepreneurship (Tortella et al. 2008). Professor Gabriel Tortella has stressed that the survival of habits, social structures, and the mentality of the Old Regime act as an impediment to the development of entrepreneurial drive (Tortella 1994). However, it is important to distinguish between different regions of Spain and the different institutional frameworks which exist in them. The Basque Country is clearly an example of the opposite being true, at least for a good part of the nineteenth and twentieth centuries.

The desire to obtain state concessions was not exclusive to Spanish businesspeople, there were foreigners who behaved in the same way, which is perhaps explained by Tortella's theory. However, there were also entrepreneurs who took risks and diversified their activities by investing in several businesses at once. Here, undoubtedly, audacity and initiative can be considered a notable value, which once again brings us back to the model of the Schumpeterian entrepreneur, where, this time, innovation plays a fundamental role.

Furthermore, another value to be considered could be social responsibility, i.e., the understanding that a company or individual has an obligation towards its fellow citizens. This responsibility can be "negative", meaning that there is a commitment to refrain from acting, or "positive", meaning an obligation to act. Positive responsibility and examples provided are of interest here, as they can be very useful. Honesty and honourability, or the absence of it, are also aspects to be taken into account. It is true that there are numerous cases of corruption and scandal, not only today but also throughout history. However, generalisations are not appropriate, as there were also honest businesspeople who were concerned with doing things properly and respecting the law.

Conclusions

The preparation and dissemination of case studies on companies and entrepreneurs are useful tools. They allow comparison of the individual with the general, help in the establishment of similarities, and provide possible examples of action when faced with similar problems. If it were not for these instruments of dissemination, today's society would not be able to take advantage of this wealth of experience and of human capital, and we would not understand the successes and failures of the past which occur cyclically in a company or country.

Today, where socialisation is normalised, and where citizens first learn in books and then in the real world, case studies are a basis for building a business culture which promotes entrepreneurship, since they indicate the values which every good entrepreneur should possess. Therefore, reading these studies on successful companies and entrepreneurs instils examples and references to be imitated by future entrepreneurs, where innovation in production processes and management styles are the pillars that enable a company to endure over time and for an economy to maintain long-term sustainable growth.

References

Anduaga, A. 2010. *La cadena vasca*. Barcelona: Ediciones del Serbal.
Arana, I. 1988. *La Liga Vizcaína de Productores y la política económica de la Restauración, 1894–1914*. Bilbao: Caja de Ahorros Vizcaína.
Ballestero, A. 2014. *José Mª de Oriol y Urquijo*. Madrid: Lid.
Calvo Caballero, P. 2003. *Asociacionismo y cultura patronales en Castilla y León durante la Restauración (1876–1923)*. Valladolid: Junta de Castilla y León.
Camprubí, L. 2017. *Los ingenieros de Franco*. Crítica: Barcelona.
Castro-Valdivia, M. 2015a. La difussion mondiale de l'œuvre de Jean-Baptiste Say. Traductions précoces et impacts sélectifs. In, E*t Jean-Baptiste Say… créa l'Entrepreneur*, ed. Société Internationale Jean-Baptiste Say, 219–245. Bruxelles: Peter Lang, doi.org/10.3726/978-3-0352-6525-5

Castro-Valdivia, M. 2015b. Money and Finance in the Wealth of Nations: Interpretations and Influences. *Journal of US-China Public Administration* 12(5): 415–429, doi.org/10.17265/1548–6591/2015.05.007

Castro-Valdivia, M. 2019. La figura del empresario y el avance historiográfico de la Historia de la Empresa. In *Empresas y empresarios en España. De mercaderes a industriales*, coord. J. M. Matés-Barco, 19–36. Madrid: Pirámide.

Castro-Valdivia, M., C. Larrinaga-Rodríguez, & J. M. Matés-Barco. 2019. La enseñanza de la Historia de la Empresa en la Era Digital. In *Educación y felicidad en las Ciencias Sociales y Humanidades. Un enfoque holístico para el desarrollo de la creatividad en la Era Digital*, coords. A. R. Fernández Paradas, M. Fernández Paradas, L. Tobar Pesántez & R. Ravina Ripoll, 469–488. Valencia: Tirant lo Blanc.

De la Torre, J. & M. García-Zúñiga. 2013. Instituciones y empresarialidad en el norte de España, 1885–2010. *Revista de Historia Industrial* 51: 141–170.

Fernández-Paradas, M. & J. M. Matés-Barco. 2016. Un recurso para la docencia y la investigación: la biografía empresarial. In *Nuevas perspectivas en la Investigación docente de la historia económica*, eds. M. A. Bringas, E. Catalán, C. Trueba & L. Remuzgo, 111–117. Santander: Editorial de la Universidad de Cantabria.

Garaizar, I. 2008. *La Escuela Especial de Ingenieros Industriales de Bilbao, 1897–1936.* Bilbao: Colegio Oficial de Ingenieros Industriales de Bizkaia y Escuela Superior de Ingeniería de Bilbao.

González González, M. J. 1995. La empresa en la historia del pensamiento económico. In *De empresas y empresarios en la España contemporánea*, coord. M. Llordén Miñambres, 13–28, Oviedo: Universidad de Oviedo.

Leyva Granados, Y. A. 2008. *Desarrollo de una cultura empresarial contra el paradigma de las agencias publicitarias*. www.repositorioinstitucional.uson.mx/handle/unison/2723 (accessed March 10, 2020).

López, S. & J. M. Valdaliso. (eds.) 1997. *¿Qué inventen ellos?* Madrid: Alianza.

Matés-Barco, J. M. & M. Castro-Valdivia. 2017. La Historia de la Empresa: herramienta para fomentar la cultura emprendedora. In, *Educación Histórica. Patrimonios olvidados y felicidad en la Didáctica de las Ciencias Sociales,* Coords. A. Fernández-Paradas, M. Fernández Paradas & G. A. Gutiérrez-Montoya, 123–150. San Salvador: Editorial Universidad Don Bosco.

Matés-Barco, J. M. (coord.) 2019. *Empresas y empresarios en España. De mercaderes a industriales,* Madrid: Pirámide.

Núñez, C. E. & G. Tortella. (coords.) 1993. *La maldición divina: ignorancia y atraso económico en perspectiva histórica.* Madrid: Alianza.

Núñez, C. E. 1992. *La fuente de la riqueza: educación y desarrollo económico en la España contemporánea.* Madrid: Alianza.

Ortiz-Villajos, J. M. 1999. *Tecnología y desarrollo económico en la historia contemporánea.* Madrid: Oficina Española de Patentes y Marcas.

Parejo, A. 2011. Introducción. In *Cien empresarios andaluces,* dir. A. Parejo, 11–23. Madrid: Lid.

Pimentel, M. 2011. Prólogo. In *Cien empresarios andaluces,* dir. A. Parejo, 9–10. Madrid: Lid.

Robbins, S. 2010. *Comportamiento organizacional* (8ª ed.). Madrid: Prentice Hall.

Schatsky, D. & J. Schwartz. 2015. *Global Human Capital Trends 2015. Leading in the new world of work.* Westlake: Deloitte University Press. www2.deloitte.com/content/dam/insights/us/articles/cognitive-technology-in-hr-human-capital-trends-2015/DUP_GlobalHumanCapitalTrends2015.pdf (accessed March 16, 2020).

Tortella, G. 1994. *El desarrollo de la España contemporánea*. Madrid: Alianza.
Tortella, G. 2000. Prólogo. In *Cien empresarios españoles del siglo XX*, dir. E. Torres, 13–18. Madrid: Lid.
Tortella, G., J. L. García Ruíz, J. M. Ortiz-Villajos López, & G. Quiroga. 2008. *Educación, Instituciones y Empresa. Los determinantes del espíritu empresarial*. Madrid: Academia Europea de Ciencias y Artes.

2 Entrepreneurship, Strategy and Networks
The Development of Commercial and Financial Companies in Early Modern Castile

David Carvajal

The Commercial and Financial World at the End of the Fifteenth and Start of the Sixteenth Centuries

In the mid-sixteenth century it was common to find Castilian merchants trading in the principal European markets and trade fairs. Antwerp, Bruges, Lyon, London, Florence, and Rome were just some of the centers where those who managed or represented large Castilian companies settled and played a relevant role. Such companies as that of Simón Ruiz, or those of the Astudillo, the Bernuy, or the Quintana *dueñas* are examples of the acquired relevance (Lapeyre 1955; Casado 2003). The Castilian presence and the success of their businesses, even though in many cases it was short-lived, was the result of a long process of consolidation and expansion of their commercial activity, encouraged by several companies and families of merchants for over a century and a half.

From the end of the fourteenth century onwards, in addition to a commercial and financial recovery, Western Europe started on a path to economic recovery which was particularly important in the centers of Northern Europe (Flanders) and the North of Italy. Having overcome the effects of the many crises that rocked the old continent during the fourteenth century, these centers continued to enjoy a privileged position and the benefits of the commercial revolution spearheaded by the great Italian companies, the great dominators of the Mediterranean, and the main commercial and financial circuits. Given their success, the Italian companies became the model to imitate.

In the case of Castile, the presence of foreigners – especially Italians – was notorious in the great commercial centers, such as Seville, and in those territories yet to be conquered, such as the Nazarí kingdom of Granada or the Canary Islands, where the expectations of profit were high (Otte 1996; González Arévalo 2012; Bello 1994). In any case, the foreign merchants and companies took advantage of the favorable climate throughout the fifteenth century and they were soon followed by the Castilian initiative. The Castilian merchants found a favorable economic context to develop their activities, expand their businesses, and start up new companies. The population passed the threshold of four million towards the end of the century and continued to grow over the first few decades of the sixteenth century; the territory increased after the incorporation of Granada and other possessions in the Atlantic and North Africa (Aznar 1983); the ratios of urbanization were around 8%, only lower than Flanders and the North of Italy; the renaissance of the urban markets and the appearance of great fairs favored the creation of commercial circuits that also took advantage of the boost in agricultural and artisanal production. All these elements are characteristic of a strong process of endogenous growth which, in addition, was accompanied by a continued opening up to abroad.

Castile was a geographically large and disperse territory in which some regions, such as the northwest coast, had remained traditionally isolated from the rest of the territory. Nevertheless, the expansion of internal trade during this period and the progressive integration of the local, regional, and peninsular markets improved the conditions so that many merchants felt they could assume the risk of doing business beyond the urban markets or the nearby trade fairs. The dense network of urban and rural markets as well as the network of trade fairs that took place throughout the year in diverse places belonging to the crown were a great opportunity for those who wished to progress in their business. This phenomenon permitted groups of merchants from such cities as Burgos to act together and become known in such centers as Seville where the local community and the Genoese had traditionally dominated the market (Otte 1996; Palenzuela 2003). To the expansion in interior trade must be added the increase in financial activities. The movement of money, the expansion of credit, and the frequent use of diverse financial instruments and operations acted as a support to promote commercial activity and, without a doubt, was also vital for encouraging investment in and the foundation of companies.

During the last decades of the fifteenth century, with an expanding economy and a relatively quiet institutional situation following the reforms of the Catholic Monarchs, the merchants knew how to take advantage of a favorable situation to create new companies, a process that came to fruition in the sixteenth century. The change of century supposed a strengthening of businesses that had been going on for decades, instigated by the Castilian merchants in other territories of the Iberian Peninsula, as well as in European centers where the great merchant families and their companies finally managed to become integrated (Casado 2003).

The Company in Castile: A Multiform Institution

The sources of the period link the term merchant to all those who trade goods. Having said that, the diversity of the merchants to be found in Castile is therefore immense. From the small rural merchants and shopkeepers to the great merchants dedicated to international trade, variety is the common characteristic, as was their interest in founding companies. Legal sources tell us that companies existed in Castile from at least the thirteenth century. Nevertheless, testimonies of commercial companies in existence before the fifteenth century are extremely scarce. It was then that companies began to appear in the wake of the economic recuperation – companies whose prime objective was to carry through their business in a relatively short period of time and to obtain a profit from doing so (Carvajal 2019).

As happened in other European territories, especially in the Italian cities (Igual & Navarro 1997; Franceschi et. al. 2007; De Ruysscher et al. 2017), the company became one of the principal associative strategies for facing up to the risks of an uncertain business with some degree of security. Essentially, the company allowed both profits and losses to be shared, thus decreasing the merchants' economic and financial risk and strengthening their capacity to generate profits. At this time, the dangers that could send a merchant into bankruptcy were many: from the uncertainty of not being able to reach business expectations when selling goods, to the risk that such activities as piracy posed, or a simple natural catastrophe which could sink a ship full of merchandise. So, sharing the risk through a company became an interesting and desirable option for the merchants. As for the benefits, we should note the convenience of associations thanks to the organizational benefits derived from a society with commercial representation in different places and the capacity to develop different types of business at the same time, thus allowing economies of scale on various different levels (Casado 2015a; 2018, p. 171).

Faced with the scarcity of company contracts or capitulations that would permit a more accurate definition, the laws of Castile allow us to make a first approximation to defining and characterizing the company as that association "which merchants and other men make with each other in order to gain something"[1]. Above and beyond that, diversity is both important and formidable (Caunedo 1993a; Carvajal 2019); even so, it is possible to characterize Castilian companies through a series of parameters such as type, number of associates, duration, strategy, etc., and which undoubtedly had an Italian influence.

At the end of the fifteenth and start of the sixteenth centuries, most Castilian companies fell into the category of what the law called "*sobre cosa señalada*" since, in their deeds of incorporation, it was usual to indicate the objective or objectives: to trade, provide a center, offer financial services or tax management, etc. Even if the objective was defined, the definition was very general, and this allowed the partners to develop one of the most interesting strategies, which we shall analyse below: diversification. Thus, the Castilian company was a multiform structure (Casado 2015a, 2018) that allowed a limited number of partners, normally between two and five, to carry out a multitude of business activities under a single legal umbrella. In addition, the different modes of participation in the company at the time and the different ways of organizing the social capital, due to the existence of senior and junior partners, commercial representatives, or partners "fuori del corpo" (copying the Italian model), gave the society's structure great flexibility. Another characteristic of these companies concerns their chronology. In general, companies lasted between one and five years. As far as we know from the existing documentation, the main activity usually influenced the association's period of validity. The shortest lived companies were created to develop a concrete, periodical activity, such as urban provisions or rent collection, which depended on an annual renovation by a Council or the Crown (Carvajal, 2020). On the other hand, if the activity were complex, involving other Peninsular or European territories where company employees had to be settled, for which a commercial network had to be set up and various different products were traded, then the company was usually created for several years (Casado 2015a, 2018; Carvajal & de la Torre 2019). None of this stopped the companies from being renewed as many times as the partners so wished if the business was successful and the partners were in favour of doing so, thus generating associations that, in some cases, could last for over two decades, as happened in the case of the Portillo family in Valladolid (Al-Hussein 1986, p. 196).

One of the great strengths of the company was its capacity to unite a large amount of capital with which to make an initial investment that, individually, would have been impossible or would have supposed an excessive risk for any Castilian merchant. The amount with which companies were founded at the start of the 16th century varied according to the purpose and range of operation (see table 2.1). We find, in general, small companies such as the Marroquín-Sánchez, whose initial capital was around 30,000 *maravedís* (3.32 kgs. of silver); other medium-sized companies such as the Medina-Calatayud, with an initial capital of 1.4 million *maravedís* (157.67 kgs. of silver); or large companies dedicated to exports, such as the company Pesquera-Silos, with an initial capital of 8.7 million *maravedís* (962.61 kgs. of silver) in 1514 (Casado 2015a, p. 79), or the Daza-Urueña, founded with 12.5 million *maravedís* (1,383.06 kgs. of silver) in 1533. To understand the value of these sums, we can compare them to some of the great mercantile fortunes of Burgos, the home of the great exporting companies. We know that in 1507 at least 11 merchants dedicated more than three million *maravedís* (331.94 kgs. of silver) to investments in commercial activities, reaching a total of 12 million in the case of Juan Alonso Salinas; therefore, individually taking on board the risks of international commerce was practically impossible, even for the richest merchants of the period (Caunedo, 1993b). In addition, these companies improved their debt capacity, something which was fundamental when first operating or during subsequent years. Having several credit-worthy partners strengthened the company's financial structure and its credit possibilities.

Another characteristic aspect of Castilian companies was their management. At the head of the company was a principal administrator – normally one of the partners who knew well the necessary mercantile techniques for registering the operations in the accounts books while also having sufficient basic knowledge to be able to develop the mercantile activity. As we shall see, the partners had to possess aptitudes for controlling the flow of information and the human resources employed by the company and had to be able negotiators. The task of management was sometimes shared by several partners who could also represent the company in the places where it operated alongside commercial representatives and commission merchants.

Finally, it is worth mentioning a fundamental question in Castilian commercial and financial companies: the profit share-out and the liquidating of the

26 David Carvajal

Table 2.1 Castilian Companies According to Initial Investment, Products & Services and Markets (1489–1538)

Year	Name	City	Initial investment (maravedis)	Initial investment (Silver Kgs.)	Products and services	Markets
1489	Daza-López de Calatayud	Valladolid	1,350,000	149.37	Trade and financial services	Iberian Pen.
1500	Marroquín-Sánchez de Toledo	Medinaceli	30,000	3.32	Wood	Regional
1500 ca.	Esquivel-Sánchez	Bilbao	130,000	14.38	Trade	International
1514	Pesquera-Silos	Burgos	8,700,000	962.61	Trade	Ireland Flanders, Italy, and France
1515	Díaz-Medina	Medina del Campo			Banking	
1517	Ruiz-Soto	San Martín de Valdeiglesias	130,000	14.38	Meat	Regional
1524	Medina-Calatayud	Medina del Campo	1,425,000	157.67	Fish	Regional
1525	Medina-Ram	Medina del Campo	2,550,000	282.15	Trade and financial services	Iberian Pen.
1528	Plazuela-Resxo	Medina de Rioseco	965,524	106.83	Trade	Regional
1522	Medina-Urueña	Medina del Campo / Valladolid	12,500,000	1,383.06	Trade and financial services	International Flanders, Italy
1532	Alcazaba-Martínez-Soto	Cuéllar / Medina del Campo	2,750,000	304.27		

Year	Partners	Location	Amount	Rate	Activity	Scope	Countries
1534	Medina-Aranda	Valladolid	4,500,000	497.90	Trade and financial services	International	Flanders, Italy, and Portugal
1535	Roquien-Mizariego-Calbet	Barcelona / Zaragoza / Medina del Campo	562,500	62.24	Trade	Iberian Pen.	Aragon
1536	Portillo-Ávila	Valladolid / Granada	975,000	107.88	Trade	Iberian Pen.	
1536	Frías-Medina-Huerta	Medina del Campo / Uceda	300,000	33.19	Trade	Iberian Pen.	
1537	Medina-Urueña	Medina del Campo / Valladolid	16,170,000	1,789.13	Trade and financial services	Iberian Pen.	Flanders, Italy
1538	Rodríguez-Román	Medina del Campo	750,000	82.98	Trade	Regional	

Sources: Author's own elaboration with data from Al-Hussein 1986; Casado 2015; Carvajal 2015a, 2018 2020; Irioja et al. 2019. Exchange rate *maravedí*-silver: 0.1001 grs./*maravedí*.

company. What profits could those who participated in a commercial and financial company expect? If we take into account the annual return with respect to the initial investment, the figures vary considerably. The known references to companies from Burgos show that a company could obtain an annual profit or interest of between 10% and 20–25% of the initial capital (Caunedo 1993a, p. 53). These margins seem attractive today, yet we must remember that not all companies managed to achieve their initial purpose and, in some cases, such dangers as pirates could result in important losses; although the principal problem was usually a delay in being paid pending debts, which was the cause of most known bankruptcies. This is a model in which the majority of decisions were taken based on the risk. At the moment of a company's liquidation and the proportional sharing out of the profits or losses according to the capital invested, the partners could decide to renew their company for a further cycle. Thus, the Castilian company showed itself to be a flexible and dynamic model in so far as its formation and dissolution are concerned, capable of taking advantage of those trading opportunities that were on the rise and of withdrawing when the expected profits did not appear. In short, a model that adapted well to an economy in constant flux and one in which the conditions for trading and mobilizing capital were ever changing in both the short and medium term.

The Keys to Castilian Entrepreneurial Success at the End of the Middle Ages and the Beginning of the Modern Age

The Castilian company was a flexible, dynamic, and multiform institution. This versatility, together with other key points, allowed the Castilian merchants to consolidate a progressive expansion through regional, peninsular, and international markets. The capacity to do business and the success of most Castilian companies resided in at least four aspects: the ability to vary the strategy between specialization and diversification, human capital and the adoption of commercial innovations, the widening and consolidation of commercial networks, and the institutional framework favourable to mercantile interests.

Between Specialization and Diversification: Products and Geographical Area

At the time of developing a company's strategy, the Castilian companies stood out for the ability of their partners and managers when deciding between specialization and diversification. Although specialization was a common strategy, as we have learned more about these companies, we have noticed how diversification became one of the keys to Castilian entrepreneurial development. Many merchants, conscious of the new opportunities offered by such businesses as the tax and financial, expanded their traditional diversification (product and markets) to enter into such areas as tax, where specialization was well known (Carretero 1999; Ortega 2012). The Castilian commercial companies also diversified towards the tax business. We know that the companies dedicated to supply could take control of the taxes levied in their activity, which allowed them to improve their potential profits. Nevertheless, on a higher level, we know that the company headed by Gonzalo de Segovia, dedicated to breeding livestock and the trading of wool and other products, also got into the tax business, securing the management of rents in several bishoprics of the north and south of the Iberian Peninsula, as well as that of the *almojarifazgo mayor* of Seville, a custom tax which was possibly one of the most succulent rents in the whole of Castile.

Between Specialization and Diversification in Products and Services

As for specialization, one of the commercial areas where this strategy can best be appreciated was in the marketing of basic products: food stuffs and raw materials. The demographic growth that took place in the cities and towns of Castile during this period and the dietary changes, more diversified and with an increase in the consumption of animal proteins, boosted the business of supplying meat and fish around which new companies arose. These companies became the hub of supply for large cities and towns such as Madrid, Cordoba, or Valladolid, as well as in medium sized towns such as Toro and small towns such as San Martín de Valdeiglesias (Bonachía 1992; Hernández 2006; Puñal 2014; Carvajal 2020). The company in San Martín in particular, founded with only 130,000 *maravedís*, is an example of specialization in the purchase of livestock (acquired in a fair 130 kilometres away), and in the sale of meat and other secondary products in the town. In spite of being small companies made up of butchers, merchants, and other capitalists, their activity demanded great organizational capacities since the purchase of animals was usually done in different places – sometimes far from the market to be supplied – and the procedure of transporting and processing the animals was long. These capacities were also necessary in the case of companies dedicated to supplying fish from the northern ports to such cities as Madrid, situated in the center of the peninsula (Puñal 2014), or the company Medina-Calatayud, founded in 1524, dedicated to supplying Medina del Campo and the surrounding area with fish (conger eel, sardine, etc.) acquired in Galicia[2].

The participation of the companies was also important in the commerce of raw materials. The boom in construction in the urban and rural world meant an increased necessity for such materials as timber. The demand generated a new business opportunity for small companies specialized in transport over forty or fifty kilometres, as well as the commercialization of important quantities of timber to such centres as Madrid or Toledo (Carvajal 2015a). Nevertheless, when we speak of raw materials, it is necessary to cite two products that stood out due to their exportation to European markets: iron and wool. Of the former, we know of the importance it had for the Basque companies, which specialized in its exportation in spite of such controversial measures as the prohibition to trade abroad at the end of the fifteenth century (Irijoa et al. 2018, p. 26).

The star product of the Castilian commercial companies was wool. Once more, an increase in the demand for textiles, as well as the rise of large productive centres such as Segovia, Toledo, Cuenca, or Palencia, boosted the production and sales of wool throughout the Iberian Peninsula. Companies such as that formed by Gonzalo de Segovia, Pedro del Campo, Álvaro de Soria, and Pedro Gómez Tapia, active between 1492 and 1519, possessed their own flocks and commercialized the production of other farmers, in their heyday possessing 2,589 sheep and commercializing 1,534 *arrobas* of wool (Casado 2000, pp. 141–145). However, if the companies dedicated to the commercialization of wool stood out for any reason, it was for exportation to the great European textile centres, which continued to grow throughout the fifteenth and the first half of the sixteenth centuries. A good measure of the size of the business are such figures as the price of 40,760 ducats paid for 537,989 pounds of wool sold by the company Pesquera-Silos in Tuscany between 1516 and 1519 (Casado 2015a, p. 88). The merchants from Burgos had a special protagonism in its exportation and they used the company as a vehicle for their trading, as we shall see later.

The companies that were dedicated to mobilizing important quantities of goods and money understood the benefits they could obtain by diversifying their business, in both products and services: reducing the risk derived from investing in a single product and the potential benefits from complementary business activities to the principal one, such as the commercialization of other goods, the transfer of money, or the control of taxes. Diversification in product within Castile could be more limited than that carried out by the large companies dedicated to exportation, yet the size and capacity of demand in the Castilian economy soon favoured the diversification of the local companies. For instance, the company Daza-Calatayud traded between 1490 and 1494 with different types of fabric, jewellery, and other products (Carvajal, 2015b); while the company of Gonzalo de Segovia, cited above, besides wool traded in cloth, canvas, silk, and dyes[3]. Meanwhile, companies oriented towards the international markets, such as the Pesquera-Silos, traded with wax, leather, anchovies, sardines, almonds, madder, or dried fruit sent from the Iberian Peninsula to Florence, while they imported high quality cloths (*velluto*, *bordetes*, etc.) or pottery. Textiles was one of the products with the greatest international projection and this company from Burgos, as did others, managed to obtain huge profits on trading them with Florencia, Lyon, or Naples, exchanging silks, Damask textiles, brocades, as well as spices such as cumin and other luxury products such as oil (Casado 2015a, pp. 83–84). In the 1530s, such companies as those of Castro-Mújica or Daza-Aranda continued on the same lines of exporting wool and trading cloth between the principal Castilian fairs and Lisbon, Flanders, and Lyon, or the Italian cities (Casado 2018; Carvajal & de la Torre 2019). In their balance sheets for 1535–36 we find Dutch linen, linen from Brabant, tablecloths, serge, linens, fustian, etc. The Castilian companies quickly understood the potential profit margin they could obtain by importing luxury goods (ivory, exotic animals, tapestries, books, miniatures, artistic objects, alabasters, weapons…) from such centres as Flanders, whose fashions were in vogue in Castile. The companies also understood that they could obtain more profit by offering their services as commercial intermediaries between the European merchants who were demanding products with a high added value, especially in Italy and Flanders. Being a commercial intermediary for foreign markets offered large returns, although it was necessary to assume many risks, as the Genoese companies had been doing for a long time, using their ships, shipowners, and foreign sailors (including Castilians) to take such luxury products as cotton, spices, or perfumes from the Aegean to Flanders[4].

If diversification in products increased in line with the greater size of the company, the same happened with the other forms of business developed by these institutions, i.e., the financial business. From the end of the fifteenth century onwards, we can find several companies in Castile dedicated to offering commercial and financial services. The partners of these companies were usually moneychangers and other businessmen with sufficient capital to be able to take the risk and offer services in exchange for currency, deposits, loans, drafts, bills of exchange, etc. Starting up a business that had not yet flourished in Castile meant taking an important risk; however, we know of such cases as the company Verdesoto-Salinas which, during the 1490s, offered its services in important financial centres of the period, such as the trade fairs of Medina del Campo and Valladolid, or even in the Royal Court[5]. These primitive mercantile-banking companies continued to grow amidst the boom in the Castilian fairs and their integration into the European financial system (Casado 2015b). The commercial companies played a key role as financial agents since they possessed the right organizational structures to foster the transfer of capital between mercantile centres, especially between the great financial markets of Europe and the Iberian Peninsula.

From Local to International Commerce

As we have seen, the Castilian companies swung between specialization, in particular the smaller companies, and diversification in the type of business and in the products. As the companies grew and the relations between the partners became more solid, many widened their radius of activity towards new territories, encouraging geographical diversification as a new strategy to deal with growth in a highly competitive environment. The merchants of Burgos, probably one of the most active and innovative groups in the kingdom, understood quite soon the necessity to extend the location of their activities and, consequently, there then appeared an important group of merchants and companies in what possibly was then the greatest economic and financial hub of Castile: the city of Seville (Palenzuela 2003). However, geographical diversification was not only limited to establishing the company in another city of the kingdom, it went beyond the borders. It involved finding partners and representatives of the established companies and negotiating in various geographical points of the Peninsula. For instance, in the fifteenth century, companies from Toledo, such as the Cota, soon appeared at great fairs and markets like that of Madrid, a place in full commercial development from where many merchants aimed to widen their links with the south (Toledo, Seville, Cordoba), the east (Cuenca) and the north (Segovia, Medina del Campo, and Burgos) (Puñal 2014, pp. 127–128). If we speak of geographical diversification as a strategy, we ought to mention the companies of Gonzalo de Segovia or Daza-Calatayud, whose partners and managers settled in various different places around the entire Iberian Peninsula. Meanwhile, the companies established in the south were not unaware of this process, although their capacity as entrepreneurs soon focused on the opportunities offered by the Atlantic Ocean, that is to say, the Canary Islands and the New World (Aznar 1983; Bello 1994). The north-south integration of the Castilian economy, by sea and by land, opened up a new opportunity for the Castilian entrepreneurs.

In a wider geographical context, during the fifteenth and sixteenth centuries the presence of Castilian companies in the principal Peninsular and European territories continued to grow. The Castilian merchants increased their commercial interests in such Peninsular kingdoms as Portugal, where companies such as that of Ruy González del Portillo and the Italians Gabriel and Mateo Pinelo traded cloth and silk (Medrano 2007, p. 346). The Crown of Aragon, as well as such centers as Valencia, became a destination for merchants from Burgos (Casado 2003, p. 59). Nevertheless, the great process of international expansion by the Castilian companies came about through the normalization of commercial routes and the establishment of Castilian merchants in Flanders, France, England, or the Italian cities, among other places. This phenomenon has been studied and defined by H. Casado (2003) for the case of the merchants of Burgos, although we know that other communities, such as the Basques from Vizcaya, also followed the same route. The community of Burgos was represented in the principal European cities through the members of the main mercantile families of the city who exercised the role of commercial representatives and commission merchants responsible for negotiating the sale of Castilian products and acquiring new products for sale in other Castilian or European ports. The presence of Castilian companies in these places mirrored what we can see of the Italian companies. Thus, a Castilian company such as the Pesquera-Silos, essentially a company of Burgos, was able to connect Castilian production, especially the Andalusian production in the south of the Peninsula with such European centers as Florence, Naples, Rome, Pisa, Lyon, or Flanders, developing up to eight routes between different points, each one specializing in demanded goods and taking the Florentine capital as its center of operations (Casado 2015a, pp. 83–84). Besides the companies of Burgos, other companies, such as Daza-Aranda from Valladolid, were capable of diversifying their business to include operations at all market levels: local, regional, peninsular, and European, through commerce between Flanders, Lisbon, Burgos, Valladolid, Toledo, Bilbao, Seville, Madrid, Granada, and many other places around the Iberian Peninsula[6].

In short, the Castilian companies were capable of adapting their strategy to the market conditions. The smallest companies tended towards specialization, but when they had the opportunity, they also went for controlled diversification.

As a company got larger as a result of its reach for new business opportunities and higher profits, diversification became a common strategy. However, they were not blind to the increased risk that diversification in products or the geographical orientation of their business supposed.

Human Capital and Changes in Management

Entrepreneurship and the founding of companies was closely linked to the existence of an important element: the human capital developed around the Castilian mercantile groups. The generation and improvement of the human capital within the mercantile world was closely linked to the formation of Castilian businessmen. At the end of the fifteenth century, the merchants were educated throughout their childhood and youth, a process that usually began with the learning of the more theoretical subjects: reading, writing, and maths were the fundamental disciplines that allowed future merchants to manage their businesses, keep their accounts books and other registers, control the companies' finances, etc. (Caunedo 2006). The second stage of learning was based on the more practical formation that the young aspirants received. In general, such formation was done within the family group or in other companies of the same city. The youths would normally undertake different roles until they became, in the best of cases, a company's agent or representative. Learning such skills as negotiation, the control of both the quality and quantity of goods, paying taxes, and managing basic operations of information allowed them to acquire, in the eyes of their peers, the condition of fully-fledged merchants. Nevertheless, it is important to state that this process of forming the human capital was followed by another of improvement through continuous learning. Those merchants who innovated and created large companies did not cease to improve their knowledge throughout their lifetimes, complementing their formation through practice or Merchant Handbooks (Caunedo 2006, p. 449).

Such changes in the generation and improvement of the human capital had a direct impact on what H. Casado called "management innovations" (Casado 2003, p. 45). The long learning process that a partner or manager of a commercial company went through resulted in them introducing important innovations in at least three aspects: information management, risk management and reduction, and improving the financial capacity through knowledge and the use of double-entry bookkeeping, used from the mid-fifteenth century by Castilians even before such European regions as England or France, or other financial knowledge linked to operational credit, insurance contracts, or such procedures as bills of exchange. We could add a fourth innovation linked to an excellent human capital that we have just examined: the capacity to manage entrepreneurial strategies concerning the specialization or diversification of products, services, and markets, both interior and exterior.

If the development of the human capital and the learning process had a notable impact on the management capacity of the partners and managers, it also had a lot to do with the skills of the companies' agents and representatives, especially if they were abroad. Although such posts were related to the merchant's learning phase, it is possible to find many merchants who, while not participating in a company as a partner, did so as contracted staff, with the possibility of entering to form part of the company. These agents, who could at the end of the fifteenth century earn between 12 and 50 thousand *maravedís*, were essential to the expansion of the Castilian international trade given their exceptional mercantile and representation skills and their ability to act as representatives of several companies if their contracts so permitted (Caunedo 1998, p. 105).

On a lower level, as far as human resources are concerned, we find the servants and temporal workers. Once more, the human capital was an essential factor since it was essential for the companies to have efficient servants, who were normally able to read and know arithmetic, as well as workers with their own skills in the business in which they were to work. For instance, the workers of the company that transported timber along the river Tagus had to have sufficient skills to move hundreds of floating timber logs while also being able to set up and take down the mills, the dams, and other hydrological infrastructures en route (Carvajal 2015a).

Finally, around the companies, there also existed many other people responsible for facilitating the mercantile and financial activity. These people were especially valued in foreign centers where contact was occasional, and they usually acted as commission merchants for several firms at the same time. We are talking here about such characters as Pedro de Arnedo (Goicolea 2018) or Arnao del Plano in Antwerp, professionals with great knowledge in mercantile and financial matters and who, thanks to their dynamism and flexibility, were of great help to the Castilian companies in their foreign trade.

The Creation of Networks

One of the most characteristic aspects of the commercial success of the Italian merchants and companies was their capacity to generate all kinds of networks that surpassed regional geography and provided them with a powerful infrastructure through which they could continue to trade and expand their interests throughout Europe. In this sense, during the fifteenth and sixteenth centuries, the Castilian merchants made great efforts to emulate this model and to generate various types of network covering both the Peninsula and Europe so as to be able to enjoy the very same benefits they observed among the merchants from Genoa, Milan, or Florence.

Before going any further, it is necessary to consider that the fundamental unit within the mercantile networks was the family. This was true in Italy (Goldthwaite 2009, pp. 105–108), but also in Castile, although the concept of family was different in the Iberian Peninsula. In any case, at the time of creating mercantile networks, the companies played an essential role as the creation of societies was one of the most common and solid connections between families of merchants who, during that period, were interested in creating networks upon which they could then consolidate their enterprises and their strategy for climbing the social ladder. Thus, it is not surprising to observe how their business connections became superimposed upon those of their existing neighbourhood, marriages between members of the families, or the joint participation in organs of urban government (Carvajal 2014). The model for these relationships in Castile can be found in Burgos (Basas 1954).

Although we know about the personal nature of many companies, such as that of Diego de Soria (Caunedo 1985), it suffices to cite some of the companies already mentioned (Daza-López de Calatayud, Daza-Aranda, Verdesoto-Salinas, Castro-Mújica, Pesquera-Silos, etc.) to understand that the company acts as a catalyst for the mercantile networks that, with the support of the agents from other merchant families, wove a dense network on both the Castilian and European levels. This support network based on the family, the neighbourhood, and the company, was one of the elements that favoured international expansion during the first half of the fifteenth century.

The potential of these mercantile networks woven through company links was reinforced by other networks that arose in a juxtaposed or parallel way. We are referring here to the financial networks and to the information networks. Concerning the former, we have already mentioned such cases as the company of Gonzalo de Segovia, capable of moving, between 1495 and 1498 from the fairs of Medina del Campo and Villalón, Burgos, and Segovia, almost 3 million *maravedís* in bills of exchange sent by Álvaro de Soria to Seville in order to pay his creditors, who were mainly Italian (Carvajal 2015b, p. 95). In the 1520s, such companies as the Medina-Ram transferred capital through exchange operations between the crowns of Castile and Aragon, moving up to 617,500 *maravedís* between Medina del Campo, Zaragoza, and Valencia[7]. These networks were the basis of a structure that soon became consolidated on a European level, thus allowing such companies as the Daza-Aranda to send money to Antwerp, in particular to the abovementioned Arnao del Plano, who offered his financial services to manage the payments and the purchase of clothing and other products for a value of 4,000 ducats (Carvajal & de la Torre 2019). The same happened with the Castro-Mújica company, although on a larger scale. This company developed an important financial business through the transfer of money, from their own business as well as that of other companies, between the Castilian fairs and the principal fairs of Europe: Antwerp, Bergen op Zoom, or Lyon. They also developed a thriving business in maritime insurance, able to divert 55,505.41 ducats from Flanders to the Castilian fairs between 1535 and1538 (Casado 2018, pp. 183–187). These financial networks formed by partners, bankers, and moneychangers provided the necessary liquidity for the business activities in the Peninsula and, perhaps more importantly, abroad, facilitating the flow of finance to the European sites and the return journey of the profits to Castile.

The second type of network was that based on the flow of information that existed between the members of a company, whatever its size: from the small company transporting timber down the Tagus river whose servants acted as messengers, carrying letters and transmitting information between partners concerning the conditions on the river and other management problems, to the flow of international information, which we know was vital to the large Italian companies (Infelise 2007). The importance of information management, particularly in such a competitive context as the international one, was such that important institutions, such as the University of Merchants, or Consulate of Burgos, developed their own postal system, which consumed around 5% of the institution's expenditure (Casado 2008, p. 47). Without a doubt, the benefits of having up to date information concerning such market conditions as prices, goods, dangers, etc., were helpful to the members of the said institution. The commercial, financial, and information networks were protected by the institutions themselves which, in turn, were fundamental for developing other tools necessary for risk management.

Risk Management: Institutions, Insurance and Justice

One last aspect that we should deal with that concerns the causes of the Castilian entrepreneurial success is risk management and the role played by the mercantile and civil institutions. In recent years, historiography has been widely debating the role played by institutions to encourage mercantile activity or, on the contrary, to defend privileges that impeded improvements in market conditions (Ogilvie 2011). In this sense, the Castilian merchants had the support of two great consulates, that of Burgos (1494), that of Bilbao (1511), or that of Seville (1543), which helped to consolidate the process of the creation of mercantile consulates during the fifteenth century in the main European markets. Having the consulates was a well-known competitive advantage that had been developed by the Italians, conscious of the reduced risk they brought to their international enterprises. Following a similar model, the network of Castilian colonies and consulates provided a certain security and support to the merchants in foreign parts, but also to those within Castile. They also reduced the high costs of transactions that small companies faced when acting individually (Casado 2003).

The consulates supported the mercantile activity and facilitated risk management through two further aspects. The first of these was the development of the insurance market. Since its creation in 1494, the Consulate of Burgos promoted legal regulations and the contracting of insurance, converting the city into one of the principal markets for contracting during the sixteenth century and promoting the development of insurance techniques, both maritime and life insurance. Thus, the merchants of Burgos in particular and the Castilian merchants in general could take advantage of the institutional infrastructure and the flow of information through the consulate to negotiate and manage the risks to their commercial expeditions through the Mediterranean, the Straits of Gibraltar, or the English Channel and, for that matter, their companies (Casado 2003). In addition, the consulates offered the merchants legal protection since most enjoyed privileges granted by the kings of Castile or by the governors of the places where the companies were situated to judge certain conflicts in which they may be immersed due to commercial and financial disputes.

Another element that helped the Castilian companies in risk management was the institutional environment. At the end of the fifteenth and start of the sixteenth centuries, the development and organization of such institutions as the civil courts or the notary's office meant that the merchants could make use of a series of institutions in case of need and lay claim to their rights. In this sense, the importance of these institutions in defending property rights should be remembered. Royal justice and the legitimacy provided by notarial documentation were beginning to be key elements in business for the Castilian companies during the 16th century (Carvajal 2018).

Finally, although it may seem fairly evident, we cannot avoid mentioning the development of modern methods of entrepreneurial management within the Castilian companies as a tool capable of improving risk management. The development of double-entry bookkeeping and registration through the preparation of diverse books, from the general ledger to the day book and other auxiliary books, and other documents such as the inventories and balance sheets allowed the partners to maintain an almost immediate control of the company's economic situation, facilitating the decisions that needed to be taken when assuming new risks or maintaining less reckless strategies.

Nevertheless, in spite of the importance of the institutions and the tools involved in risk management, it was impossible to eliminate this component completely from mercantile negotiations. At this point, one last aspect came into play: the need to establish a relationship based on trust. This concept only reflects how the good name, fame, and honor of a merchant and his company could be key elements for improving their negotiating capacity, increasing the possibility of obtaining greater profits, and reducing the risks to their operations. Although never a certainty, negotiating with other merchants with whom one maintained a relationship built on trust was always a good resource for reducing risks and assuring success in business.

Conclusions

Starting up a business has never been and is not an easy task – it requires many different ingredients. The Castilian merchant has traditionally been characterized as a conservative individual averse to risk. Nevertheless, the example of the Castilian merchants and companies in the fifteenth and sixteenth centuries demonstrates that there was a time in which launching a business and participating in the great international markets was relatively frequent in Castile. In fact, it was done with quite a lot of success. Besides the Castilian merchants who acted individually, we have also focused on those who took the trouble to found companies with the purpose of increasing profits by gaining access to regional, peninsular, and international markets.

It was a complex process. A merchant did not take risks just for the adrenaline rush, nor could he create a company out of nothing. As has been pointed out over recent years, there are diverse factors acting in favor of entrepreneurship in Castile. Without a doubt, the expansive dynamic of the Castilian economy (demography, production, exchanges, etc.) made for a fertile breeding ground that was ideal to foster entrepreneurship. However, other factors intrinsic to the Castilian mercantile world, such as the facility to create companies or the attempts to emulate the corporate model of the Italian cities, which had proven to be the most modern by leaving behind the medieval company. The Castilian companies knew how to adapt and generate an adequate organizational model for the time and for their expectations. The success of this model was based on the capacity to develop different specialization and diversification strategies; on the generation and improvement of the human capital which, in turn, imposed changes and innovations in management; on the creation of mercantile, financial, and information networks to act as safer foundations for the activity; and, finally, on an institutional environment capable of improving risk management, reducing it through support among merchants or the signing of insurance contracts, in addition to promoting trust between merchants and their companies.

In short, Castile lived an unparalleled moment as far as innovation and successful entrepreneurship is concerned, both within Castile's frontiers and in the wide world beyond, where competitiveness continued to grow. During the second half of the sixteenth century, the situation began to change. Castile's economic boom began to lose pace and the bankruptcies among Castilian merchants and their companies began – merchants and companies who, until that moment, had enjoyed entrepreneurial success (Al-Hussein 1986, 260). In any case, the Castilian merchants and companies gave a boost to the first globalization from its initial moments and the geographical discoveries that came with it (Lapeyre 1955).

Notes

1 Thirteenth century legal compilation: *Las Partidas*, Partida V, Título X.
2 Archivo Municipal de Valladolid (=AMVa), Fondo H. de Esgueva, c. 404–78. Reg. 97, 1524, julio 23, Medina del Campo.
3 Archivo de la Real Chancillería de Valladolid (=ARChV), Pleitos Civiles, Pérez Alonso (F), 103-1 and 104-1.
4 For example, companies like the one founded by the Genoese merchant Giorgio de Cazana and the shipowner Martín de Uriste in 1492 (ARChV, RE, c. 141–6) or the company stablished by Francisco de Riberol and the shipowner Juan Martínez de Amezqueta in 1505, trading with goods valued at 10,000 ducats (ARChV, Registro de Ejecutoria, c. 197-41).
5 ARChV, PC, Masas (F), c. 3174-3; Archivo General de Simancas, Regitro General del Sello, leg. 1499-10, 96.
6 AMVa, Fondo H. de Esgueva, c. 404–97. Reg. 182.
7 AMVa, Fondo H. de Esgueva, c. 404–45. Reg. 98.

References

Al-Hussein, F. H. A. 1986. "Las compañías o asociaciones de mercaderes." In *Historia de Medina del Campo y su tierra*, vol 2, edited by Eufemio Lorenzo, 191–220. Valladolid: Ayto. de Medina del Campo – Excma. Diputación Provincial de Valladolid – Consejería de Educación y Cultura.
Aznar, E. 1983. *La integración de las islas Canarias en la Corona de Castilla (1478–1526): aspectos administrativos, sociales y económicos*. La Laguna: Universidad de La Laguna.

Basas, M. 1954. "Mercaderes burgaleses en el siglo XVI." *Boletín de la Institución Fernán González* 126: 156–169.
Bello, J. M. 1994. *Extranjeros en Castilla (1474–1501). Notas y documentos para el estudio de su presencia en el reino a finales del siglo XV*. La Laguna: Universidad de La Laguna.
Bonachía, J. A. 1992. "Abastecimiento urbano, mercado local y control municipal: La provisión y comercialización de carne en Burgos (Siglo XV)." *Espacio, Tiempo y Forma, Serie III. Historia Medieval* 5: 85–162.
Carretero, J. M. 1999. "Los arrendadores de la hacienda de Castilla a comienzos del siglo XVI (1517–1525)." *Studia Historica. Historia Moderna* 21: 153–190.
Carvajal, D. 2014. "Merchant Networks in the Crown of Castile Cities between Medieval and Early Modern Age." In *Commercial Networks and European Cities, 1400–1800*, edited by Andrea Caracausi and Christoff Jeggle, 137–152. London: Pickering & Chatto.
Carvajal, D. 2015a. "Compañías y comercio de la madera en Castilla a fines del siglo XV e inicios del XVI." *Espacio, Tiempo y Forma. Serie III* 28: 201–219.
Carvajal, D. 2015b. "Flujos financieros norte-sur en Castilla a fines de la Edad Media." *Anales de Historia Medieval de la Europa Atlántica* 2: 81–104.
Carvajal, D. 2018. "Ley, justicia y cambio económico en Castilla a fines de la Edad Media e inicios de la Edad Moderna." *Ricerche di Storia Economica e Sociale* 2: 35–60.
Carvajal, D. 2019. "Compañías y negocios en Castilla (siglos XV-XVI)." In *Empresas y Empresarios en España*, edited by Juan Manuel Matés, 37–56. Madrid: Ediciones Pirámide.
Carvajal, D. 2020. "Los carniceros y sus negocios en el mundo rural castellano a fines del siglo XV e inicios del XVI." In *Les bouchers et leurs affaires entre villes et campagnes XIIIe-XVe siècles*, edited by Catherine Verna, Sandrine Victor and Ramón Banegas, 279–301. Valencia: University of Valencia.
Carvajal, D. & S. de la Torre. 2019. "Los Daza: mercaderes aragoneses en Medina del Campo." *Revista de Historia Jerónimo Zurita* 95: 153–175.
Casado, H. 2000. "Comercio, crédito y finanzas públicas en Castilla en la época de los Reyes Católicos." In *Dinero, moneda y crédito en la monarquía hispánica*, edited by Antonio Miguel Bernal, 135–156. Madrid: ICO–Marcial Pons.
Casado, H. 2003. *El Triunfo de Mercurio. La presencia castellana en Europa (Siglos XV y XVI)*. Burgos: Caja Círculo.
Casado, H. 2008. "Los flujos de información en las redes comerciales castellanas de los siglos XV y XVI." *Investigaciones de Historia Económica* 10: 35–68.
Casado, H. 2015a. "Los negocios de la compañía Pesquera-Silos en Florencia en los inicios del siglo XVI." In *Hacienda, Mercado y Poder al norte de la Corona de Castilla en el transito del Medievo a la Modernidad*, edited by Ernesto García and Juan Antonio Bonachía, 69–97. Valladolid: Castilla Ediciones.
Casado, H. 2015b. "Circuitos comerciales y flujos financieros en Castilla a fines de la Edad Media e inicios de la Modernidad." In *Estados y mercados financieros en el occidente cristiano (siglos XIII- XVI): XLI Semana de Estudios Medievales, Estella, 15–18 de julio de 2014*: 273–307. Pamplona: Gobierno de Navarra
Casado, H. 2018. "Comercio y finanzas castellanas en los Países Bajos en la primera mitad del siglo XVI: el ejemplo de la compañía Castro-Mújica." In *Comercio, finanzas y fiscalidad en Castilla (siglos XV-XVI)*, edited by Hilario Casado, 165–198. Valladolid: Castilla Ediciones.
Caunedo, B. 1985. "Los negocios de Diego de Soria: mercader burgalés." In *La ciudad de Burgos: actas del Congreso de Historia de Burgos: MC aniversario de la fundación de la ciudad*, 163–172. Valladolid: Junta de Castilla y León.

Caunedo, B. 1993a. "Compañías mercantiles castellanas a fines de la Edad Media." *Medievalismo* 3: 39–57.
Caunedo, B. 1993b. "Acerca de la riqueza de los mercaderes burgaleses: Aproximación a su nivel de vida." *En la España medieval* 16: 97–118.
Caunedo, B. 1998. "Factores burgaleses, ¿privilegiados o postergados?" *En la España medieval* 21: 97–114.
Caunedo, B. 2006. "La formación y educación del mercader." In *El comercio en la Edad Media: XVI Semana de Estudios Medievales*, edited by José Ángel García de Cortázar et al. 417–454. Logroño: IER.
De Ruysscher, D., A. Cordes, S. Dauchy, & H. Pihlajamäki (eds.). 2017. *The Company in Law and Practice: Did Size Matter? (Middle Ages-19th century)*. Leiden-Boston: Brill.
Franceschi, F., R. Goldthwaite, & R. Mueller (eds.). 2007. *Commercio e cultura mercantile. Il Rinascimento italiano e l'Europa*. Vol. IV. Treviso-Costabissara: Fondazione Cassamarca-Angelo Colla.
Goicolea, F. J. 2018. "Castilian Trade in the Low Countries in the early 16th century. The activities of the merchant Pedro de Arnedo in the town of Middleburg." *Annales Mercaturae* 3: 51–83.
Goldthwaite, R. A. 2009. *The Economy of Renaissance Florence*. Baltimore: The Johns Hopkins University Press.
González Arévalo, R. 2012. "Apuntes para una relación comercial velada: la República de Florencia y el Reino de Granada en la Baja Edad Media." *Investigaciones de Historia Económica* 8-2: 83–93.
Hernández, P. 2006. "Abastecimiento y comercialización de la carne en Córdoba a fines de la Edad Media." *Meridies: Revista de historia medieval* 8: 73–120.
Infelise, M. 2007. "La circolazione dell'informazione commerciale". In Commercio e cultura mercantile. Il Rinascimento italiano e l'Europa, Vol IV, edited by Franco Franceschi et al., 499–522. Treviso-Costabissara: Fondazione Cassamarca-Angelo Colla.
Igual, D. & G. Navarro. 1997. "Los genoveses en España en el tránsito del siglo XV al XVI." *Historia. Instituciones. Documentos* 24: 261–332.
Irijoa, I., F. J. Goicolea, & E. García. 2018. *Mercaderes y financieros vascos y riojanos en Castilla y Europa en el tránsito de la Edad Media a la Moderna*. Valladolid: Castilla Ediciones.
Lapeyre, H. 1955. *Une famille de marchands: les Ruiz*. Paris: SEPVEN.
Medrano, V. 2007. "El comercio terrestre castellano-portugués a finales de la Edad Media." *Edad Media. Revista de Historia* 8: 331–356.
Ogilvie, S. 2011. *Institutions and European Trade. Merchant Guilds, 1000–1800*. Cambridge: Cambridge University Press.
Ortega, Á. 2012. "Estrategias, dinero y poder. Compañías financieras castellanas a finales de la Edad Media: Una primera propuesta metodológica." In *Los negocios del hombre. Comercio y rentas en Castilla. Siglos XV y XVI*, edited by Juan Antonio Bonachía and David Carvajal, 261–286. Valladolid: Castilla Ediciones.
Otte, E. 1996. *Sevilla y sus mercaderes a fines de la Edad Media*. Sevilla: Universidad de Sevilla.
Palenzuela, N. 2003. *Los mercaderes burgaleses en Sevilla a fines de la Edad Media*. Sevilla: Universidad de Sevilla.
Puñal, T. 2014. "El comercio madrileño en el entorno territorial y urbano de la Baja Edad Media." *Edad Media: revista de historia* 15: 115–133.

3 Windmills, Not Giants. Competition and Monopoly on the Reinosa Route

Rafael Barquín Gil

Introduction

There is surely no statement on which all economists in the world can agree. But if there were, it might well be the following: the closest we come to perfectly competitive market conditions is in the market for wheat. Of course, such conditions are unattainable. Economic theory identifies six conditions for perfect competition: a large number of buyers and sellers; a homogeneous product; complete, free and symmetrical information; an absence of barriers to entry; an absence of transaction costs; and perfect mobility. Several of these are clearly impossible to achieve (which could also be said of the opposite conditions for the perfect monopoly). However, the wheat market is a good candidate, even if it meets the conditions imperfectly. Indeed, standard economic theory textbooks in universities use this case as an illustration of perfect competition (Krugman 2006: 207; Hall & Lieberman 2005: 236; Mankiw 2004: 40; Samuelson et al. 1996: 126).

The circumstances under which the Spanish wheat market operated in the nineteenth century were not very different from those in the rest of Europe. It can therefore be assumed that economic relations were governed by "imperfect perfect competition". And yet there are historians who believe that this market was characterized by the most extreme forms of collusive practices. In what follows, I will refer to this belief as the "collusion hypothesis" (Moreno 1995: 244–46; 1996: 189–90; Moreno 2006: 318; 2018; Hoyo 1993: 189–90; 1999). The setting for it is the so-called "Reinosa route" in the north of the historical region of Old Castile. This in itself is striking. One could imagine that there were collusive structures in place in remote areas, where a small number of landowners controlled isolated markets thanks to their political influence and inadequate communication. But the characteristics of this region at that time were quite the opposite. The north of Castile had good transport routes and the ownership of the land was widely dispersed. Not coincidentally, it has been a devout, politically conservative area, although it is not reactionary.

The aim of this work is to confirm what we would expect to find; that is, that the wheat and flour market at that time and place was fairly competitive (Barquín 1999, 2000, 2011, and 2019). While this is a necessary task, it may not be particularly interesting. Disentangling the obvious never is. The really thought-provoking issue is to find out why the obvious interpretation has been called into question. Therefore, before addressing the core, "uninteresting" part of this topic, I propose a possible explanation of how the implausible interpretation came to be seen as the truth. Moreover, this will provide us with the historical context.

One of the most successful interpretations of Spain's contemporary economic history relies on what is referred to as the "nationalist path of Spanish capitalism" (Serrano et al. 1978). It has enjoyed such a degree of success that it forms part of the basic corpus of educational texts on this subject and is even used as a heading for a standard section in university textbooks. The contention is that from the late nineteenth century to the mid-twentieth century, the Spanish bourgeoisie often turned to the State to protect themselves from threats and secure their hold on the domestic market. This was accomplished by means of three instruments: trade policy, cartelization, and state regulation of the markets. The problems of economic growth that Spain faced in those years, especially during the early Francoist period (1936–1959), can be explained by this convergence of unfortunate policies.

In my opinion, this interpretation is essentially correct. But I also think it should be treated with a degree of circumspection as these elements do not all occur at the same time in the same place. Indeed, state intervention in the functioning of the markets is only seen during the Franco years (in the case of cereals, Barciela 1986). The earlier appearance of cartels has been demonstrated in some sectors, such as steel (Fraile 1991), but not in others, such as banking (Pueyo 2006). In any case, with the exception of the railways and a few other industries, cartelization was virtually nonexistent before 1914. The scope of application of the "nationalist path" is somewhat limited. It is significant that the dire first twenty years of Franco's dictatorship were preceded by a remarkable economic transformation and modernization (Beascoechea & Otero 2015). If the Spanish economy underwent a radical change with Francoism it is likely because the economic policies of the late Restoration period, the Primo de Rivera dictatorship, and the Second Spanish Republic were so substantially different.

The problem with research built around the idea of the "nationalist path" is that it has at times entailed an unconstrained search for precedents in ever more distant periods. It was certainly warranted at times. For example, there was not a free-trade period in the history of Spain before the current democracy (Serrano Sanz, 1987). But it is not easy to find precedents for the other two pillars of the "nationalist path". With few exceptions, the liberal governments of the nineteenth century did not fix prices or foster monopolies. Ultimately, the Spanish Liberal State was no different from those of the rest of Europe. As such, the evolution of the Spanish economy in the nineteenth century did not diverge from that of other European countries, unlike the economy in Francoist Spain.

Therefore, suspicions about how free the market for wheat and flour was in nineteenth-century Spain are an unfortunate example of this search for such precedents. It is underpinned by a pessimistic and atavistic view of Spanish history, according to which the disaster of the Francoist period can be traced back to liberal Spain. But the reality is that the massive intervention in the economy of the Franco years, similar to that of any communist economy, is the antithesis of liberalism. The particular history of the flour millers and merchants of northern Castile is a success story because it occurred in an environment of free competition, albeit limited to the national scope. This success could well have been even greater if Spanish producers had not only competed with each other, but also with foreign producers. But that is something we will never know.

The Flour Traffic between Castile and Santander in the Mid-Nineteenth Century

Between 1820 and 1880, the regions linking the wheat plains of Tierra de Campos with the Port of Santander — the Reinosa route — witnessed large volumes of commercial traffic. The cereal from Castile was transported in carts and barges to the mills and "flour factories" of the Pisuerga River and the foothills of the Cantabrian Mountains. There, the flour was bagged and transported to Santander, from where it was sent to three destinations: Cuba (and also Puerto Rico), Catalonia (and the rest of the Spanish coast), and Europe (especially France and Great Britain). There was also a significant traffic of wheat to Catalonia and Europe, but not to America.

This trade was supported by highly protectionist trade legislation. In Cuba, the duties levied on imports of non-Spanish flour were equivalent to its price in the United States[1]. In the Spanish mainland and the Balearic Islands, imports of wheat and flour had been banned since 1820 (in reality, 1826; see Barquín 2003: 129), unless their price was above certain levels, which were clearly exceeded only in 1856 and 1857. It was only after 1869 (in actual fact, from the preceding year) that this *prohibitionism* was replaced by a less restrictive trade regime, the Figuerola Tariff. As a result, Cantabrian flour almost completely dominated the Cuban market, while in Catalonia and the rest of Spain the only competitors were the Levantine, Andalusian, and Aragonese flours.

The trade and industrial activity on the Reinosa route started to emerge in the final decades of the eighteenth century (Moreno 1991b) but did not reach particularly notable levels until the 1820s. The amounts involved were never very remarkable[2]. Flour exports to America increased from about 5,000 tonnes in the 1820s and 1830s, reaching peaks of 40,000 and 50,000 tonnes in 1866 and 1873, respectively. Trade with Catalonia registered similar albeit more stable volumes. Although flour was not normally sold to the rest of Europe, in some years those exports surpassed the two former shipments combined. All together, these trade flows were small relative to total wheat production – not just relative to national production but now also to regional production. Although we do not have data on wheat harvests until the end of the nineteenth century (GEHR 1991, Barquín 2002), on the basis of the available statistics we can estimate the harvest of the two most active provinces in this regard — Valladolid and Palencia — at about 200,000 tonnes, and the combined harvests of the Duero Basin at about 600,000 tonnes. Thus, the largest volumes shipped out represent less than half of the production of these two provinces, and a fifth of that of Castile and León.

One of the most striking aspects of the collusion hypothesis is that, if true, it would run counter to the spirit of the times. In the early decades of the nineteenth century, a radical transformation of Spain's institutional framework took place, a process known as the Liberal Revolution. At the economic level, it meant the dismantling of the system of privileges, regulations, and restrictions of the Ancien Régime, and the affirmation of freedom as a legal and economic principle. Apart from the Spanish Constitution of Cádiz of 1812, and the even more important associated legislation (both suspended but not ignored), various liberalization measures were adopted during the reign of Ferdinand VII. At the beginning of the reign of Isabel II, Spain was already part of the ever-growing group of nations adhering to liberalism. This applied to domestic trade in wheat and flour, but not to foreign trade, as we have seen.

This economic freedom (and precisely because it was free) allowed for the legal existence of collusive organizations such as monopolies or cartels. Nothing in the Spanish legal system of those decades prevented merchants and industrialists from joining forces to defend their interests. Indeed, business alliances were sometimes created, albeit only on a temporary basis. Thus, in 1839 several flour manufacturers put forward a joint proposal for supplying the army, which seems to have been viewed unfavourably by the Treasury and the Military Quartermaster (Moreno, 1995: 240). However, that initiative did not result in the founding of a cartel. It was only much later, in 1887, that the Spanish Agrarian League was created. This was the first lobby of agricultural producers and it included the cereal farmers. In short, there was never a cartel per se, or at least not as a formal structure. But if lobbies, cartels, and other associations were not prohibited, and we even know of their existence in other sectors, why were they not present in the flour industry or in wheat farming?

The formal and legal existence of a cartel is relevant because appearances are more important than the reality in this matter. Any cartel member may be tempted to break collusion agreements and make sales behind the backs of the others. As such, there must be sanctioned mechanisms for which courts and laws are needed. But if these do not exist, or cannot be applied, the group must exert pressure on the splitter through informal mechanisms, such as said associations. To fill this gap, researchers have turned to inter-family relationships, but this hypothesis is weak because there are families in all the companies and institutions and their presence often means nothing.

But before we go any further, where was such a cartel supposedly located? There is not one but two possible answers here. On the one hand, there were the flour manufacturers in the south of the province of Palencia, specifically in the town of Grijota and its surrounding region. These would be the so-called (in an unfortunate neologism) *"flourcrats"*. On the other hand, there were the large trading houses of Santander. It is interesting to note that the research on these two groups addresses them independently, and that only recently (Moreno 2018) has their vertical integration been considered, but never a true merger or takeover. In any case, all indications point in the opposite direction. For example, only eight matches are found between the 80 surnames of Cantabrian merchants in the period 1828–76 (Hoyo, 1993: 113 and 288) and the 57 surnames of flour manufacturers from Palencia and Valladolid in the period 1853–60 (Moreno, 1991a: 175–80). Nor do contemporary testimonies support this argument. According to Sierra (1845: 94–98) "there are many more shipowners who do not have factories than those who do" (which nevertheless indicates that some did have factories). Another indication is the sporadic nature of purchases of country estates or crops by flour manufacturers and merchants (Moreno, 1991a: 178–83 and Hoyo, 1993: 256–63). We also know that many of the flour trading operations in Santander for shipment were freely contracted and were published in the "Revista Semanal", a section in the *Boletín de Comercio*. The transparency of these operations also underlines the lack of vertical integration[3]. In short, neither group dominated the other, and there was no combined entity governing them. They were two different groups in terms of where they came from and what they did, with discrete relationships maintained between the two, and the preeminent figures in each were different. It is a genuine challenge to determine how one cartel might be organized around two separate cartels (which are not in fact cartels).

There is another important question: how many individuals-families-companies made up these alleged cartels? This is an issue of particular relevance when it comes to the "flourcrats" because we first have to establish which territory we are referring to. Grijota was a small town (1,170 inhabitants according to the Diccionario de *Madoz* of 1845) with a few large flour factories, which would obviously have no problem reaching an agreement. However, only a fraction of the flour shipped from Santander came from Grijota. If we extend the scope to all the towns that, more or less regularly, supplied that port, we should include not only the provinces of Cantabria and Palencia but also those of Valladolid, Burgos, and León. This lack of precision explains why the lists of flour factories are sometimes limited to the Reinosa route (although never only to Grijota) and sometimes extend far beyond that. Thus, Luis Ratier (1848: 24–30) cited 26 factories in Cantabria (with 124 millstones), 21 on the Canal of Castile (123 millstones), and 14 outside of those two areas (64 millstones)[4]. In total, there were 61, of which only two belonged to the same person. For the five-year period of 1855–60, Moreno (1991a: 175–80) identifies about 60 owners of flour factories only in the provinces of Palencia and Valladolid. If we add the 26 of Cantabria from 10 years earlier, we have at least 86 owners (Barquín 2011: 269).

The issue of territorial scope is much less problematic when it comes to the Cantabrian merchants because we can safely assume that all of them – or almost all – lived in Santander. Hoyo (1993: 108–26 and 1999: 278) speaks of 55 "surnames", and of course, being spatially concentrated would make it easier for them to coordinate. The problem is that in Santander cartelization is unlikely for mere technical reasons. Firstly, ships entering the port came from so many different places. Indeed, there were many more foreign flags on ships than Spanish ones. Thus, even if all the Santander merchants and shipping companies were able to collude in some way, they would still face competition from foreign merchants and shipping companies.

But there is a second reason. Storage and speculation was a very risky activity with wheat and flour as both were perishable goods. Nobody could store these products without incurring losses due to their deterioration or the measures that would have to be taken to reduce that deterioration. Therefore, storing them and waiting for prices to rise could be a disastrous strategy. This was such a serious problem that it constitutes a definitive argument ruling out any type of long-term speculative storage, at least until the invention of efficient, inexpensive procedures to do so (Barquín 2019: 109–110). However, flour does not deteriorate in the same way as wheat. While it may be economically viable to store wheat for a year, since any losses can be borne over such a short timeframe, speculating with flour is entirely unfeasible because it is a very delicate commodity. That is why it was never stored in warehouses except immediately prior to being shipped. In short, the collusion hypothesis can only be constructed on the basis of stockpiling wheat, not flour. But this represented a major complication for Cantabrian merchants for two reasons. First, because they lived far away from the production centres in Castile. Second, because transporting the wheat to Santander was less appealing than converting it into flour in Castile, since flour weighs less and takes up less space, making it more economical to transport. This is why on the Reinosa route there were almost no mills near Santander.

In both of these supposed cartels, small-scale capitalists predominated. For example, in Santander in 1874, the largest trading house – and the one that had the closest relationships with the other families, the house of López-Dóriga – accounted for only 13.2% of the total commercial investment (Moreno 2018: 14). As for the Spanish ships (which were only part of the total), in 1845 there were 66 registered, of which 7, accounting for 8.2% of the total tonnage, belonged to the largest trader (Sierra 1845: 94–98, Ratier 1848: 120–124). Regarding the Reinosa route, and as Sierra pointed out (1845: 89), "there are factories that belong to respectable capitals, more generally, the owners are of middling fortunes and [in] some cases very small". This is not surprising because, as we have seen, there were more than fifty different owners of mills and factories. Even more interesting is the fact that there was much greater milling capacity than production capacity (Sierra 1845: 85, 89 and 101). Thus, a hypothetical "flourcrat" cartel would become unworkable if two or three of them were not part of it.

We can identify another difficulty: the absence of barriers to entry. From the production of wheat to the export of the flour, all these businesses were open to anyone. Of course, the initial stages were completely free: there were countless farmers and mills in Castile. This was also true of the carts: the transportation of grains and flour had also been liberalized since the beginning of the nineteenth century, if not before. The construction of the railways brought about a major change by replacing the myriad of roads with a single carrier. But the line was not completed until 1862; more importantly, the company that held the concession, *Norte*, never distributed or stored wheat, nor did it hold any ownership stake in the companies that did. Rail fares were based on rational criteria of quantity, distance, and price, and were always well below the legal limits (imposed on the carrier by law), both for large-scale traders and for small-scale vendors.

As a matter of fact, the only restrictions in this area prior to the Liberal Regime were on the manufacture, storage, and sale of flour. The Cortes de Cádiz abolished *water rights* at the same time as the feudal lordships. But, unlike the feudal system, this abolition of water rights still held under the restoration of absolutism (Maluquer de Motes 1983: 85–86). Later, the law of 8th May 1822 on Promoting Industry and Trade recognized millers' right to stockpile wheat for processing into flour. But perhaps the most important piece of legislation was the decree of 26th February 1824 which, while reiterating the ban on the import of wheat and flour, declared the freedom of this trade in mainland Spain, implicitly including its storage. This freedom was later confirmed in The Commercial Code of 1829 and the Royal Decree of 19th November 1835. In fact, it seems that by that time there had long been a tacit understanding of the freedom of trade and industry (Castro, 1987: 748–49).

Thus, these activities were permitted according to both the legal framework and the customs of the time, a fact that contemporaries viewed as so obvious it did not merit further comment. For example, Sierra (1845: 85) states that flour manufacturers "mill and sell flour according to market prices". Similarly, Torrente (1852: 365) claims that "it is not thought, however, that it is at the discretion of [sellers and buyers] to raise or drive down the prices to an excessive degree". In other words, they both assumed that flour manufacturers were price-takers rather than monopolistic. And the same could be said for the rest of the participants in other activities. In the same vein, this transparency in business is reflected in the notices in the *Boletín Oficial del Comercio de Santander* where we find numerous sales of all kinds of industrial goods (Barquín 1999: 295). The existence of a futures market in Valladolid also confirms the extent and depth of the goods and factor markets (Moreno 2018, 15).

Thus, the cartel did not formally exist, – we cannot identify a clear stage in which it could have been established, there was no vertical integration, contemporaries saw only a fragmented market, and there were no legal conditions to foster the emergence of a cartel. In short, there is absolutely no evidence to support the collusion hypothesis. Let us now look at three findings that point in the same direction.

Brokerage Revenues on the Reinosa Route

The first is what we can refer to as brokerage revenues, which could also be considered a cost if we regard it as an additional component of the final price rather than the income of one of the participants, (Hoyo 1993, Barquín 1999, and 2011). Whichever way we look at it, this figure would be calculated as the difference between the sale price of the good (flour) and the purchase price of the raw material (wheat) and all the inputs needed to transport and process it. High brokerage revenues could be due to either the existence of monopsonistic

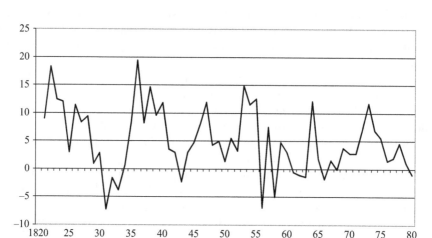

Figure 3.1 Trading Income on the Reinosa Route (Percentage)
Source: author's own elaboration with data from Barquín 2011: 272–276

practices that depressed wheat prices in Castile or monopolistic practices that inflated flour prices in Santander. Note that evidence of high brokerage revenues does not necessarily indicate that such practices were in place, but it does open up the possibility of their existence. On the other hand, if brokerage revenues are low we can safely say that there was no cartel (or that it was useless, which is essentially the same).

Calculating this cost on the Reinosa route is a complicated task because we need to know the costs of the various activities involved. The result is shown in Figure 3.1 (Barquín 2011, 2000, and 1999). Each datum is the percentage that the broker would receive with respect to the income from the sale of the three quality classes of flour as well as the bran. The average for the period from 1821 to 1882 is 4.8%, with some years registering negative values (the end of the reign of Ferdinand VII) and others high values (during the Carlist War). There is a slight downward trend. The key thing is that brokerage revenues are low.

These figures are confirmed by four pieces of information from the Reinosa route (Barquín 2011: 275–76). In chronological order, the first is evidence from a certain road transport company that emerged in 1840. According to its rate chart, partners of that company benefitted from a small discount compared to external clients. This discount, which could be equated with brokerage revenues, ranged from 1.0% to 2.7% of the price of the goods. A second piece of information is provided by Sierra in 1845, who stated that the commission and brokerage fees paid for transported flour amounted to 2.1% of its price (without specifying where the flour came from). The third such finding was reported by Hoyo (1999: 282–83), drawn from his review of the various notarial records of merchants operating between Herrera de Pisuerga and Santander in late 1853; their commission amounted to 2.5%

of the final price of the flour. The last is from the "Revista Semanal" of the *Boletín de Comercio* appearing on 6th August 1877. It reported a sales transaction for the export to America of 2,000 sacks of flour priced at 18.75 *reales/arroba*, which had been purchased for 18 *reales* at the railway station, "without charges for the seller". In short, the commission for this broker would have been 2% of the final price. A similar conclusion can be drawn from the limited information available for other geographical areas. In summary, the collusion hypothesis is refuted on the basis of both indirect calculations and the documentary review.

Wheat Prices in Castile

Simply by observing the prices of wheat along the Reinosa route, we can confirm the sub-hypothesis that the "flourcrats" did not exercise a monopsony. These prices are shown in Table 3.1. The prices for Palencia (A), Herrera De Pisuerga, and Reinosa are weekly statements compiled by the Army Quartermaster (AHN file 1357). Those of Medina de Rioseco come from its *Mercurial* (official commodity price list). For the sake of comparability with the previous set of figures, only the months present in both series have been used. The prices of Palencia (B) are those paid by the flour manufacturers for the purchase of wheat, according to Sierra (1845: 82).

There are two relevant facts. First, except for the first year (in which prices were almost equal), the prices at which the flour manufacturers bought the wheat in Palencia were higher than those listed for Rioseco, by between 1.4 and 6 *reales*. In other words, these "flourcrats" paid about three *reales* above the market price for a bushel of wheat, contrary to what one might expect from a monopsony.

Table 3.1 Wheat Prices on the Reinosa Route. Reales/Fanega

	Military Intendancy			Mercurial	Sierra
	Palencia A	Herrera	Reinosa	Rioseco	Palencia B
1828 (jan-apr)	22.2	23.3	30.7	19.9	–
1830 (jun-dec)	18.7	22.9	26.9	19.8	–
1831 (jan-jul)	21.9	23.9	31.5	20	–
1834	–	–	–	26.6	26
1835	–	–	–	22.7	27
1836	–	–	–	29.3	35.3
1837	–	–	–	35.6	37
1838	–	–	–	36.3	41
1839	–	–	–	26.6	33.3

Sources: author's own elaboration with data from AHN . leg. 1357; Sierra 1845: 82; Mercurial de Medina de Rioseco. See text.

Note: Four *reales* is one *peseta*. *Fanega* equals 55.5 litres.

Second, wheat prices rose from Rioseco to Reinosa, with increases above the rise in transport costs. Rioseco, Palencia, and Herrera are located close together on the plains crossed by the Canal of Castile. They are all considered *"tierras de pan llevar"* (land that brings forth bread; in other words, cereal-growing lands). Nonetheless, there is a slight difference in prices, increasing with their proximity to the sea. There is then a substantial jump in prices between Herrera and Reinosa of about six *reales* per *fanega*. The distance between these locations — 60 kilometres — is similar to the distance between the aforementioned localities, but passing through more challenging terrain, where there was no canal. However, there was a suitable road, which had been open since the eighteenth century. Thus, although the transport conditions were worse, they were still fairly good.

These price differences — the small gap between Rioseco and Herrera, and large one between Herrera and Reinosa — can primarily be explained by the influence of the flour trade. The competition among flour manufacturers and merchants to gain possession of the wheat drove up prices, as Sierra points out (1845: 92). Incidentally, Grijota, located close to Palencia, does not seem to have exerted any particular influence in any regard. The collusion hypothesis fails.

The Flour Traffic from Santander

A solution to the problem of the deterioration of goods due to prolonged storage could be found in the foreign market. It would act as a "safety valve" to prevent the sale of goods at a loss. The "flourcrats" would act as follows: when the price of wheat in Castile was low they would buy it, not to make and sell flour, but rather to store it as a basis for speculation. This would create shortages in the local market. When the price was high enough, they would sell that wheat, or the flour made from it, generating a significant profit. The problem is that a good harvest could prevent the price from rising. Or even if it did rise, the local market could be unable to absorb all the goods that had been stored. To solve this problem, the external markets (Catalonia, Cuba, and Europe) would act as a "safety valve", providing a market for wheat and flour at a remunerative price. What is interesting is that, if all this is indeed true, exports and sales would move in the same direction as the prices. In the years when prices were high in Castile, there would be a lot of traffic from Santander; in the years of low prices, there would not be.

Table 3.2 shows the coefficients of correlation (r) between the quantities of flour shipped to these three destinations and their prices in Santander, in contemporary series and lagged one year back and one year forward. In this way, we seek to determine whether these shipments affected prices or vice versa, and by how much. To see its interpretation, we can consider the highest coefficient, 0.67, which is the one between sales to mainland Spain (Catalonia) and the prices in Santander a year earlier. Since these relations are a function of a single variable, r equals the square root of the coefficient of determination (R^2), which is 0.444. Thus, this result can be interpreted as indicating that flour prices in Santander explain 44.4% of the variance in sales to Catalonia. It is

Table 3.2 Correlation Coefficients (r) between Flour Exports by Destination and the Price of Flour in Santander, 1848–1882

	America	Europe	Mainland Spain	Total
q(t) / p(t)	−0.25	0.38	−0.57	−0.24
q(t+1) / p(t)	−0.35	0.17	−0.67	−0.49
q(t-1) / p(t)	−0.02	0.23	−0.18	0.09

Sources: author's own elaboration with data from Boletín Oficial de Comercio de Santander, Boletín Oficial de la Provincia de Santander, Comisión creada por el Real Decreto de 7 de julio de 1887, Mercurial de Santander and own elaboration (data in www.uned.es/cee/rbarquin)

an inverse relationship (the sign of the correlation coefficient is negative): the lower the prices in Santander, the more flour was sent to Catalonia. Similarly, the highest positive coefficient r in the third row, 0.23, which is equivalent to an R^2 of 0.054, can be interpreted as indicating that shipments of flour to Europe would explain 5.4% of the increase in its price in Santander.

Looking at the table as a whole, the conclusions that can be drawn are as follows. First, in general, the causal relationships are weak or non-existent. This should not be surprising given that this analysis overlooks at least one important variable: the price of flour in Europe and the other markets. Second, the relationships in q(t-1)/p(t) are much weaker than in q(t+1)/p(t). That is, the price explains the sales better than the sales explain the price. Third, the mainland market is the one that is most influenced by Santander, followed by the American market, in both cases showing an inverse relationship. The European market is the only one that registers a direct (positive) relationship, albeit weaker than that with mainland Spain and of a similar strength to the relationship with the American market.

In short, it may be the case that a decline in flour prices in Santander favoured sales to the three markets (and, above all, to mainland Spain). But the inverse relationship is much weaker or even non-existent: flour sales hardly affected its price in Santander. Storage and speculation do not explain the prices and movements of flour. Once again, the collusion hypothesis fails.

Conclusions

The underlying question raised in these pages is whether Spain differed from the rest of Europe in the nineteenth century. That is, were the wheat and flour markets of Palencia-Santander different, and were they dominated by obscure business interests? The answer is no. There is no indication to suggest such a thing. Hundreds of companies and thousands of workers with beliefs and attitudes similar to those in the rest of Europe participated in all the related activities carried out between the fields of Castile and the Port of Santander. The legal framework was similar to that of France, Italy, or even Great Britain. There were no barriers to entry into any of the businesses. Nobody possessed market power because nobody controlled a significant part of any of the businesses. In fact, the very notion of controlling that market is meaningless because of the inevitable deterioration that wheat and flour would suffer over the long term. Of course, this does not mean that the conditions for perfect competition were precisely met. That never happens. What it means is that, within the constraints of an imperfect market, with transport costs, transaction costs, incomplete information, etc., the agents operated with relative freedom, and the price of the goods was reasonably aligned with supply and demand. Exactly as would be expected.

So why do some see giants where there are only windmills? It is my belief, in line with Steven Pinker's wonderful book *Enlightenment Now* (2018: 55–71), that the time has come to question the psychological causes behind untenable economic theories. My explanation for the case addressed here, and which I put forward only as a possible hypothesis, is that it is due to the continued presence in Spain of historiographical traditions born during the late Francoist period and the transition to democracy seeking to explain the immediately preceding period. But long before that, during the nineteenth century, Spain had a liberal economic system; this was even true in the time of Ferdinand VII, the epigone of Spain's absolutist monarchs. And this liberalism applied to every aspect of economic life except one: foreign trade policy. Spaniards' economic relations with one other were based on the prevailing rules of liberal capitalism – undoubtedly the most successful economic system of all time. It was the system that made it possible to establish the flour factories on the Reinosa route, and that assured the prosperity of the city of Santander.

Notes

1 Garrabou and Sanz 1985: 22. Moyano 1880: 15. Torrente 1845: 19 and 20. Sierra 1833: 61. The beginning of this policy can be dated to 1824, when the tariff of 1818 came into effect (Moreno 1995: 232).
2 Official statistics on the export of wheat and flour after 1849 have been published on several occasions, for example, GEHR 1985: 356–57. Most of the figures prior to that year can be obtained from the "Tariff Information" published in the *Gaceta de Madrid* (BOE) of 17/4/1848. Moreno (1995) and Barquín (2003) have reduced and standardized them using very similar criteria. Figures specifically from the Port of Santander, which was by far the most important, can be downloaded at www.uned.es/cee/rbarquin, for both annual and monthly figures (in this case, since 1858).
3 And anyway, the statement to the contrary would not be true. In other words, if we had no notice of such trading, even if it was carried out through supply or forward contracts, it would not mean that there was vertical integration, just as such integration is not necessarily present between an industry and its upstream suppliers. It is noteworthy that Moreno (2018: 14) claims that the flour sold "from hand to hand" between flour makers and shipowners accounted for less than 10% of the total. Admittedly, the public information reviewed does not seem to suggest that the percentage was so low, but at any rate the figure does not really matter as it proves nothing. Santander monthly flour and wheat exports database is in www.uned.es/cee/rbarquin
4 Sierra 1845: 84 and Ratier 1848: 24–31. There may have been more flour factories. One indication of this is, for example, the news that appeared in the *Boletín Oficial de la Provincia de Santander* on 18th April 1838, which referred to the destruction

caused by flooding. Eight flour factories in Cantabria suffered damages. Among them were two in Rionansa and one in Hermandad del Campo de Suso, which do not appear on Ratier's list.

References

Archivo Histórico Nacional (AHN). Fondos Contemporáneos. Sección del Ministerio de Hacienda. Serie General. Legajo 1357.

Barciela, C. 1986. Introducción (segunda parte). In *Historia agraria de la España contemporánea, Vol. 3, El fin de la agricultura tradicional (1900–1960)* ed. by R. Garrabou, C. Barciela, and J. I. Jiménez: 383–454. Barcelona: Crítica.

Barquín, R. 1999. El comercio de la harina entre Castilla y Santander y la crisis de subsistencia de 1856/57. In *Consumo, condiciones de vida y comercialización* ed. by B. Yun and J. Torras. Junta de Castilla y León, Valladolid: 293–309.

Barquín, R. 2000. El mercado español del trigo en el siglo XIX. PhD diss. Universidad de Burgos. doi.org/10.36443/10259/134

Barquín, R. 2002. La producción de trigo en España en el último tercio del siglo XIX. Una comparación internacional. *Revista de Historia Económica*, 20, 1: 9–36 doi.org/10.1017/s0212610900009654

Barquín, R. 2003. El comercio exterior de trigo y harina y las crisis de subsistencia en España. *Tst: Transportes, Servicios y telecomunicaciones*. 5: 127–148.

Barquín, R. 2011. El comercio de harina entre Castilla, Santander, Barcelona y Cuba: ¿Cártel o libre comercio? *Revista de la historia de la economía y de la empresa*, 5: 265–86.

Barquín, R. 2019. Teoría, mito y realidad del acopio y la especulación el comercio de trigo y harina en el norte de Castilla. In *Empresas y empresarios en España: de mercaderes a industriales*, coord. by J. M. Matés: 99–117. Madrid: Pirámide.

Beascoechea, J. M. & L. E. Otero (eds). 2015. *Las nuevas clases medias urbanas: transformación y cambio social en España, 1900–1936*. Madrid: Los libros de la catarata.

Boletín Oficial del Comercio de Santander. Cámara Oficial de Comercio Industria y Navegación. Biblioteca Municipal de Santander.

Boletín Oficial de la Provincia de Santander. Biblioteca Municipal de Santander.

Castro, C. 1987. *El pan de Madrid*. Madrid: Alianza.

Comisión creada por el Real Decreto de día 7 de julio de 1887. 1887–1889. *La Crisis Agrícola y Pecuaria*. Madrid: Sucesores de Rivadeneyra.

Fraile, P. 1991. *Industrialización y grupos de presión*. Madrid: Alianza.

Garrabou, R. & J. Sanz. 1985. Introducción. La agricultura española durante el siglo XIX. ¿Inmovilismo o cambio? In *Historia agraria de la España contemporánea, Vol. 2, (Expansión y crisis 1850–1900)*, ed. by R. Garrabou and J. Sanz: 7–192. Barcelona: Crítica.

Grupo de Estudios de Historia Rural (GEHR). 1985. Los precios del trigo y la cebada. In *Historia Agraria de la España Contemporánea, Vol. 2, (Expansión y crisis 1850–1900)*, ed. by R. Garrabou and J. Sanz: 321–68. Barcelona: Crítica.

Grupo de Estudios de Historia Rural (GEHR). 1991. *Estadísticas históricas de la producción agraria española, 1859–1935*. Madrid: Ministerio de Agricultura, Pesca y Alimentación.

Hall, R. E. & M. Lieberman. 2005. *Microeconomia: Principios y Aplicaciones*. Thomson.

Hoyo, A. 1993. *Todo mudó de repente*. Santander: Universidad de Cantabria.

Hoyo, A. 1999. Gestión comercial, precios y crisis de subsistencias en Castilla, 1820–1874. In *Consumo, condiciones de vida y comercialización* ed. by B. Yun and J. Torras. Valladolid: Junta de Castilla y León: 275–91.
Krugman, P. R. 2006. *Introducción a la economía. Microeconomía*. Reverte.
Maluquer de Motes, J. 1983. La despatrimonialización del agua: movilización de un recurso natural fundamental. *Revista de Historia Económica*, I, 2: 79–96.
Mankiw, N. G. 2004. *Principios de economía*. Madrid: Mc Graw Hill.
Mercurial de Medina de Rioseco. Archivo del Ayuntamiento de Medina de Rioseco.
Mercurial de Santander. Archivo del Ayuntamiento de Santander.
Moreno, J. 1991a. La fiebre harinera castellana. La historia de un sueño industrial (1841–1864). In *Estudios sobre capitalismo agrario, crédito e industria en Castilla (siglos XIX y XX)*, ed. by B. Yun. Valladolid: Junta de Castilla y León.
Moreno, J. 1991b. La fábrica de Monzón de Campos (1786–1805): La primera harinera de España *Investigaciones históricas: Época moderna y contemporánea*, 11: 109–30.
Moreno, J. 1995. Protección arancelaria, distorsiones de mercado y beneficios extraordinarios: La producción de harinas en Castilla la Vieja. 1820–1841. *Revista de Historia Económica*, XIII, 2: 227–50.
Moreno, J. 1996. Empresas y empresarios castellanos en el negocio de la harina, 1778–1913. In *La empresa en la Historia de España* ed. by F. Comín and P. Martín. Madrid: Civitas: 187–202.
Moreno, J. 2006. Factor empresarial y atraso económico en Castilla y León (siglos XIX y XX). In *Historia Empresarial de España. Un enfoque regional en profundidad* dir. by J. L. García and C. Manera. Madrid, LID: 315–36.
Moreno, J. 2018. Los harinócratas. Organizaciones, mercado e inquietudes inversoras de los empresarios de Castilla la Vieja y León, 1820–1868. *Investigaciones de Historia Económica* 14: 11–22. doi.org/10.1016/j.ihe.2016.06.003
Moyano, C. 1880. Informe sobre el comercio de harinas de trigo con nuestras Antillas... *Gaceta Agrícola del Ministerio de Fomento*, 1880-I: 11–20.
Pinker, S. 2018. *Enlightenment Now: The Case for Reason, Science, Humanism, and Progress*. Penguin.
Pueyo, J. 2006. Relaciones interempresariales y consejeros comunes en la banca española del siglo XX., *Investigaciones de Historia Económica* 6 (6): 137–162
Ratier, L. 1848. *Anuario Estadístico de la Administración y el Comercio de la Provincia de Santander*. Valladolid.
Samuelson, P. A., W. D. Nordhaus, & M. J. Mandel. 1996. *Economía*. Madrid: McGraw-Hill.
Serrano, A., S. Roldán, & J. Muñoz. 1978. La involución nacionalista y la vertebración del capitalismo español. *Cuadernos económicos de ICE* 5: 13–221.
Sierra, L. M. 1833. *Memoria sobre el estado del comercio que publica la Real Junta de Santander*. Santander.
Sierra, L. M. 1845. *Cuestión de harinas. Contestación al Sr. D. Mariano Torrente*. Santander: Imprenta de Martínez.
Torrente, M. 1845. *Memoria sobre la cuestión de harinas*. Madrid: Imprenta de J. Martín Alegría.
Torrente, M. 1852. *Bosquejo económico político de la Isla de Cuba*. Madrid: Manuel Pita.

4 *Lacave & Echecopar*
Strategies and Businesses in the Second Half of the Nineteenth Century

María Vázquez Fariñas

Introduction

Throughout its history, Cádiz has been recognized as an important city of trade and commerce. Among other reasons, this is due to its strategic geographical position, which has been one of the key factors in its development. Likewise, the wine business has traditionally been one of the most important economic activities in Andalusia, particularly in Cádiz, which acted as a bridge between producers in the wine region of Marco de Jerez[1] and European wine importers (Maldonado Rosso 1999, pp. 35–40).

Thus, the wine business has always played a particularly significant role in Cádiz, especially between the mid-eighteenth and nineteenth centuries during which time there was a gradual transformation of the traditional viticulture into a modern winemaking agribusiness in Marco de Jerez. The end of the eighteenth century saw the introduction of a number of advances that led to a major boom in the wine industry. These included the ageing of the wines, storage, the vertical integration of the business, and the construction of a great many wineries. The wine industry of Marco de Jerez thus experienced a huge concentration of capital with an increase in the number of Spanish exporters (Maldonado Rosso 1996, pp. 17–21).

In the nineteenth century, intermediaries (agents and *almacenistas*[2]) played an increasingly important role in the business, although the process of change was enormously complex and contentious (Maldonado Rosso 1999, pp. 79–99). According to studies by Maldonado Rosso (1999, pp. 159–181), for years there had been various clashes between grape-grower associations, the merchants, the coopers, and even the government. On the one hand, the winemaking bourgeoisie defended the freedom to set prices and the sale of wines year-round; in order to meet the demand of its main market—the British—it was in favour of producing aged wines by incorporating foreign wines and blending them with those from the area. On the other hand, the grape-grower oligarchy preferred to maintain the production of basic wine products, prohibit the introduction of foreign wines, set minimum prices, and sell wines on a seasonal basis. This conflict between proponents of traditional viticulture and those pushing for the modern approach was one of the main obstacles to the development of the sector. Eventually, after the government had enacted several provisions aimed at liberalizing the production and trade of wines, several notable transformations occurred in the sector. These included the widespread implementation of the *criaderas* and *soleras* system for the ageing of sherry wines, the construction of large wineries, the creation of new types of winemaking companies, and the emergence of new business relationships. All these innovations, together with the improvement of the transport network in the mid-nineteenth century, contributed to a significant increase in overseas wine sales.

But the city of Cádiz did not become a centre of the wine industry until the second or third decade of the nineteenth century. During the city's modern history (fifteenth to eighteenth centuries), it was, along with other regional port towns (El Puerto de Santa María, Sanlúcar de Barrameda, Rota, Chiclana…), the commercial and financial centre of sherry wines destined for the British Isles, northern continental Europe, the area of the Strait of Gibraltar, and the Spanish colonies in America. However, in all this time there is no record of wines being aged in the city of Cádiz. The functions of Cádiz with regard to this branch of business were brokering (mainly between British importers and representatives of the winemaking localities and as a port linking Europe and India), financial services (discounting bills of exchange, providing monetary services…), and shipping agency services for the shipment of wines (Vázquez Fariñas & Maldonado Rosso 2017, pp. 114–115).

It was during the nineteenth century when large winemaking houses appeared in the provincial capital Cádiz, involved in the ageing and exporting of wines in addition to the abovementioned brokering and shipping. In this regard, it is worth pointing out the prosperous businesses of three specific families of the Cádiz winemaking bourgeoisie: the Lacave, the Gómez, and the Abarzuza families. All three enjoyed a leading position in the national and international markets and had a wide variety of wines in their products portfolio.

In this chapter, we focus on the Lacave family, and more specifically, on the role played by the company *Lacave & Echecopar* in the latter half of the nineteenth century. To that end, the main sources used were the company's internal information, stored in a private archive donated by the family to the Historical Wine Studies Unit of the University of Cádiz; documentary records found in the Provincial Historical Archive of Cádiz (the deeds for the foundation, renewal, and dissolution of companies, wills, divisions of assets, and deeds of sale, among others); contemporary press reports; official reports; and various statistics that provide information on the historical context, the company, and the individuals associated with it.

Drawing on these sources, it is interesting to analyse the activity of this wine company, the different businesses in which it invested, and strategies it adopted to maintain its position in a constantly changing market. Furthermore, by studying this Cádiz-based wine company we can add to the knowledge on the business and economic life of the city of Cádiz in the nineteenth century. Therefore, following this introduction, we analyse the origins of the commercial company *Lacave & Echecopar* in the first third of the nineteenth century. In so doing, we seek to provide an understanding of the structure of the company's share capital and the partners who had a stake in it before then detailing its main activities with a particular focus on the wine business as the company's most important activity. We then analyse the strategies developed by the company during the latter half of the nineteenth century, a period of growth and expansion in the wine sector. Finally, by examining the last surviving years of this company, we can gain an understanding of how it faced up to the Andalusian viticulture crisis in the last third of the century.

The Origins of *Lacave & Echecopar*

The history of this company begins with Pedro Lacave Miramont, descended from a family of farmers from Navarrenx, a French town in the Department of Basses-Pyrénées[3]. At the end of the eighteenth century, at just 11 years of age, he came to Cádiz to join his uncle and cousin, Juan and Lucas Miramont, in trading. After several years in this world of business, he took the bold step of starting his own company (Vázquez Fariñas 2018a, p. 75). Thus, in 1810, *Lacave & Company* was born. It was dedicated to the trade of colonial products and shipping agency services, especially for English ships (Retegui y Bensusan 1992, p. 48), which allowed it to establish trading relations with the rest of Europe and expand its network of contacts. To do so, Pedro Lacave partnered with Hugo Macdermot until the latter's death in 1824 (Greiner y Gindroz 1897, p. 18). He then continued his business alone until 1830, when he founded, along with his fellow countryman Juan-Pablo Echecopar, the commercial company *Lacave & Echecopar*, dedicated to general trade and the commission business[4]. Thanks to his association first with Hugo Macdermot and later with Juan-Pablo Echecopar, Pedro Lacave achieved considerable business growth in the first half of the nineteenth century.

In these years, he was already involved in the wine sector. In addition, his marriage in December 1821 to Ana María Lacoste Salazar, the daughter of a renowned winemaker from Jerez, helped to improve his business and socioeconomic standing (Vázquez Fariñas 2018a, p. 75). Since the eighteenth century, matrimonial alliances had become increasingly important in mercantile Cádiz, as marriage was a fundamental way of securing financing, integrating into society, and gaining a degree of credibility and trust for business dealings (De la Pascua Sanchez 2009, p. 161). Thus, establishing matrimonial ties between members of the more economically and socially prestigious families became a strategy widely used by the business-owning bourgeoisie to reinforce the power of their companies and prevent the dispersion of the family fortune (Cózar Navarro 2007, pp. 42–43). As such, this union was a notable indication of the social prestige and economic level achieved by Pedro Lacave, who not only strengthened his relationships and interests, but also linked himself to a family with a history and prominent position in mercantile Cádiz (Maldonado Rosso 1999, p. 261).

Through their company *Lacave & Echecopar*, the partners would go on to develop a prominent wine business from the city of Cádiz while at the same time participating in other businesses such as shipping agency services, banking, salt, timber and staves[5], textiles, and mining, among others; they thus developed a clear strategy of business diversification that expanded far beyond the province of Cádiz (Vázquez Fariñas 2020, pp. 39–50).

The company grew so much towards the middle of the nineteenth century that the partners decided to bring in the nephews of Pedro Lacave Miramont, who between 1824 and 1850 had come from France to join the family business. Pedro Lacave Mulé, and Pedro-Luis and Juan-Pedro Lacave Soulé[6] would specialize in the wine business, playing a decisive role in the expansion of this family business. At that time, the person selected to succeed a business owner was prepared for the role by sending him to university, abroad, to a company outside the family, or introducing him to the family business from a young age (Díaz Morlán 2013, p. 27). This last practice was the one most commonly used by the Lacave family, with the relationship between the partners constituting an element of trust, security, loyalty, and allegiance, which guaranteed the future of the business.

At the beginning of the 1840s, Cádiz continued to be at the forefront of Spanish commercial activity. The products that made up the largest share of the Cádiz economy at the time were wine and salt (Cózar Navarro 2007, p. 37). Those years witnessed a rise in foreign demand for wines, which, together with the ongoing modernization of maritime and land transport, greatly accelerated the trade in these products from the Bay of Cádiz (Maldonado Rosso 1992, pp. 25–26). Riding this economic boom that the city was experiencing, the partners—like many contemporary businessmen—adopted a diversification strategy to secure their capital, make their investments profitable and reduce their risk. Pedro Lacave and his partners thus created the company *Juan Pablo Echecopar & Company* in Gibraltar to engage in the business of commissions in general, and particularly of wines, spirits, iron, staves, cash, and goods shipped to America as well as *Echecopar & Company*, established in El Puerto de Santa María and dedicated to the trade and export of wines (Vázquez Fariñas & Maldonado Rosso 2017, p. 102). In addition to the wine business, the commissions, the banking activity, and the shipping agency services, they held an ownership stake in a very diverse group of companies: a cork and oil factory in Seville named *Juan Pedro Lacave & Company*; the famous Sevillian pottery manufacturing company, *Pickman & Company*; a mining company called *La Gaditana*; *Los Amigos*, a spinning mill, also in Seville; *Empresa Gaditana del Trocadero*; *Empresa Fabril Gaditana*, *Empresa del camino de hierro de Jerez al Puerto, Rota y Sanlúcar* and *Tabacos Ygueravide*[7], among others.

However, by 1860 the company's wine exports had reached such levels that the partners decided to specialize in the production and sale of this product (Greiner y Gindroz 1897, p. 21). In order to focus their efforts on this activity, they established a clear strategy of vertical integration in the wine business, which they would further develop in later years, spanning the process from extraction to the sale of their wines in a large business complex in an area known as La Segunda Aguada in the outer part of the city of Cádiz (Vázquez Fariñas 2018b, p. 242). To that end, they purchased various plots of land and real estate, with their combined properties reaching extraordinary dimensions.

These two strategies made the company extremely dynamic and better able to adapt to changes in the market and take on the competition in the sector, while also generating substantial profits. Moreover, they constitute a clear precedent for modern-day business organization.

In 1851, with this business expansion phase in full swing, Pedro Lacave Miramont died (Vázquez Fariñas 2017). The role of the founder had been fundamental to the success of the company, but his death did not mean the end of business, as we will see in the next section.

The Commercial Expansion of *Lacave & Echecopar* (1852–1862)

After the death of Pedro Lacave Miramont, his widow, Ana María Lacoste Salazar, came into the company to represent him, as stipulated in the company's deeds. This fact highlights the role that women had started to play in business by that time. The Commercial Code of 1829 expressly permitted a wife to participate in a commercial activity, provided that her husband had previously given his explicit authorization (Commercial Code 1829, art. 5). We have not found any such authorization among the notarial records of Cádiz, but Ana María Lacoste spent some years involved in the family business helping her husband, and her experience in the organization of the work would explain why it was she who succeeded him as the head of the company after his death, just as other women did at that time (Solà Parera 2012).

The heirs of Pedro Lacave Miramont (his wife and the nephews he had brought over from France years earlier to get them involved in the family business) decided to use their inheritance to continue the mercantile arm of the company. So, in January 1853, Ana María Lacoste, Pedro Lacave Mulé, Pedro-Luis Lacave Soulé, and Juan-Pablo Echecopar formally established before a notary a new business partnership under the same name of *Lacave & Echecopar*[8]. The company would deal in the business of commissions, wines, staves, iron, spirits, and any other short-term speculation.

In those years, the company continued to develop its diversification strategy by taking an ownership stake in various companies. In March 1851, it consolidated its stake in the pottery factory in La Cartuja de Sevilla, *Pickman & Company*. This ownership continued until 1868, when the four partners liquidated the company, leaving only Carlos Pickman and his son Ricardo at the head of the company (Maestre de León 1993, pp. 27–29).

In addition, *Lacave & Echecopar* continued its banking activity, which covered three main areas: providing credit or granting loans; investments in the share capital of other companies; and the provision of financial services such as wire transfers, collections, and payments (Sánchez Casado 2001, p. 12). It became one of the ten most important banking companies in the city of Cádiz. In Cádiz, there was a long tradition of owners and merchants who, in addition to their private business, provided banking services. Among them were the partners of *Lacave & Echecopar*, as well as other renowned merchants such as Francisco Paúl, Benito Picardo, Juan de Dios Lasanta, and the Aramburu brothers (Ruiz Vélez-Frías 1977, p.80). These businessmen received amounts of money from individuals and administered them within their business, periodically paying out fixed amounts to depositors; this activity was underpinned by the trust the merchants enjoyed due to their honesty and prestige (Ramos Santana 1987, pp. 95–97). The expansion of these financial activities is also a reflection of the economic and commercial prosperity that the city was experiencing during those years.

Lacave & Echecopar also continued to work as shipping agents in the port of Cádiz. From the press of that time, we learn that they acted as intermediaries for the French company *Gauthier Brothers & Company* in 1857, and that they sent ships from the port of Cádiz to Havana, with port of calls in Santa Cruz de Tenerife and Puerto Rico[9].

As far as their investments in real estate are concerned, most of them were basically aimed at expanding the facilities in La Segunda Aguada. To that end, they purchased several farms and plots of land and carried out works on those that they already owned. They built several wineries, warehouses, and even their own iron quay with a crane, which was to be used exclusively at the service of their warehouses and wineries[10]. They shipped their goods for sale in foreign markets directly from there, meaning that the boxes and barrels left the wineries just in time to be shipped. This ensured that the wines were not left out in the open at the docks awaiting loading. In addition to investing in real estate, they sold part of their land for the construction of the railways, which, together with the construction of their own dock, would give them an enormous advantage over their competitors. Their strategically advantageous location—by the sea, and with the railway running right past their wineries and warehouses—enabled them to easily send out their products and acquire raw materials and other goods without having to rely on intermediaries.

All these investments show the company's move towards vertical integration, as these acquisitions were made in order to control the entire wine production process from the sourcing of raw materials, through the production and preparation of wines, to the transport, distribution, and sale of the end product in the different markets. By bringing the warehouses and external elements together in one place, they reduced costs, making the production process more efficient and increasing business profits. Moreover, *Lacave & Echecopar* was similar in this regard to most of the region's wine companies created in the nineteenth century, where the businessmen entering the wine industry ended up becoming involved in all the stages of the production process (Ramos Santana 1996, pp. 170–171; Maldonado Rosso 2011, p. 182). Examples of such cases include the renowned winery owners Osborne, Domecq, Terry, Garvey, Gordon, Williams, Humbert, and Sandeman, among others (Fuentes García et al. 2020, p. 46). Against the backdrop of the growth in the wine business, these businessmen invested in the purchase of rural and urban land. The partners of *Lacave & Echecopar* did likewise; as mentioned above, they considerably increased their investments in real estate in these years. After entering the wine business, they also became producers through the purchase of vineyards[11] and ended up establishing their own wineries and facilities for the sale of wines. In little over 30 years, they gradually managed to integrate all the stages of the wine production process into a single business.

The production method used in the wineries also represented an important advantage for the company (Vázquez Fariñas & Maldonado Rosso 2017, p. 104). By the end of the century, operations had been mechanized, with two gas engines, three steam engines, and two large boilers. In addition, they used tubes that crossed the wineries in all directions and enabled the wines to be efficiently transported from one place to another. All of these innovations further consolidated their strong position in the wine sector.

In addition, for the production of some of their wines, the Lacaves used the traditional *criaderas* and *soleras* system that was typical of Marco del Jerez. At this point it should be noted that *Lacave & Echecopar* did not only sell sherries. According to the information extracted from the company's accounting ledgers, they also produced and sold wines from other regions as authentic; these included Málaga, Alicante, and Bordeaux wines, as well as port and marsala[12]. They probably sold them directly, as well as using them to add to their mixtures and to create various kinds of imitations. Thus, the company was involved in the sale of very different types of wines: not only did they produce sherry wines, they also imitated wines from other regions, and at times, they focused only on the sale of these wines, primarily acting as a distributor.

By this time, most of the wines the company processed came from other companies, because according to their ledgers, the only land they had was in Rota. By sourcing the grapes for the production of their varieties of Moscatel and Tintilla de Rota directly from Rota, they accomplished their strategy of vertical integration, while they bought the rest of the grapes they needed to prepare their wines from suppliers throughout the Andalusian territory (Greiner y Gindroz 1897, p. 64).

Thanks to *El Álbum Nacional* (Greiner y Gindroz 1897, p. 78), we have been able to determine the volume of the company's wine exports, which generally show a clear upward trend in the period under study (Table 4.1). Although there was a slight decline in exports from 1851 to 1853, between 1853 and 1857 foreign sales rose from 9,820 to 15,205 hectolitres (hl) per year, an increase of 5,385 hl in just four years. Throughout this period (1851–1857), *Lacave & Echecopar* exported a total of 92,146 hl.

We have data that allow us to compare the sales made by this Cádiz company during that time with those of other Andalusian wineries. By way of example, the Córdoba company *Bodegas Alvear*, which specialized in the production of Montilla wines, exported a total of 332.53 hl between 1851 and 1857 (Fuentes García 1995, p. 122), a very small figure compared with that of *Lacave & Echecopar*. On the other hand, two wineries in Jerez, *González Byass* and *Domecq*, recorded higher export figures in those years, with foreign sales of 87,834.38 hl and 93,561.99 hl, respectively (Lignon-Darmaillac 2004, p. 464). Unfortunately, however, we do not have a breakdown of these sales, so we cannot analyse the percentage that corresponds to sherries and

Table 4.1 Wine Exports by *Lacave & Echecopar*, 1850–1857

	Hectolitres
1850	10,340
1851	10,675
1852	10,535
1853	9,820
1854	10,235
1855	11,696
1856	13,640
1857	15,205
Total	92,146

Source: authors, based on Greiner 1897, p. 78.

what proportion is made up of other wines. Generally speaking, though, it can be said that *Lacave & Echecopar* occupied an important position in the Andalusian wine sector by this time.

Due to the expansion of the business during those years, on 1st January 1858 the partners went before a notary to set up a new trading company. It was established under the same name of *Lacave & Echecopar* and included Eduardo Echecopar, the eldest son of Juan-Pablo Echecopar, as an industrial partner[13]. Furthermore, for the first time in its history, the share capital was stated in the articles of association, amounting to 8,500,000 *reales de vellón* (henceforth, rv). Of that total, Ana María Lacoste, as the senior partner, contributed 2,500,000 rv, while Juan-Pablo Echecopar, Pedro Lacave Mulé, and Pedro-Luis Lacave Soulé accounted for 2,000,000 rv each. Regarding the distribution of profits, 22% was allocated to each of the capitalist partners, while Eduardo Echecopar received 6%. Finally, the remaining 6% was to be shared equally among several of the company's employees.

In those years, the process of infrastructure expansion in La Segunda Aguada continued. The businesses had developed to such an extent and their wineries had become so enormous that the *Guía de Cádiz* of 1862 highlighted the prominence of these facilities, pointing out that[14]:

> [...] the wineries of Mr. Pedro Lacave, which are established in La Segunda Aguada, represent great wealth, and are at all times stocked with large supplies of wines ready for shipping. In one of them, there is a remarkable vessel; it is a monstrous barrel in terms of its size and capacity. It was built inside the winery itself, occupies the middle of it, and stands alone, bearing the words "First in Andalusia". It measures 2,144 Castilian arrobas. June 1852. [...]

The creation of a large winery complex in Cádiz had already become reality towards the last third of the nineteenth century. But investments in real estate were not limited exclusively to the area of La Segunda Aguada. At that time, the partners also purchased several properties in the city centre, thus expanding the company's headquarters and the family home where the owner lived with her nephews and partners in the company. Moreover, the acquisition of real estate highlights the capital that the partners were accumulating as a result of their business activity. It therefore reflects the remarkable boost given to the business by the founder's nephews, Pedro, Pedro-Luis, and Juan-Pedro. Their exceptional work and dedication were recognized by the press of the time, which noted how this company's business dealings had developed so much in those years that they had to expand their scope of action, requiring expansion works on their wineries in order to meet the demand from their clients (Rahola, 1910, p. 309).

On 12th January 1862, Ana María Lacoste, the widow of Pedro Lacave Miramont, died. The other partners consequently signed and notarized a new deed on 28th June of that year to continue the business they had been developing up to that point[15].

The Last Years of *Lacave & Echecopar* (1862–1870)

After the death of Ana María Lacoste in January 1862, Juan-Pablo Echecopar, Pedro Lacave Mulé, Pedro-Luis Lacave Soulé, and Eduardo Echecopar agreed to continue on together in the mercantile arm of the business, so in June of that same year they formed a new general partnership[16]. The first three continued as capitalist partners, with Eduardo Echecopar as industrial partner, and they kept the same name and corporate purpose as they had been using up to then. The biggest change was the reduction in the share capital, which was set at 7,500,000 rv, with the three capitalist partners contributing equal shares of 2,500,000 rv. Regarding the distribution of profits, Juan-Pablo Echecopar, Pedro Lacave Mulé, and Pedro-Luis Lacave Soulé, as capitalist partners, were each to receive 27% of the profits; Eduardo Echecopar was to receive 8%; and the remaining 11% was to be divided between the company's four longest-standing employees for as long as they continued working there. With these changes incorporated, the term of the partnership was set at four years, which would last until 31st December 1865.

In June 1866, after the previous deed had expired, the same partners decided to renew it and increase the share capital, so that it now amounted to 12,000,000 rv. The three senior partners, Juan-Pablo Echecopar, Pedro Lacave Mulé, and Pedro-Luis Lacave Soulé, contributed to this total in the same proportion as before; that is, 4,000,000 rv each. The division of profits continued as before, and once again a four-year term was set for the entity[17].

They were tough years for the business. The port of Cádiz was experiencing a drop in exports due to the decline in trade with the former overseas dominions and the difficulties already being felt in the wine sector (Sánchez Albornoz 1970, pp. 90–92). Exports from Cádiz fell by 25% between 1856 and 1858, with their value dropping from 266,008,544 rv to 200,863,459 rv in just two years[18]. On top of all this, there was the monetary crisis that struck in 1864 and the banking crisis of 1866, which further exacerbated the problems of the Cádiz trade (Cózar Navarro 1998, p. 32).

The greatest problems for winemaking began in 1867, due to the fall in the price of wine and the drop in exports. There were several reasons behind the decline in exports: the high cost of farming the vineyards, strong competition in the sector, British customs duties, the lack of protection from the State, and the propaganda against sherry that had emerged due to the rise in exports from Marco de Jerez to England in the preceding years. Said rise had led to a fall in other countries' sales, and those countries now set about belittling sherry (González Gordon 1970, pp. 165–166). In those years, there was a sharp decline in the preference for Spanish wines in the British market, and as a result demand stagnated. To cope with this situation, sherry producers tried to cut costs in order to be able to lower prices and thus boost their market share. But profits fell while, in these ever shifting circumstances, the position of the region's wines in the international market worsened relative to that of other wines (Simpson 1985, pp. 171–173; Jiménez Blanco 2008–2009, p. 139).

As such, they were not good years for the wine sector. This was evident in the company *Lacave & Echecopar*, as their wine exports appear rather unstable around those times (Table 4.2). Specifically, between 1858 and 1860, their sales abroad increased from 16,325 hl to 19,630 hl, but declined slightly the following year, then remained steady at around 18,100 hl a year until 1863. In 1864, exports rose to 20,690 hl, and although sales declined in the following years, they rose again in 1867, when the highest figure of this period was recorded, with this Cádiz winery selling 24,115 hl of wines to overseas markets. At the end of the 1860s, *Lacave & Echecopar* was struck hard by the economic troubles of the time, with its exports dropping to 15,215 hl in 1870.

Table 4.2 Wine Exports by *Lacave & Echecopar*, 1858–1870

	Hectolitres
1858	16,325
1859	18,625
1860	19,630
1861	18,570
1862	18,215
1863	17,610
1864	20,690
1865	20,205
1866	17,310
1867	24,115
1868	21,085
1869	15,784
1870	15,215
Total	243,379

Source: authors, based on Greiner 1897, p. 78.

The analysis carried out shows that *Lacave & Echecopar*'s foreign sales followed a similar trend to that of Spanish exports of wine from Jerez and El Puerto de Santa María in those years. Between 1858 and 1860, Spanish exports also grew, although more notably so than *Lacave & Echecopar*'s exports, rising from 160,632.33 hl to 238,883.47 hl in two years. In 1864, there was a marked increase, with 316,532.24 hl sold to overseas markets, a figure that fell sharply the following year to 240,849.45 hl[19]. This reflects the downward trend in the Spanish wine market towards the end of the 1860s, and the drastic decrease in foreign sales of sherry and similar wines, which ended up affecting *Lacave & Echecopar*.

The sector sought out different ways of mitigating these problems. Particularly notable in this regard is the opening up of two new markets: the domestic market—demand from Spain grew slightly—and foreign markets in Cuba, Puerto Rico, the Philippines, and South America (Simpson 1985, p. 183). Although demand from these new markets was not enough to alleviate all the problems in the sector, they did help to defuse some of the difficulties. In those years, *Lacave & Echecopar* sent their wines from Cádiz to Barcelona, San Sebastián, Le Havre (France), Bristol (Great Britain), Havana (Cuba), Hamburg (Germany), and New York (USA)[20].

The prevailing economic crisis worsened as it coincided with the revolution of 1868—known as the *Glorious Revolution*—which broke out in Cádiz, with major social and economic consequences for the city. Several authors agree that the fact it began there was very likely due to the general dissatisfaction and distress felt by the people of Cádiz, who were going through economically challenging times and thought that political change could improve their situation (Ramos Santana 1992, p. 220). It is worth noting the bourgeoisie's loss of wealth and the demise of many exporting industries in the years following the revolution (Sánchez Albornoz 1970, p. 100), which increasingly underlined the decline of the port of Cádiz, seriously hindered the growth of commercial activity in the city.

Against this backdrop, there was an important shift in the direction of the company, as the partners decided to separate and dissolve the company to continue the businesses separately, thus bringing an end to 40 years of joint commercial activity in Cádiz (Vázquez Fariñas 2018a, p. 84). Although the available information does not unequivocally indicate the causes behind this dissolution, the partners were likely prompted to make this decision due to the path the business was on, the economic and political instability, and the crisis that had emerged in the wine sector. In addition, there were very probably certain rifts between them, since the end of the company did not mark the cessation of commercial activities for any of the families. From that point on, the Lacaves agreed to take on the business they had been developing until then, retaking the original company name of *Lacave & Company*, while Juan-Pablo Echecopar and his son Eduardo continued to devote themselves to the commissions business through a new company called *J. P. Echecopar*, created with the capital that the two withdrew from the dissolved company[21].

In parallel, the Lacaves established another company in Seville under the same name of *Lacave & Company*, to continue to engage in the commissions business, cork, cooperage, and wine storage in the Andalusian capital (Vázquez Fariñas 2018b, p. 243).

The growth of this new company, *Lacave & Company*, with offices in Cádiz and Seville, continued throughout the twentieth century, as they entered more and more markets and exported their products all over the world. During its more than 100-year history, the company was always headed by members of the Lacave family. They managed to become one of the region's most important winemaking groups, to the point where they became part of the so-called Sherry Triangle (highest category) after the creation of the Regulatory Council of the Designation of Origin "Jerez-Xérès-Sherry" in 1933 (Vázquez Fariñas 2016).

Conclusions

Over the course of this chapter, we have seen that the Lacave family developed an important business in the wine sector throughout the nineteenth century. *Lacave & Echecopar* presents a family business model that, thanks to the management of human capital and the strategies developed, was able to endure in a constantly changing market.

To that end, the partners adopted a clear strategy of diversifying their businesses in an attempt to secure their capital and gain higher incomes. This strategy made the company extremely dynamic over the span of the century (with involvement in businesses such as the cork and oil factory in Seville, *Juan Pedro Lacave & Company*; the Sevillian pottery manufacturing company, *Pickman & Company*; the mining company, *La Gaditana*; and the spinning mill in Seville called *Los Amigos*, among others). At the same time, they strove to integrate the wine business, controlling the extraction, production, transport, and market distribution.

Despite the death of the main partner, which is usually a major setback for any company, the other partners managed fairly easily to continue the business and diversification strategy, dedicating themselves to the commission business and speculation in staves, iron, wines, and spirits, while developing the banking business and shipping agency services. They also continued their acquisition of warehouses and wineries that had begun before the founder's death, with the aim of creating their large business complex in Cádiz. By the mid-nineteenth century, the growth of their facilities was truly remarkable, and the company had managed to integrate in one place the entire process of wine production, from the winemaking to the distribution and sale of the final product. In addition, by grouping the wineries and external elements in one place, they saved costs, allowing them to carry out the production process more efficiently and increase corporate profits. The growth in the company's wine production and exports from the middle of the century reflects the fact that the company already occupied a prominent position in mercantile Cádiz, and more specifically in the wine sector.

The expansion of the company in those years runs parallel to the favourable trends in Cádiz and Spain as a whole. However, towards the last third of the century, this heyday was interrupted by several events, leading to the split between the Lacave and Echecopar families, who decided to go on with their businesses separately. Nevertheless, the new company, *Lacave & Company*, created in 1871, managed to tackle the challenges facing the sector and continued to grow from the late nineteenth century. Their notable development in the wine sector continued throughout the twentieth century, as they entered into ever more markets and exported their products all over the world, becoming a hugely important wine exporter with a weighty historical tradition.

Notes

1 The Sherry Wine Region, where sherry wines are produced. This area of wine production includes the towns of Jerez de la Frontera, El Puerto de Santa María, Sanlúcar de Barrameda, Chiclana de la Frontera, Chipiona, Puerto Real, Rota, Trebujena, and Lebrija; the latter two are in the province of Seville and the rest are in the province of Cádiz.
2 Companies that produced wine but did not distribute their products on the market or export them, rather they supplied the larger wineries with wines for blending and ageing.
3 You can learn more about Pedro Lacave Miramont in Vázquez Fariñas 2017, 2018a, 2020; and Vázquez Fariñas & Maldonado Rosso 2017.
4 Provincial Historical Archive of Cádiz (hereinafter PHAC). Notary of Joaquín Rubio, 1830, file no. 3,206, pp. 452–453.
5 Staves: any of the narrow strips of wood placed edge to edge to form the curved sides of a vessel (such as a barrel or cask) (Merriam-Webster Dictionary).
6 Juan-Pedro Lacave Soulé moved from France to settle in Seville, taking on the family's businesses in the Andalusian capital.
7 *Lacave & Echecopar General Ledger*, 1845–1849.
8 PHAC. Notary of Joaquín Rubio, 1853, file no. 3,272, pp. 470–473.
9 *El Clamor Público, newspaper of the Liberal Party* (6th May 1857).
10 *La Época* (21st August 1857).
11 In the various articles of association and renewal of the company, it is noted that the partners contributed vineyards for the development of the business activity, without detailing their location or size.
12 *Inventory ledgers from Aguada*.
13 PHAC. Notary of Joaquín Rubio, 1858, file no. 3,284, pp. 66–71.
14 *Guía de Cádiz*, 1862, p. 72.
15 PHAC. Notary of Joaquín Rubio, 1862, file no. 3,292, pp. 409–415.
16 PHAC. Notary of Joaquín Rubio, 1862, file no. 3,292, pp. 783–787.
17 PHAC. Notary of Joaquín Rubio, 1866, file no. 3,305, pp. 561–566.
18 *Statistical Yearbook of Spain*, 1856–1857, 1859–1860.
19 *Statistical Yearbook of Spain*, 1856–1857, 1859–1860, 1860–1861, 1862–1865.
20 *Official Gazette of the Province of Cádiz* (29th March, 8th April, 15th May, and 24th November 1866).
21 PHAC. Notary of Ramón María Pardillo, 1870, file no. 591, pp. 4,724–4,734.

Sources and References

Manuscripts

Lacave's Archive (Historical Wine Studies Unit of the University of Cádiz):

- *Lacave & Echecopar General Ledger*, 1845–1849.
- Inventory ledgers from Aguada.

Provincial Historical Archive of Cádiz:

- Notary no. 2: file no. 591.
- Notary no 14: files no. 3.206, 3.272, 3.284, 3.292, 3.305.

Print Documents

Commercial Code, 1829.
Official Gazette of the Province of Cádiz. 29th March, 8th April, 15th May, and 24th November 1866. Historical Archive of the Provincial Government of Cádiz, Cádiz.
El Clamor Público, newspaper of the Liberal Party, 1857.
Office for National Statistics (1858): *Statistical Yearbook of Spain for 1856 and 1857*, Madrid, Kingdom General Statistics Commission.
Office for National Statistics (1860): *Statistical Yearbook of Spain for 1859 and 1860*, Madrid, Kingdom General Statistics Commission.
Office for National Statistics (1863): *Statistical Yearbook of Spain for 1860 and 1861*, Madrid, General Statistical Board.
Office for National Statistics (1867): *Statistical Yearbook of Spain for 1862 and 1865*, Madrid, General Statistical Board.
La Época (Madrid, 1849): 21st August 1857, no. 2.580. National Library of Spain (Digital Newspaper Library).
Rosetty, J. 1862. *Guía de Cádiz, El Puerto de Santa María, San Fernando y su departamento*. Biblioteca Municipal José Celestino Mutis, Cádiz.

References

Cózar Navarro, M. C. 1998. *Ignacio Fernández de Castro y Cía. Una empresa naviera gaditana*. Cádiz: Servicio de publicaciones de la Universidad de Cádiz.
Cózar Navarro, M. C. 2007. La actividad comercial en la bahía de Cádiz durante el reinado de Isabel II. *Revista de Historia TST. Transportes, Servicios y Telecomunicaciones* 13: 34–60.
De la Pascua Sánchez, M. J. 2009. Familia, matrimonio y redes de poder entre la élite social gaditana de los siglos XVII y XVIII. In *Las élites en la época moderna: la Monarquía española. Vol. 1: Nuevas perspectivas*, ed. E. Soria Mesa, J. J. Bravo Caro, and J. M. Delgado Barrado, 157–174. Córdoba: Servicio de Publicaciones de la Universidad de Córdoba.
Díaz Morlán, P. 2013. La sucesión de las empresas familiares británicas y españolas en los siglos XIX y XX. El papel del mérito, la formación y el aprendizaje. In *La profesionalización de las empresas familiares*, coord. P. Fernández-Pérez, 17–33. Madrid: LID Editorial, Colección Historia Empresarial.

Fuentes García, F. J. 1995. Viñedo y comercio de vinos en Córdoba: Las bodegas Alvear en el siglo XIX. *Revista de Estudios Regionales* 42: 87–129.

Fuentes García, F. J., L. J. Cabeza Ramírez, & S. Sánchez Cañizares. 2020. *Alvear. La empresa familiar decana de las exportadoras andaluzas.* Valencia: Tirant lo Blanch.

González Gordon, M. M. 1970. *Jerez-Xerez-Sherish Saris: noticias sobre el origen de esta ciudad, su historia y su vino.* Jerez de la Frontera (Cádiz): Fundación Manuel Mª González Ángel González Byass.

Greiner y Gindroz, E. (dir.). 1897. Los vinos finos de España y la Casa Lacave y Compañía, Cádiz. *El Álbum Nacional, revista ilustrada. Serie de números dedicados a la industria y al fomento de la producción española.*

Jiménez Blanco, J. I. 2008–2009. Capital español, beneficios británicos. Una gran bodega jerezana del siglo XIX. *Revista de Historia de Jerez* 14–15: 133–156.

Lignon-Darmaillac, S. 2004. *Les grandes maisons du vignoble de Jerez (1834–1992).* Madrid: Casa de Velázquez.

Maestre de León, B. 1993. *La Cartuja de Sevilla: Fábrica de Cerámica.* Seville: Pickman S.A.

Maldonado Rosso, J. 1992. Consideraciones sobre la participación del vino en la economía del Marco del Jerez y de la Bahía de Cádiz. In *Solera: Exposición sobre los Vinos de Nuestra Tierra. Catálogo,* dir. J. Maldonado Rosso and A. Ramos Santana, 18–28. Seville: Consejería de Cultura de la Junta de Andalucía.

Maldonado Rosso, J. 1996. Génesis de las vinaterías jerezana y sanluqueña contemporáneas. In *El jerez-xérès-sherry en los tres últimos siglos,* coord. A. Ramos Santana and J. Maldonado Rosso, 11–28. Cádiz: Ayuntamiento de El Puerto de Santa María.

Maldonado Rosso, J. 1999. *La formación del capitalismo en el marco del Jerez: de la vitivinicultura tradicional a la agroindustria vinatera moderna (siglos XVIII y XIX).* Madrid: Huerga y Fierro Editores.

Maldonado Rosso, J. 2011. Pedro Domecq Loustau (1824–1894). In *Cien empresarios andaluces,* dir. A. Parejo Barranco, 180–185. Madrid: LID Editorial.

Rahola, F. (dir.). 1910. *Mercurio: Revista Comercial Iberoamericana,* año X, n° 106.

Ramos Santana, A. 1987. *La burguesía gaditana en la época Isabelina.* Cádiz: Cátedra Adolfo de Castro, Fundación Municipal de Cultura.

Ramos Santana, A. 1992. *Historia de Cádiz, vol. III. Cádiz en el siglo XIX. De ciudad soberana a capital de provincia.* Madrid: Sílex Ediciones.

Ramos Santana, A. 1996. Los bodegueros del Marco de Jerez: actitudes y mentalidad. In *El jerez-xérès-sherry en los tres últimos siglos,* coord. A. Ramos Santana and J. Maldonado Rosso, 159–182. Cádiz: Ayuntamiento de El Puerto de Santa María.

Retegui y Bensusan, M. de. 1992. *Cádiz en 1820. Estudio histórico y defensa de su comercio marítimo.* Cádiz: Cámara Oficial de Comercio, Industria y Navegación.

Ruiz Vélez-Frías, F. 1977. *Los bancos de emisión de Cádiz en el siglo XIX.* Córdoba: Universidad de Córdoba, Instituto de Historia de Andalucía.

Sánchez Albornoz, N. 1970. Cádiz, capital revolucionaria en la encrucijada económica. In *La Revolución de 1868: Historia, Pensamiento, Literatura,* selec. C. E. Lida and I. M. Zavala, 80–108. New York: Las Américas Publishing Company.

Sánchez Casado, J. L. 2001. Mercados locales de capital y prácticas bancarias: el ámbito mercantil y financiero de Cádiz-Sevilla, 1845–1890. Paper presented at the VII Congreso de la Asociación de Historia Económica, Zaragoza, Spain.

Simpson, J. 1985. La producción de vinos en Jerez de la Frontera, 1850–1900. In *La nueva historia económica en España,* ed. P. Martín Aceña and L. Prados de la Escosura, 166–191. Madrid: Tecnos.

Solà Parera, A. 2012. Las mujeres como partícipes, usufructuarias y propietarias de negocios en la Barcelona de los siglos XVIII y XIX según la documentación notarial. *Revista de Historia Contemporánea* 44: 109–144.

Vázquez Fariñas, M. 2016. Las bodegas en Cádiz amparadas por el Marco del jerez. In *Actas del Congreso científico El vino de Jerez en los 80 años de la denominación de origen 1935–2015*, coord. C. Saldaña Sánchez, 303–314. Jerez de la Frontera (Cádiz): Consejo Regulador de las Denominaciones de Origen "Jerez-Xérès-Sherry", "Manzanilla-Sanlúcar de Barrameda" and "Vinagre de Jerez".

Vázquez Fariñas, M. 2017. El negocio del vino en el Cádiz del siglo XIX: las Bodegas Lacave. PhD diss., Univ. of Cádiz.

Vázquez Fariñas, M. 2018a. La industria vinícola en el Cádiz decimonónico. Lacave y Echecopar: bodegueros y consignatarios marítimos. *Revista de Historia TST. Transportes, Servicios y Telecomunicaciones* 37: 70–90.

Vázquez Fariñas, M. 2018b. Los vinos de la casa gaditana Lacave y Compañía hacia finales del siglo XIX: ventas y áreas de mercado. In *Tres siglos bebiendo Jerez. Comercio y consumo (XVIII-XX)*, ed. A. Ramos Santana and L. Lozano Salado, 241–265. Cádiz: Ediciones Suroeste.

Vázquez Fariñas, M. 2020. *El negocio del vino en la ciudad de Cádiz. Historia empresarial de Lacave y Compañía, 1810–1927*. Madrid: Marcial Pons.

Vázquez Fariñas, M. & J. Maldonado Rosso. 2017. Cádiz, ciudad vinatera entre mediados de los siglos XIX y XX. *Revista de Estudios Regionales* 109: 95–119.

5 The *Sociedad Azucarera Antequerana*, a Successful Company in Late Nineteenth-Century Spain

Mercedes Fernández-Paradas and
Francisco José García Ariza

Introduction[1]

The presence of sugar cane in the Iberian Peninsula can be traced back to the ninth century. The first attempts at beet cultivation in Spain date back to 1874 and took place in the region of Andalusia, specifically Vega de Granada and Guadix in the province of Granada (Martín Rodríguez 1982, p.125; Marrón Gaite 1992, pp. 20–27; Almansa 2005; Martín Rodríguez 2011). In 1882 and 1883, the first two sugar beet factories began operating in the provinces of Córdoba and Granada (Martín Rodríguez 1982). At the end of the 1891–1892 season, the provinces of Almería and Málaga also became involved. In that season, two companies were created, one of which was the Sociedad Azucarera Antequerana —the focus of this research. In the decades around the turn of the century, the sugar beet sector grew notably, to the point where there were 151 sugar factories in 1910 (Marrón Gaite 2011, p. 106).

The Sociedad Azucarera Antequerana was established on 18th November 1890 in Antequera, an Andalusian municipality in the north of the province of Málaga. It was an important company: in the early twentieth century it accounted for 5.8% of national production and 13.7% of Andalusian production of beet sugar (Parejo Barranco 1997, p. 230).

This research, based on primary sources —in particular, the Sociedad Azucarera Antequerana Archive— seeks to analyse the process of creating the company and its early years, with a special focus on its promoters and managers. It also examines the construction of the San José sugar factory in Antequera. Furthermore, this study presents an overview of the company's trajectory, characterized in its early years —particularly the 1890s— by the growth in sugar production, revenues, and profits.

Antequera, a Different Sort of Municipality

The Sociedad Azucarera Antequerana was created to respond to the fin-de-siècle crisis, which we will address later. Antequera has long been a unique municipality. Although it has always been one of Andalusia's mid-sized cities, it has not always participated in the productive features of other such cities, referred to as agricultural cities. This was the case from the sixteenth century until the

1960s, when Antequera's economy started to shift towards a predominance of the service sector. Its distinctiveness lies in the coexistence between its agrarian nature and its trade and manufacturing activities, which have capitalized on its advantageous geographical location in the heart of the Andalusia region in southern Spain. It has also benefited from its proximity to cities such as Málaga and Seville, which have played a major role in distributing goods from their respective ports.

At a time when the Spanish and Andalusian economies were becoming more open, the municipality of Antequera was able to generate endogenous growth models based on one or more productive activities; this was the case with the textile industry for part of the nineteenth century (Gómez Moreno & Parejo Barranco 2009).

At the turn of the nineteenth century, of all the mid-sized Andalusian cities that had been involved in the textile business prior to industrialization, Antequera was the only one that managed to consolidate, eventually becoming home to one of the nation's most important woollen industries. Over the course of that century, its textile industry went through two different stages. The first lasted until around 1875 and was a phase of consolidation and expansion. The second, up until the end of the century, was one of stagnation and crisis. The Sociedad Azucarera Antequerana was founded as a response to the fin-de-siècle crisis in general, and the crisis afflicting the textile industry in particular.

In 1861, Antequera was 15th in the ranking of Spain's industrial cities. In that year, approximately 2,000 people, or 20% of its working population, worked in textile factories. This made it the most industrialized municipality in the province of Málaga and one of the most in Andalusia as a whole (Parejo Barranco 1998, p. 148).

In the 1870s, it began to experience an economic recession. In addition to the demand drying up, it was technologically backward and faced domestic and international competition in fabrics, whether wool or cotton. Another underlying factor was that Antequera's business owners had more interest in agriculture, especially olive cultivation.

Between 1875 and 1900, more than 50% of the looms were shut down. At the end of the nineteenth century, the textile industry attempted to modernize by manufacturing blankets and introducing technological improvements. From the turn of the twentieth century until 1914, blankets from Antequera were sent as far as North Africa, South America, and Japan (Parejo Barranco 1987a, p. 335, 1987b). However, these initiatives were not enough. The main cause of the decline was globalization, which led to new territories becoming involved in the competition for markets, which in turn triggered a fall in prices of agricultural products and land rent (Garrabou 1985; Jiménez Blanco 1986). An additional contributing factor was the greater connectedness of the internal market brought about by the expansion of the railway network, which meant the Antequera textile industry faced more competition. By 1887, Antequera was no longer among the group of industrialized Spanish cities (Gómez Moreno & Parejo Barranco 2009, pp. 16–17).

The Antequera economy achieved a recovery in the early twentieth century, based on a different model grounded in the Second Industrial Revolution and the development of other industrial activities, such as oil, electricity, metallurgy, and sugar production. It also made progress in agriculture, with an increase in productivity relying on crops or fruits for export, such as olive oil. The agri-food sector was gradually assuming a greater role, with one of the key activities being the production of beet sugar by the Sociedad Azucarera Antequerana (Parejo Barranco 1987a, pp. 338–339).

The Founders

The Sociedad Azucarera Antequerana was founded in November 1890, by ten men who agreed to contribute capital of 1,500,000 pesetas, with the aim of producing and selling beet sugar. Most of these men were members of Antequera's high society, and some of them were related to each other. Some were heavily involved in national politics, in the ranks of the conservative political parties, and some were notable political leaders.

Of these, the most important was Francisco Romero Robledo (1838–1906), who was the driving force behind the founding of the company, as well as its president and largest shareholder until his death. At first, he subscribed to 250 shares for a total value of 125,000 pesetas, which in the following years he increased to 315,000 pesetas. It is also worth mentioning his political career and family ties, particularly his marriage to Josefa Zulueta Samá, daughter of Julián Zuluela y Amondo. The latter was a wealthy landowner in Cuba and owner of several sugar mills; Romero Robledo's wife inherited a quarter part of one of these mills[2]. He was therefore familiar with this business activity, which in large part explains why he took the initiative to promote it in Antequera. In addition, he had inside information thanks to his political responsibilities; he was a large landowner and he knew how successful beet farming had become in Vega de Granada. During his very active political life as a member of conservative parties, mainly during the last quarter of the nineteenth century and early twentieth century, he held a number of important positions. For example, he was Minister of Overseas Territories and Minister of the Interior on several occasions, as well as President of the Congress of Deputies. He held total political dominance over the municipality of Antequera and the province of Málaga (Ayala Pérez 1974; Parejo Barranco 1987a, p. 373, 2006; Ramos Rovi 2013, pp. 452–453).

The other founders were Luis Vasconi Cano, Lorenzo Borrego Gómez, Fernando Moreno González del Pino, Francisco Bergamín García, Ramón Checa Moreno, Antonio Luna Rodríguez, Juan Franquelo Díaz, José Casco Romero, Ramón Checa Moreno, and José García Sarmiento.

When the Sociedad Azucarera Antequerana was formed, Lorenzo Borrego, who was born not in Antequera but in the municipality of Montejaque, was obliged to subscribe to 200 shares worth 100,000 pesetas[3]. He was on the first Board of Directors and remained a member until July 1894, when he submitted his resignation on the basis that he did not live in Antequera and due to his role as a Member of Congress as he was also a senator (Ramos Rovi 2013, p. 111)[4].

Francisco Bergamín García, born in the municipality of Campillos in Málaga, was a Member of Congress and also on the first Board of Directors. Although he pledged to subscribe to 150 shares with a capital of 75,000 pesetas, in the end he bought 50 shares. He was appointed secretary at the first meeting of the Board of Directors on 18th November 1890, a position he held until the beginning of 1899. His contribution to the company also entailed drawing up contracts for the expropriation of the properties through which the pipes and aqueduct supplying water to the mill would run, as well as preparing the plans for the corresponding construction works. In addition, he represented the Sociedad Azucarera Antequerana in the lawsuit that it filed against the government, opposing the latter's decision to terminate the contracts agreed upon with the sugar producers on paying taxes equivalent to the consumption tax. He excelled as a writer, lawyer, intellectual and politician. He was professor of Political Economics, Commercial Law and Statistics, and also of International Law, as well as being Dean of the Bar Associations of Madrid and Málaga. He was Minister of the Interior, of Education and of Finance, a senator, and Vice President of the Congress of Deputies (Ramos Rovi 2013, pp. 100–101).

Luis Vasconi Cano took 90 shares and was also appointed to lead the first Board of Directors. His participation in the company was due to his being a civil engineer and his experience in the construction of dams, as well as his personal and professional ties with José María Bores Romero, nephew of Francisco Romero. Vasconi Cano drew up the plan for the construction of the Antequera sugar factory and, together with José María Bores, directed the construction works. The two men were also, along with Bergamín, responsible for the survey and implementation of the works on the aqueduct to supply water to the factory. With José García Sarmiento, Luis Vasconi took care of the contract signed with the Compañía de Ferrocarriles Andaluces (Andalusian Railway Company) for the transport of coal to the factory. The collaboration between Luis Vasconi and José María Bores went even further. For example, in the late 1890s they were involved in the expansion works of the Port of Málaga, and in 1902 they formed the Sociedad de Aguas del Cerneja to produce hydroelectricity, and the Sociedad Iberia Concesionaria (Heredia Flores 2014)[5].

Fernando Moreno González del Pino, born in Antequera, committed to 50 shares, contributing a total capital of 25,000 pesetas. He was also a member of the Board of Directors. His most important role in the company was that of substitute chairman at the meetings of the Board of Directors and of the General Shareholders' Meetings, standing in for Romero Robledo, who was often absent. Another of his contributions was his industrial experience, as he was the son of José Moreno Burgos, who, along with his uncle, had been among the largest textile manufacturers in the city. In 1851, Fernando Moreno went to Belgium and France to close the deal on the purchase of machinery for the cotton factory of his father and his uncle, and to gain technical and managerial experience in a French textile factory in Reims. Fernando was not able take over the family factory because the company was dissolved. He opted to diversify his activities, with the purchase and development of land playing a key role, to which end he created an agricultural colony. From his father, he inherited the flour factory, La Concepción, which he gave a technological overhaul. Together with his involvement in the Sociedad Azucarera Antequerana, this shows his innovative spirit (Parejo Barranco 1987a, pp. 331–339, 1995).

José García Sarmiento was born in Antequera. When the company was created, he had to subscribe to 100 shares for a value of 50,000 pesetas. He was a member of the first Board of Directors and all successive boards until his death in 1912. He led the company from his positions of manager and administrative director, which he held from January 1891. He gradually gained control, buying shares himself and through the sale of shares to several nephews by marriage, while also placing relatives in key positions (Fernández-Paradas & García Ariza 2019, pp. 165–166). For example, his nephew Luis Morales was the technical director and accountant from the 1895–1896 season on. Furthermore, after the death of Francisco Romero on 3rd March 1906, José García Sarmiento —who at that time held 250 shares— was selected in the General Shareholders' Meeting to be "effective president" of the company. Immediately afterwards, his son, José García Berdoy, was appointed deputy director[6]. The García Berdoy family took over from Romero Robledo at the head of the city's conservative ranks. Garcia Berdoy controlled the Sociedad Azucarera Antequerana from 1912 until his death in 1953. His role as a businessman went even further: he founded Antequera Cinema in 1932, as well as a woollen fabrics company and a fertilizer company. In addition, he was one of the promoters of the Caja de Ahorros y Préstamos de Antequera (Antequera Savings and Loans Bank) (1903), of which he was president, while also being on the board of the Banco de España in Antequera (Campos Rodríguez 2003).

Ramón Checa Moreno, a native of Antequera, took 30 shares for 15,000 pesetas. Unlike the abovementioned founders, he was not on the Board of Directors. His surname Checa links him to the family of Francisco Romero's mother, Teresa Robledo Checa. It is worth noting that he was one of the few textile manufacturers who attempted to modernize his factory, introducing Jacquard machines and specializing in the production of blankets.

José Casco Romero, also from Antequera, was an agricultural landowner. He was not a member of the Board of Directors. We do not know if he took all the shares he had committed to buy —a total of 40 for 20,000 pesetas— since he died shortly after the founding of the company; in early 1892, his heirs held 30 shares. His second surname, Romero, suggests that he may have been related to Francisco Romero.

Antonio Luna Rodríguez was not from Antequera. He was an alternate director on the first Board of Directors. He bought 30 shares for 15,000 pesetas. A lawyer by trade, he was Dean of the Antequera Bar Association. When Francisco Bergamín was away, Luna Rodríguez stood in as secretary of the Board of Directors, and when the former gave up his position as secretary, he was replaced by the latter. After the death of Francisco Romero, he held the presidency of the Conservative Party of Antequera. His family was related to the García Sarmiento family: his son, José de Luna Pérez, married Carmen

García Berdoy, daughter of José García Berdoy (Postigo Durán 2011, pp. 63 and 76)[7].

Lastly, there was the property registrar, Juan Franquelo Díaz. He bought 30 shares for 15,000 pesetas. He was appointed alternate director on the first Board of Directors. His involvement in the company may have come about due to the fact that he was a property registrar, which would facilitate the task of registering company properties.

The Other Managers

A number of other people also participated in the management of the Sociedad Azucarera Antequerana. We focus here on the most relevant: José María Bores Romero, Diego Wladimir Guerrero de Smirnoff, Ezequiel Ordóñez y González, Luis Morales Bordoy, and Manuel Morales Ruiz.

Diego Wladimir Guerrero de Smirnoff held 100 shares. Shortly after the foundation of the Sociedad Azucarera Antequerana, he was hired as an agricultural engineer. Having qualified abroad, he is considered one of the foremost experts in the cultivation and processing of beet sugar of the late nineteenth and early twentieth centuries. His father was a French engineer, who established a sugar factory in the municipality of Atarfe in the province of Granada, which his son managed. Guerrero stood out for his technological contributions: he applied for the patent for what is known as "triple carbonation". He also wrote several works; it is worth mentioning some of those published in 1893 and 1894 were considered reference works at the time: *La remolacha y la Hacienda. Episodio Nacional*; *La remolacha y la Hacienda. Episodio Nacional: segunda parte*, *Cultivo de la remolacha pobre y cultivo de la remolacha rica*, *¡No más fraude en los abonos! ¡Notas prácticas sobre el empleo económico de los abonos químicos y la adquisición de los materiales fertilizantes*, y *Cómo se obtiene y se cultiva la remolacha azucarera. La remolacha y la Hacienda. Episodio Nacional*. He also translated the renowned book by George Dureau (1891), *Tratado del cultivo de la remolacha azucarera* (A Treatise on the Cultivation of Sugar Beet).

Although José María Bores Romero was not a founding partner of Sociedad Azucarera Antequera, he acquired 50 shares for a capital of 25,000 pesetas shortly after its formation. He was Francisco Romero's nephew. In addition to his family ties to the latter, his involvement in the company can also be explained by his qualifications as a lawyer and a civil engineer. As mentioned above, he drew up the plans for the construction of the factory along with Vasconi, as well as the planning and implementation of the works for the factory aqueduct. Like his uncle and father, he was also engaged in politics. In the 1890s, he was twice elected a member of parliament. From 1898 on, he opted to devote himself exclusively to his professional activity as an engineer and to managing and promoting companies. In addition to the abovementioned companies he promoted with Vasconi, he had a stake in Hidroeléctrica Ibérica, founded in 1901. He also participated in the founding of the Sociedad Electrohidráulica Industrial, which made use of waterfalls in the province of

Granada, he installed electric lighting in Baza, and he set up an esparto fibre factory for paper. His most important project was for the metro in Madrid, but it did not come to fruition. Another project that was implemented was his plan to improve the supply of drinking water to the city of Málaga. With regard to his activity in the electricity sector, it is worth highlighting his writings on the so-called hydroelectric issue. Towards the end of his life he returned to politics; in November 1929, he was elected as a member of the National Assembly in the Primo de Rivera dictatorship and he stood as a candidate in the constitutional elections of June 1931, although he did not win a seat (Pinto Tortosa 2009; Ramos Rovi 2013, p. 110; Heredia Flores 2014).

Ezequiel Ordonez y González was a lawyer and politician in the conservative party. His son, Mariano Ordóñez García, married Francisca Romero Robledo y Zulueta, one of the daughters of Francisco Romero. He subscribed to 50 shares in the Sociedad Azucarera Antequerana for an amount of 25,000 pesetas. His main contribution to the company was as a creditor. After Romero Robledo's death, the Board of Directors appointed him honorary president[8].

Luis Morales Berdoy was the son of Isabel Berdoy, the sister-in-law of José García Sarmiento and Manuel Morales Ruiz (Talavera Quirós 2014, p.181), a worker in the factory. He was technical director of the factory. In late 1895, he travelled to France to improve his professional skills; in particular, he worked with new beet milling machines and in a laboratory. He returned to Antequera in 1896, before going back to France to finish his training. From 1898, he was also in charge of the accounting. In 1902, he travelled to Germany, Austria, Belgium, France, the Netherlands, and Sweden to find out about implementing the Steffen system, concluding that it was not appropriate as it was suitable for places with abundant water and low temperatures, conditions that were not met in Antequera[9].

The Construction of the Sugar Factory

Romero Robledo provided the land for the construction of the factory, transferring it from his Antequera country estate, Casarón de Casablanca, as well as the water, an essential element in sugar manufacturing, in exchange for shares.

As commented above, Luis Vasconi and José María Bores were in charge of the planning and construction of the factory. Antonio María Luna Quartin was responsible for carrying out the building works, and the pipes for the water supply were entrusted to José Morales Cosso, both of whom were shareholders.

The French company Fives-Lille was commissioned to provide the machinery for the factory, as was common practice among this type of company in Andalusia at that time (Piñar Samos & Giménez Yanguas 2013, p. 60). It had the capacity to process 250 tonnes of beets per day, placing it among the largest in the country. Responsibility for assembling the machinery was assigned to Felix Gardin, a French engineer appointed by Fives-Lille, who was also in charge of the sugar production until the end of 1891. Materials for building the factory also had to be bought, including iron girders from Málaga, fire bricks from Glasgow, roof tiles from Marseille, and electrical equipment from Paris. Up to the beginning of 1892, the Sociedad Azucarera Antequerana spent more than 1,230,000 pesetas on equipment. The factory began operating on 4th October 1891[10].

In addition, the company needed a railway siding alongside the tracks from where it would receive coal and machinery and from where the sugar would be sent out. To that end, it signed a contract with the Compañía de Ferrocarriles Andaluces, which was responsible for constructing it[11].

A Growing Company

In the 1891–1892 season, the Sociedad Azucarera Antequerana produced 387,308.50 kilograms (kg) of sugar, which represented 2.7% of national production and 3.7% of Andalusian production. Relative to this first season, production was 1.7 times higher in the 1892–1893 season, reaching 678,585.50 kg, which went up to 1,642,327.40 kg in 1894–1895, that is, it multiplied by 2.4. In 1895–1896, it dropped to 839,199.50 kg. In 1896–1897, it increased to 1,398,630 kg, in 1897–1898 it was 1,594,140 kg and in 1898–1899 it reached 1,883,710 kg, the highest figure of the decade. The last increase can be attributed to Spain's loss of Cuba, a territory where sugar was also produced. In other words, Cuban sugar no longer reached Spain, which boosted production in the factories on the Spanish mainland in order to meet domestic demand[12]. In all but a few seasons, sugar production at the San José factory accounted for the majority of the sugar coming from the province of Málaga (Casado Bellagarza 2015, p.490).

The sale price of sugar per kilogram in 1891–1892 was 0.71 pesetas. In the following years —except in 1897–1898— the price was above 0.80, and in 1899–1900 it was 1.11 pesetas, with this increase being due to the lack of sugar from Cuba. The rise in sugar production and its sale price also had a positive impact on sugar revenues. In 1891–1892, the company generated revenues of 273,976.50 pesetas; five years later, in 1896–1897, the corresponding figure was 1,202,893.80 pesetas, with this amount continuing to rise to 3,403,281.40 in 1899–1900.

These revenues were generated thanks to the company's successful sales strategy, based on hiring representatives to sell their sugar, which enabled it to create a distribution network. In this way, it managed to send its sugar to a large part of the country. In the first campaign of 1891–1892, Antequera sugar was mainly sold in Andalusia; specifically, in Antequera, the Córdoban municipalities of Lucena and Montilla, Cádiz and Málaga. Outside of Andalusia, their product reached Barcelona, Madrid, Murcia and Valencia. In later seasons, more places were able to enjoy the sugar, including La Coruña, Almería, Granada, Huelva, Santander, Seville, Tarragona and Vigo.

As expenses were substantially lower than revenues —in some seasons more than 34% lower— the growth in sugar sales was accompanied by a remarkable rise in the company's profits. In 1891–1892 they totalled 99,196.80 pesetas; two seasons later they had more than doubled, totalling 218,178.20 pesetas.

Compared to the first season, this total was quadrupled in 1896-1894 and in 1899–1900 it was 13.5 times higher[13].

Conclusions

The Sociedad Azucarera Antequerana was founded in Antequera in late 1890, in response to the fin-de-siècle crisis that was afflicting the municipality. This crisis was caused by the greater competition stemming from globalization and the progress of the railway in Spain, which especially affected its textile industry. Promoted by the Antequera politician Francisco Romero Robledo, it became an important company in Andalusia and in Spain.

The group that founded it consisted of ten men, most of whom had family ties with others in the group, and some of whom excelled in various facets of national life, especially politics. Romero Robledo also chose them because their professional profile allowed them to contribute in some way. The same was true of the other managers who were not founders. The infrastructure that enabled the production of the sugar was built quickly, in less than a year. French technology was used, which at the time was considered cutting-edge.

The company's successful trajectory is reflected in the data on sugar production, revenues, and profits from the 1890s.

Notes

1 This study is part of the INGEURSUR, Thematic Network, financed by the University of Malaga.
2 Municipal Historical Archive of Antequera (MHAA), Company Archives (CA), Sociedad Azucarera Antequerana Archive (SAAA), file 226, Division of assets upon the death of Josefa Zulueta, 26th February 1897.
3 To identify the share capital contributed by the partners, we have relied on MHAA, CA, SAAA, file 339, folder 2.
4 MHAA, CA, SAAA, file 336, Sociedad Azucarera Antequerana Annual Report 1893-1894.
5 MHAA, CA, SAAA, Minutes of the Board of Directors, 12th January 1895.
6 MHAA, CA, SAAA, ledger 140.
7 MHAA, CA, SAAA, file 140.
8 MHAA, CA, SAAA, ledger 141, Minutes of the Board of Directors, 30th April 1906.
9 MHAA, CA, SAAA, ledger 141, Minutes of the Board of Directors, 18th November 1890, and file 337, Sociedad Azucarera Antequerana Annual Report 1902–1903.
10 MHAA, CA, SAAA, files 309–310 and 337.
11 MHAA, CA, SAAA, file 253, folder 3.
12 MHAA, CA, SAAA, files 336–338.
13 MHAA, CA, SAAA, files 336–338.

References

Almansa, R. Mª. 2005. Familia, tierra y poder en la Córdoba de la Restauración. Bases económicas, poder político y actuación social de algunos miembros de la élite. Córdoba: Universidad de Córdoba.

Ayala Pérez, J. 1974. Un político de la Restauración Romero Robledo. Antequera: Publicaciones de la Biblioteca Antequerana de la Caja de Ahorros de Antequera.

Campos Rodríguez, J. 2003. José García Berdoy. In 20 Antequeranos del siglo XX, dir., J. M. González Córdoba, 30–32. Antequera: Escuela de Artes Gráficas.

Casado Bellagarza, J. L. (2015). La Colonia Agrícola de San Pedro Alcántara 1857–1910. PhD diss. Universidad de Málaga.

Fernández-Paradas, M., & García Ariza, F. J. 2019. La Sociedad Azucarera Antequerana: una respuesta a la crisis finisecular (1890–1906). In Empresas y empresarios en España. De mercaderes a industriales, coord., J. M. Matés Barco, 153–179. Madrid: Pirámide.

Garrabou, R. 1985. La crisis agraria española de finales del siglo XIX: una etapa de desarrollo al capitalismo. In Historia agraria de la España Contemporánea. 2. Expansión y crisis (1850–1900), eds., R. Garrabou, and J. Sanz Fernández, 477–542. Barcelona: Crítica.

Gómez Moreno, Mª. L. & Parejo Barranco, A. 2009. La economía en transformación: Antequera entre los siglos XX y XXI. El Ejido: Fundación Cajamar.

Guerrero de Smirnoff, D. W. 1893a, Cómo se obtiene y se cultiva la remolacha azucarera. Granada: Tipografía Hospital de Santa Ana.

Guerrero de Smirnoff, D. W. 1893b. Cultivo de la remolacha pobre y cultivo de la remolacha rica. Granada: Tipografía Hospital de Santa Ana.

Guerrero de Smirnoff, D. W. 1894a. La remolacha y la hacienda. Granada: Imprenta de D. José López Guevara.

Guerrero de Smirnoff, D. W. 1894b. La remolacha y la hacienda. Episodio Nacional. Granada: Imprenta de D. José López Guevara.

Guerrero de Smirnoff, D. W. 1894c. ¡No más fraude en los abonos!¡Notas prácticas sobre el empleo económico de los abonos químicos y la adquisición de los materiales fertilizantes. Granada: Establecimiento tipográfico de F. Gómez de la Cruz.

Heredia Flores, V. M. 2014. José Bores Romero, un ingeniero en la España de la Restauración. In Pensar con la Historia desde el siglo XXI, Actas del XII Congreso de la Asociación de Historia Contemporánea, eds., Folguera, P. et al. Madrid: Universidad Autónoma de Madrid Ediciones.

Jiménez Blanco, J. I. 1986. La producción agraria de Andalucía Oriental, 1874–1914. Madrid: Universidad Complutense de Madrid.

Marrón Gaite, Mª. J. 1992. La adopción y expansión de la remolacha azucarera en España (de los orígenes al momento actual). Madrid: Ministerio de Agricultura, Pesca y Alimentación.

Marrón Gaite, Mª. J. 2011. La adopción de una innovación agraria en España: los orígenes del cultivo de la remolacha azucarera. Experiencias pioneras y su repercusión económica y territorial. Estudios Geográficos 270: 103–134.

Martín Rodríguez, M. 1982. Azúcar y descolonización. Origen y desenlace de una crisis agraria en la Vega de Granada. El "Ingenio de San Juan, 1882–1904". Granada: Universidad de Granada.

Martín Rodríguez, M. 2011. Juan López-Rubio Pérez (1829–1913). In Grandes empresarios andaluces, coord. A. Parejo Barranco, 214–221. Madrid: Lid Editorial.

Parejo Barranco, A. 1987a. Historia de Antequera. Antequera: Publicaciones de la Biblioteca Antequerana de la Caja de Ahorros de Antequera.

Parejo Barranco, A. 1987b. Industria dispersa e industrialización en Andalucía: el ejemplo del textil antequerano (1750–1900). Málaga: Universidad de Málaga.

Parejo Barranco, A. 1995. Los viajes europeos de un burgués antequerano: José Moreno Burgos en Bélgica e Inglaterra (1842 y 1851). Revista de Estudios Antequeranos 1: 209–250.

Parejo Barranco, A. 1997. La producción industrial en Andalucía (1830–1935). Sevilla: Instituto de Desarrollo Regional.

Parejo Barranco, A. 1998. Revolución liberal y élites locales. Dos ejemplos antequeranos de la segunda mitad del siglo XIX. In De economía e historia: estudios en homenaje a José Antonio Muñoz Rojas, coords., A. Gómez Mendoza, and A. Parejo Barranco, 139–184. Málaga: Diputación Provincial de Málaga.

Parejo Barranco, A. 2006. Francisco Romero Robledo. Último político romántico. Ingenio de la Restauración (Antequera, 1838-Madrid, 1906). Antequera: Ayuntamiento de Antequera.

Pinto Tortosa, A. J. 2009. El medio agrario andaluz ante la llegada del liberalismo: las revoluciones de 1835 y 1836 en Antequera. Antequera: Ayuntamiento de Antequera.

Postigo Durán, I. 2011. Origen de la industria del azúcar de remolacha en Antequera: las primeras campañas del Ingenio de San José, 1890–1910. Revista de Estudios Antequeranos 15, 53–78.

Piñar Samos, J. & Giménez Yanguas, M. 2013. Motril y el azúcar: paisaje, historia, patrimonio. Granada: Fundación El Legado Andalusí.

Ramos Rovi, M.J. 2013. Diccionario biográfico de parlamentarios andaluces (1876-1923), Sevilla.

Talavera Quirós, R. 2014. Familias Antequeranas. Antequera.

6 Small, Medium and Large Companies in the Supply of Water in Spain (1840–1940)

Juan Manuel Matés-Barco

Introduction

The study of water supply companies confirms the importance that private enterprise has had in the development of public utilities. It also provides information on the types of companies that have emerged to provide these activities and the long-term evolution of the management model. In Spain there is no clear preponderance of the private or public sector in the management of local public utilities (Fernández 2009). For this reason, it is useful to learn about the emergence in the nineteenth century of those companies that would become major players in a sector that has expanded greatly both nationally and internationally (Larrinaga 2008).

In the same vein, several reasons bolster the importance of studying the history of drinking water supply companies in Spain. Firstly, there is the concentration of investment, both national and foreign, that these companies monopolised in order to commence their business activity (Matés-Barco 2002; Castro-Valdivia & Fernández-Paradas 2019, 2020; Martínez 2020). Secondly, the unique typology generated by this business phenomenon allows us to obtain knowledge of matters related to the History of the Company. Finally, there is the fact that these firms burst onto the scene throughout the nineteenth century and became highly prominent, while at the same time pursuing significant advances from a technological point of view. On the other hand, they moved within a legislative framework characterised by the appearance of management techniques such as *natural monopoly* and *administrative concession*, which have played a predominant role in the development of public utilities and in the improvement of public health (Núñez 2000; Matés-Barco, 2004 ; Ruiz-Villaverde 2013).

The historical perspective allows us to glimpse a changing policy on the management model of municipal services (Mirás 2006, p. 1). In the second half of the nineteenth century, the transformation that took place in public utilities had significant impacts that affected the economy and technological development. The study of the regulation of *administrative concessions* and the confluence of public and private interests are issues that illustrate the search for solutions to the problems caused by urban growth (Ferreira da Silva & Cardoso de Matos 2004, p. 3; Matés-Barco 2018b).

However, despite the importance of the sector, it has been one of the most forgotten by historiography. Within the analysis of public utilities, much attention has been paid to other sectors – especially electricity, gas, and trams – but interest in the business development of the supply of household drinking water has been side-lined. The reasons may be related to the linkage of those other sectors with banking – which has been much studied – and the large investments required for power plants and railways. In countries such as Great Britain, France, and Italy, there are abundant studies on the management of water supply services, both from the perspective of companies and municipalities, as well as with respect to the evolution of the sector itself.

Between 1840 and 1939, one can observe the creation of a significant number of private companies dedicated to the supply of water. After this period of expansion, a new stage (1940–1980) saw their progressive disappearance from the business panorama. Only a few companies resisted the interventionist policies of the successive governments of the time. More recently (1981–2012), there has been a resurgence of private management in the water supply sector, marked by an essentially integrative dynamic both vertically and horizontally. There are various reasons for municipalities to adopt this trend. Firstly, there is the existence of a dynamic that wishes to take advantage of the managerial and financial capacity of large private groups. Secondly, there is the strategy of breaking free from the power of the unions in public companies. Finally, there is the manifest desire to reduce local government and generate income for municipal treasuries (Bel 2006, p. 43; González-Gómez 2006, p. 142). However, in recent years, the call to establish legal norms that permit the "re-municipalisation" of these services has been heard once again in certain municipal spheres. As can be seen, the trend with respect to the management of this public service is cyclical and shifting. Some authors have called it a "to-and-fro process".

In order to highlight the importance that private companies have had in the development of the sector in Spain, it may be useful to make a brief reference to the situation in other countries. In Western Europe, public management of the drinking water supply service predominates, and in some countries such as Austria, Denmark, Greece, Holland, and Luxembourg it is absolutely dominant. In others such as Portugal, Sweden, Italy, Belgium, Finland, and Germany, the management by private companies is negligible and almost irrelevant. This pattern is broken by France and Great Britain, where the presence of private water supply companies has a long tradition, to the point that in the first years of the twenty-first century the figures were 75% and 88% of the municipalities, respectively. On the other hand, in the United States, private ownership of this sector dropped throughout the nineteenth century. While at the beginning of the eighteenth century the predominance of private ownership was overwhelming, by 1915 only 31.4% of water supply services were in private hands, and by 2002, after decades of dithering, only 10% of U.S. municipalities had a privately-run water supply. (Bel 2006, pp. 78, 119 and 121; Matés-Barco 2013, 2019b).

This research has been based on abundant source documents that provide fairly complete information on these companies. Among these are the *Revista de Obras Públicas, Memorias y Estadísticas Diversas* (Journal of Public Works, Reports and Miscellaneous Statistics), the financial yearbooks, and the abundant documentation in the municipal and state archives. Likewise, the *Catálogo de Sociedades de abastecimiento de agua potable* (Catalogue of Drinking Water Supply Companies) presents an exhaustive study of the existing bibliography and detailed information on each of the 273 companies that appeared in Spain between 1840 and 1990 (Matés-Barco 1997, 2014).

In this chapter, after this brief introduction, the next section deals with the context of water supply companies in relation to other public utilities such as electricity. The third and fourth sections analyse the different types of companies according to the size of their investments. In the fifth section, a brief overview is made with respect to the notions of risk and uncertainty that existed in this business at the beginning of its establishment in the cities. Finally, some brief conclusions are drawn, and the sources and bibliography are included.

Public Utilities in Spain

In the second half of the nineteenth century, many of these companies emerged thanks to the investment of foreign capital, especially British, French, and Belgian (Castro-Valdivia & Matés-Barco, 2020). These investors contributed their knowledge, technology, and industrial material to the development of this business sector. As Fernández-Paradas (2009, p. 110) indicates, this phenomenon was not limited to water supply companies, but was the result of a trend that was occurring in some public utilities, most notably the railways and the first gas, tram, and electricity companies (Bartolomé 2007, p. 31).

To compare the size of the water supply companies with other sectors, the choice was made on the basis of the size of the investment (railways), their novelty and connection to urban services (electricity), and similarity in investment parameters (textiles). It is clear that the railway companies were at a very high level, which does not allow for any kind of meaningful comparison with water companies.

Electricity companies, despite being above the investment capacity of the water companies and being much more numerous, operated at a relatively similar level. Isabel Bartolomé (2007, pp. 30–35 and 103–107), has highlighted the continued existence of a significant number of small companies, most of which had equity of less than five million pesetas around 1925. She notes the existence of large companies along with other very small ones. In 1935, the basic resources of the standard electricity company did not exceed ten million pesetas. In any case, the upward trend of the electricity companies can be observed, thanks to the process of consolidation they were undergoing, while the water companies remained almost static during this decade.

The situation of textile companies was the same; although they enjoyed a slightly higher investment than water companies, their profile was almost parallel to them. For gas companies, Mercedes Fernández-Paradas (2009, pp. 121–122) describes that there were more small companies and that their basic resources did not exceed five million pesetas. Among the large gas companies, which were in the minority, the differences in the volume of their resources were very noticeable and could range from 10 to 390 million pesetas.

This brief comparison shows that the water companies operated at a similar level to other industrial sectors and were fairly well established in the 1920s and 1930s, with very stable development in the medium term. In essence, it had become a sector that was not experiencing major shocks, where investments were coming in that were perhaps not very large – in comparison with other areas – but which ensured a certain subsistence.

The Large Companies

Were these water supply businesses large companies or were they more in line with the hesitant beginnings of small, family-run businesses? In order to understand the size of the water companies in context, and to glimpse the degree of integration that existed with the development of the company in Spain, the work carried out by Carreras and Tafunell (1994) has been used as a model. While the special attention that these authors dedicate to large industrial companies, banks, and insurance companies means that they do not include the performance of any water company, it does serve as a reference for this comparative analysis. In order to establish a basic classification, a division has been made in order to ascertain the size of the companies: (a) small, with a capital of less than 0.2 million pesetas; (b) medium-sized, between 0.2 and 1.9 million pesetas; and (c) large, with an investment of more than two million pesetas.

This segmentation was made on the basis of various criteria. The first is due to the fact that the data available for the first decades of the twentieth century have been taken as a reference, since it is the period in which the greatest number of water supply businesses were set up and can be considered the expansion years of the sector. The second refers to a better understanding of the business behaviour of other sectors, and therefore it is possible to establish the level at which the water companies operated. Finally, during this period there are better statistical inputs, allowing us to know the trends and progress of each company. These data make it possible to ascertain the average capital of a water company for a series of years; between 1922 and 1934, investment moved between 1.64 and 1.78 million pesetas, with a peak in 1930 that reached 1.93 million pesetas. For this reason, a company with more than two million pesetas in capital could be considered one of the largest in the sector.

In general, these water companies did not particularly stand out for their large size. The very structure of the supplies determined the existence of a wide variety of situations. Before 1880, it was common for small companies to emerge, even in the larger cities, as the practice of monopolies was not yet very well established; however, between 1881 and 1900, the appearance of companies of considerable size began (Villar-Chamorro et al., 2019).

The data on total assets refer for the most part to the most profitable and longest-lasting companies. Most companies had total assets of between four and eight million pesetas at their peak in the 1920s. Of course, the two biggest companies in the sector, Aguas de Barcelona and Aguas Potables y Mejoras de Valencia, were much larger than this.

Between 1860 and 1899, a small number of large companies was established in the water market, but this occurrence took place very slowly. It is evident that the size of the town determined to a great extent the size of the company, and in Spain large cities were not very abundant. It is not easy to specify the level of investment per capita in the different towns since it did not meet uniform criteria. However, what is clear is that the growing demand, not only in terms of quantity but also in the quality of the service provided, encouraged the establishment of these companies. They were trying to reach an optimum demand point that would guarantee their viability over the medium and long term. Barcelona stood out because of the rapid and massive incorporation of private companies into the management of the water supply, but in Madrid the same effect did not occur; there it was the state that initially undertook the management of the service (Matés-Barco 2018a, 2019a). Until the twentieth century, the capital of the kingdom was an administrative city with little private enterprise. This situation explains to some extent the absence of private companies in the water sector. Private water supply companies emerged in Valencia and Alicante somewhat later than Barcelona.

The source documents show two companies at the beginning of the sector, Aguas de Morón y Carmona (1853) and Aguas de Jerez (1868), which were set up with 1.1 and 8.7 million pesetas of nominal capital, respectively. This meant an investment of 37 and 166 pesetas per inhabitant which, despite the differences between the two, were significant amounts. Comparing the nominal capital with the classification of the main public limited companies made by Carreras and Tafunell (1994, p. 92) for 1866–1867, the Jerez company would be approximately at number 33, on par with a solid group of insurance, finance, and gas lighting companies. It should be remembered that, of the fifteen largest companies, thirteen were railway companies, and water supply was a sector that was just beginning to emerge at this time.

In the last decades of the nineteenth century, 1870–1899, the existence of seven companies of this type is observed, which established themselves in the business thanks to the expansion and strong growth of the sector. In 1871, Aguas Subterráneas del Río Llobregat was created and in 1882 Aguas de Barcelona emerged. The latter company, which was backed by foreign capital, took advantage of a large number of small companies that had paved the way in the city and gradually absorbed them over the following years. Sevilla Water Works (1881) dates from this period and also made a significant investment: 8.7 million pesetas, making it the third largest company in the sector at that time. Somewhat later were Aguas Potables y Mejoras de Valencia (1890) and Aguas de Alicante (1898), with 7.5 and five million pesetas in capital, respectively. From these years, we must highlight the appearance of La Hondura (1898) in Puerto de la Cruz on the island of Tenerife, and Fomento Agrícola Castellonense (1888), which despite its name had among its objectives the supply of drinking water. Both companies stand out, the first for the size of its investment, five million pesetas, large for a small island town; the second, with an investment of 1.1 million, is notable for its early combination of supplying water for domestic consumption and for irrigation.

There is a very significant peculiarity; the largest companies were concentrated in towns with more than 30,000 inhabitants and there seems to be a certain relationship with the rate of population growth. Except for Jerez and Seville, which had annual rates of less than 1%, the rest of the cities were growing faster than this, even at double that rate. The reason for this trend seems obvious; large companies were interested first in those cities with the greatest customer potential in order to take advantage of economies of scale. As can be seen in Table 6.1, the date of the establishment of companies in capitals such as Barcelona, Valencia, Seville, Alicante, Valladolid, and Santander are tangible examples (Matés-Barco 2006 and 2008d).

Obviously, the small and medium-sized cities were an interesting market in the second phase, once the best prospects had been developed. These towns, because of their size, did not require such a big investment as the previous ones. Furthermore, in the medium-sized urban centres, small entrepreneurs often emerged, interested in developing local businesses that did not require too great an investment. On the other hand, there was no tendency for these

Table 6.1 Large Water Supply Companies (1933)

Company	Year founded	Municipality	Nominal capital (ptas.)
Aguas de Barcelona	1882	Barcelona	40,000,000
Aguas Subterráneas del Río Llobregat	1871	Barcelona	10,000,000
Sevilla Water Works	1881	Sevilla	8,750,000
Aguas de Jerez	1868	Jerez de la Frontera	7,500,000
Aguas Potables y Mejoras de Valencia	1890	Valencia	7,500,000
Aguas de Alicante	1898	Alicante	5,000,000
La Hondura	1898	Puerto de la Cruz	5,000,000
Aguas de Ceuta	1911	Ceuta	4,000,000
Empresas Hidráulicas de Canarias	1933	Las Palmas	3,765,000
Omnium Ibérico	1902	Alcira	3,200,000
City of Las Palmas Water & Power	1913	Las Palmas	3,125,000
Arandina de Aguas Potables	1933	Aranda de Duero	2,562,500
Aguas de La Coruña	1903	Coruña	2,500,000
Aguas de León	1923	León	1,500,000
Hidráulica Santillana	1905	Madrid	2,000,000
Canal de la Huerta de Alicante	1907	Alicante	2,000,000
Suministro de Aguas Potables	1924	Tarrasa	2,000,000

Source: prepared by author with data from: *Estadística de la Contribución de utilidades de la Riqueza Mobiliaria* (1905, 1910, and 1915); *Anuario Técnico e Industrial de España* (1913), *Anuario Financiero y de Sociedades Anónimas de España* (1922–1970); *Anuario Financiero de Bilbao* (1930–1934)

firms to merge; urban supply was a very compartmentalised market with a clear predilection for each town to have its own company.

The balance sheet for the period 1840–1940 shows that it was not usual to find large companies involved in the water sector. In the total calculation they represent 18.08%. The period that saw the greatest appearance of this type of company was between 1868 and 1900, but from then on much of this trend faded away. In the first decades of the twentieth century, some companies were set up that can be included in this group, but their individual importance was relatively low compared to companies in other sectors.

Small and Medium-Sized Companies

In the large group of medium-sized companies, 46.8% of the total, it is difficult to establish criteria that mark the profile of this type of company. They were established in both large and medium-sized cities, and even in some small ones. The population growth rates were very diverse, but it can be seen that these municipalities became very dynamic nuclei. We can mention the cases of Linares, Motril, Cartagena, Reus, Córdoba, and Manzanares, among others. Despite the chronological differences, there was a tendency to set up these companies in the first decades of the twentieth century, once the potential of the sector had been identified.

Large companies were not interested in markets that lacked potential, and sometimes there were no local entrepreneurs with sufficient financial or technical capacity to devote themselves to water management. Nevertheless, companies emerged that came about through the contribution of a group of local people, as was the case of Aguas de Arteta in Pamplona. The low nominal value of the shares – 100, 75, 50 pesetas, and sometimes even up to 25 pesetas per share – and the company names they adopted such as "Popular Ovetense", "Hijos de…", "Viuda de…" show the local and family nature of these initiatives.

Most of these companies managed the service for many years. This data allows us to assume that the business had to provide a certain return or at least break even. Some of these companies, equipped with financial resources, managed to establish themselves and grow in the sector (Matés-Barco 2009). That would include Aguas del Canto (1923), which supplied Elda, and Aguas Potables de Barbastro (1905), which, despite having very limited initial capital, managed to keep their business operating for over fifty years. Table 6.2 includes the companies that can be considered medium-sized, according to the capital invested. At the beginning of the sector it was not a very numerous group, but it began to grow in the first decades of the twentieth century and became practically the most represented.

As for small companies, 35.1% of the total, their significance cannot be overlooked. Firstly, they have enormous aggregate importance as they form a considerable group in terms of the total number of companies established. Individually they did not contribute very much investment, but all together they were a force to be reckoned with. Secondly, these companies had the

Table 6.2 Medium-Sized Water Supply Companies (1933)

Company	Year founded	Municipality	Nominal capital (ptas.)
Aguas de Reus	1913	Reus	1,600,000
Aguas Potables de la Murtra	1927	Barcelona	1,600,000
Aguas y alcantarillado de Manzanares	1918	Manzanares	1,500,000
Servicios Públicos	1926	Madrid	1,500,000
Hidráulica de Villarrobledo	1926	Villarrobledo	1,500,000
Aguas y Fuerzas del Brugent	1927	Barcelona	1,500,000
Aguas de Almendralejo	1927	Almendralejo	1,500,000
Fomento Agrícola Castellonense	1888	Castellón de la Plana	1,400,000
Aguas de Morón y Carmona	1853	Morón de la Frontera	1,125,000
Acueducto Príncipe Alfonso	1912	Villanueva y Geltrú	1,113,500
Abastecimiento de Sabadell	1903	Sabadell	1,000,000
Aguas Potables de Valdepeñas	1923	Valdepeñas	1,000,000
Aguas de Huelva	1925	Huelva	1,000,000
Cartagena Mining & Water C. Ltd.	1889	Cartagena	750,000
Aguas de Ciudad Real	1919	Ciudad Real	750,000
Aguas Potables de Córdoba	1891	Córdoba	725,000
Aguas de Linares	1908	Linares	620,000
Aguas del Gévora	1878	Badajoz	618,000
Aguas Potables de Alcázar de San Juan	1908	Alcázar de San Juan	600,000
Acueducto Vilanovés	1912	Villanueva y Geltrú	600,000
Aguas Potables de Barcelona	1924	Barcelona	600,000
Aguas de Cataluña	1927	Barcelona	600,000
Aguas de Argentona a Mataró	1922	Mataró	552,000
Aguas de Motril	1902	Motril	535,000
Aguas Potables de San Felíu de Guixols	1923	San Felíu de Guixols	510,000
Aguas de Santa Bárbara	1887	Cartagena	500,000
Aguas del Tibidabo	1928	Barcelona	500,000
Aguas Yerem Tomás	1929	Masnou	500,000
Empresa Hidrofórica	1848	Reus	473,500
Andalusia Water C. Ltd.	1912	Algeciras	437,500
Aguas de Lugo	1905	Lugo	350,000
Aguas Potables de Barbastro	1905	Barbastro	300,000
Aguas de Tafalla	1914	Tafalla	300,000
Aguas Potables y Riegos	1923	Valencia	300,000
La Salud	1910	Castro del Río	282,275
Aguas Potables de Cádiz	1885	Cádiz	250,000
Urbanizaciones	1925	San Cugat del Vallés	250,000
Aguas y Mejoras de Alcácer	1928	Alcácer	250,000
La Estrella	1918	Villa del Río	234,250
Aguas del Canto	1923	Elda	225,000
Aguas de Denia	1870	Denia	200,000
La Fraternidad	1900	Martos	200,000
La Alameda	1909	Bujalance	200,000
La Constancia	1923	Espejo	200,000

Source: prepared by author with data from: *Estadística de la Contribución de utilidades de la Riqueza Mobiliaria* (1905, 1910, and 1915); *Anuario Técnico e Industrial de España* (1913); *Anuario Financiero y de Sociedades Anónimas de España* (1922–1970); *Anuario Financiero de Bilbao* (1930–1934).

capacity to adapt to markets that were not very expansive, possessed little economic dynamism, and were unattractive to large companies, but which demanded the provision of the service: small rural towns, isolated enclaves, etc. These companies played a significant role, since they facilitated the installation of a residential water supply in locations that would otherwise have taken many years to adopt this public service.

Small-sized companies began to spring up in small and medium-sized towns, thanks to the gap left by the large companies, which were more interested in focusing on larger markets with greater growth potential. These small companies emerged essentially at two times: in the early stages of the sector, between 1860 and 1890, especially in large towns but linked to the supply of a neighbourhood or a small area of the city; and in the early years of the twentieth century, once the potential of the business had been recognised and it had been observed that the large companies were not very interested in the small markets far removed from their radius of activity. In Table 6.3, companies with low levels of capital have been included. Their low investment capacity soon forced them to transfer their concession rights to other firms that could afford the costs of the first installations. These small businessmen were of little importance, and disappeared quickly, but the significance they had as precursors and forerunners of the water business should be emphasised. While their attempts were mostly in vain due to the high investments required for the supplies, they were pioneers who marked a clear path forward in the implementation of the service.

Before 1890, the best examples were the companies that appeared in Barcelona; numerous companies were registered in the *Registro Mercantil*, some with a capital of just 5,000 pesetas (Matés-Barco 2019a). These initiatives were a faithful reflection of the attempts by many small entrepreneurs to enter the water business, but also of their limited reach. Of course, this situation was repeated in other places in Spain with similar characteristics; companies with limited capital emerged in small communities, with few pretensions from local investors and a minuscule and shaky profile. Frustrated actions such as *La Aurora* (1846) in Madrid, which could not even come up with the guarantee bond, led to state intervention with the creation of the *Canal de Isabel II*. A similar situation can be seen in Valencia with the creation of *Aguas de Bufilla* (1848), and in La Coruña, with initiatives such as those of *Jean Bouchard* (1860) and *Luis Petit* (1863). The absence of large companies in this first stage can be attributed to the poverty of the Spanish economy, which was not able to take on the necessary investments for the acquisition of new technologies. Everything seems to indicate that the economic backwardness meant that the markets were very small, and that, since there were no large urban and industrial concentrations with sufficient demand to attract this type of service, it became very challenging to set up these companies (González-Ruiz 2013; Garrido-González 2015).

The cooperation and merging of many of these small and medium-sized companies would have provided a smoother entry into the water business, but the transaction costs involved in these agreements made that solution difficult to

Table 6.3 Small Water Supply Companies (1933)

Company	Year founded	Municipality	Nominal capital (ptas.)
Aguas de Aldaya	1909	Aldaya	190,000
Aguas Potables de Ripollet-Sardañola	1917	Barcelona	180,000
Aguas Potables de Palamós	1903	Palamós	157,600
Aguas de los Molinos	1923	Los Molinos	150,000
Aguas de Villafranca	1924	Villafranca del Penedés	150,000
La Crevillentina	1903	Crevillente	100,000
La Esperanza	1913	Segorbe	100,000
Hidráulica San Pascual	1914	Yecla	100,000
Agua Potable de Seo de Urgel	1918	Seo de Urgel	100,000
Aguas de San Pedro de Ribas	1924	San Pedro de Ribas	100,000
Citi, Aguas Subterráneas	1927	Valencia	100,000
Aguas de San Vicente de Castellet	1914	San Vicente de Castellet	90,000
Hidráulica Carpense	1923	El Carpio	90,000
Aguas de las Hortichuelas	1925	Berja	90,000
La Abastecedora	1927	Angulo	90,000
Aguas de Valmaseda	1898	Valmaseda	75,000
Aguas de Cangas de Onís	1913	Cangas de Onís	75,000
Aguas de Urduliz	1926	Urduliz	75,000
El Llano	1926	San Sebastián de Gomera	75,000
San Juan	1917	Lobosillo	50,000
Riegos de Moró	1926	Villafamés	50,000
Aguas Potables de Caudé	1927	Zaragoza	50,000
Sondeos y Explotaciones	1904	Las Palmas	47,500
Aguas Potables de Zamora	1868	Mazarrón	45,000
Los Cartageneros	1896	Cartagena	40,000
Aguas Potables de Santa Catalina del Monte	1887	Murcia	30,000
La Antisequía	1894	Elche	30,000
Aguas Potables de Callús	1925	Callús	30,000
Aguas Potables de Aspe	1927	Aspe	25,000
Aguas Potables de Guisona	1910	Guisona	20,500
Aguas Potables de Cáceres	1899	Cáceres	20,000
El Progreso de Cieza	1914	Cieza	2,000
El Carranchalet	1894	San Vicente de Raspeig	1,000

Source: prepared by author with data from: *Estadística de la Contribución de utilidades de la Riqueza Mobiliaria* (1905, 1910, and 1915); *Anuario Técnico e Industrial de España* (1913), *Anuario Financiero y de Sociedades Anónimas de España* (1922–1970); *Anuario Financiero de Bilbao* (1930–1934).

achieve. In addition, the inexperience of the entrepreneurs was compounded by the uncertainty inherent in the lack of knowledge of the business and the primitivism of the cooperative spirit. Large foreign investors or entrepreneurs more willing to invest ended up with many of these concessions. This process, which was repeated in several cities – Barcelona, Cádiz, Seville, Jerez, La Coruña, and Alicante – is a significant example of the trend that prevailed in the early stages of the sector (Mirás 2004). When entrepreneurs discovered that it was actually possible to set up a profitable and stable business – during the final decades of the nineteenth century and the first decades of the twentieth century – and that the organisational technique of the *administrative concession* respected private management, nothing prevented Spanish developers from entering the sector to the full extent of their abilities. In any case, the dynamism of large cities like Barcelona continued to exert a very powerful draw on all types of companies, and it was common for the number of companies to continue to grow despite the presence of the largest company in the sector. The two small companies that emerged well into the twentieth century – *Aguas Potables de Barcelona* (1924) and *Aigües de Catalunya* (1927) – are clear examples.

In the large cities, and especially in the late nineteenth century, small companies did not have great potential for the future. These markets were very much in demand by the large companies, which quickly asserted themselves. Moreover, the pace of demand was growing very rapidly in these cities and small companies could not cope with the large investments that were needed in a very short time period. It was logical, therefore, that their role was merely anecdotal, as they were simply trailblazers without sufficient capacity to satisfy the market.

From 1900 onwards, however, the tables seem to have turned and there was a new flowering of small businesses, especially in smaller towns, which were unappetising markets for large firms. In these places, once the business was established, it does not seem that the future was particularly dark for small companies. During this period, companies emerged that settled in second- and third-tier towns: *Aguas Potables de Cieza, Aguas Potables de Tobarra* in Hellín, *Augusto Burgos* in Moguer, *Ramón Gorasabel* in Toro, *Aguas Potables de Talavera de la Reina*, etc. Even in the *Anuario* of 1930, for example, there were companies of this size that had been managing the water business for many years: *La Crevillentina* (1903), *Aguas de Denia* (1870), *La Antisequía* (1894), *Aguas de San Vicente de Castellet* (1914), *Aguas de Villafranca* (1914), *Aguas Potables de Barbastro* (1905), *La Fraternidad* (1900), *Aguas de Lugo* (1905), etc. In the end, these companies survived if there was no competition, otherwise they were doomed to vanish or be absorbed by a larger company.

In short, faced with the continuous failed attempts of other initiatives or of the municipal authorities themselves, in the late nineteenth century new companies began to emerge to deal with the problem of water supply. These were small companies promoted by some local leaders, which issued shares at a very low nominal value (25 or 50 pesetas), in order to attract small savers, and which included terms such as "cooperative" or "popular" in their company name as an expression of their local and family nature. In general, the small size of the companies was combined with a limited capacity for medium-term growth as they supplied small population bases. The progressive interventionism that was exercised on the sector limited its potential even more, to the point that the only alternative that remained was to accept municipalisation, although in this respect they were not too different from other larger companies.

Risk and Uncertainty in the Water Business

Water utilities can be considered a low-risk, stable business and when well-managed they attracted the investment of the small saver. But if the differences between short-, medium-, and long-term risks are analysed in detail, it can be seen that the establishment of this type of company was not easy. The case studies show that these companies faced the type of risk existing in any business, which was generally related to the unforeseen events that occurred during the installation of the service (Knight 1921).

On the other hand, companies were often faced with low demand and serious difficulties in attracting new subscribers. The plight that the pioneering companies in the sector encountered when establishing themselves in a city was not uncommon. Theirs was a completely new service that the public was not used to paying for, and there was clear resistance from the neighbours to paying a fee. The introduction of new hygiene practices facilitated the extension of the water supply service, but the public was very slow to adopt them. Technical obstacles also generated uncertainty in this business; for example, there were often problems in finding sufficient water flows and the large capital investment required for the initial installation was challenging. However, once the business had been established in a city for some time, demand tended to increase, which ensured medium- and long-term profits. In other words, once consolidated, companies were usually able to survive and found no major impediments to managing the water supply over a long period of time (González & Núñez 2008, p. 300).

To limit the effects of possible risks, companies employed a variety of techniques. In the 1870s and 1880s, small companies often coped by limiting their initial investments as much as possible and practising a very slow growth policy. On many occasions this strategy was a failure because other more dynamic companies with deeper pockets ended up absorbing them and dominating the market. For their part, the larger firms, in addition to the strong economic backing they enjoyed, tended to make large bond issues in order to obtain resources and attract investors seeking a secure income and as a means of reducing risk (Núñez & Segreto 1994).

Once these problems had been solved, the operating risks over the medium-term were small, except for the so-called "institutional risk", i.e. a change of attitude on the part of the public authorities which could make it very challenging for companies to operate, and which in the end proved to be insurmountable. A good example is the interventionist policies practiced from about 1924, which regulated the water supply service with tariff controls and the obligation to extend the supply to the entire population (Fernández 2007, p. 299; Mirás 2003, p. 41; Núñez 2004, p. 210).

On the other hand, there was a group of companies that lagged behind or had difficulties in offering a certain level of profitability in the short term. Slow growth in demand in some areas, supply difficulties, and the lack of knowledge of the sector may have been the causes of their weak performance. In turn, the rise in industrial wages would help explain why the profit margins were low and the level of investment fell until the start of the twentieth century. Making these companies profitable involved a medium- to long-term approach since it was difficult for demand to grow immediately and automatically. It was necessary to break old habits and outdated supply models and to overcome the inertia and resistance among the population, goals that could not be achieved in months or even a few years.

The data available from some companies in their early stages – even if they are from the first years of the twentieth century – show slow but positive growth; only after several years – a decade or more – do the advantages of economies of scale begin to appear. A detailed analysis reveals an interesting fact: once the initial years had passed – with the attraction generated by a completely new product and the reactivation of the demand that came about starting in 1917–1918 – water supply was seen as a fairly profitable business from 1920 onwards. The enormous number of companies that were founded during these years is another good example of what has been said. The shallowness of the crisis of the early 1930s must be mentioned. Profits did not collapse during the Republic (Tafunell 1996, p. 40), as might be assumed. In fact, the supply of water was a very stable business once it had been consolidated, due to the inelasticity of demand and the existing monopoly on supply. An example of this is *Aguas de Arteta* (1893), which despite its rocky start, was earning profits in 1930 and paying a dividend of 9.5%.

In this context, one can understand why some companies diversified their business activities and attempted to make the supply of drinking water compatible with other undertakings. This strategy was prompted by the uncertainty that existed in the early stages of the sector, when it was not clear whether selling water to households would be profitable. For this reason, the interest in the production and distribution of electrical energy was combined with the digging of wells for irrigation.

To sum up, there was an initial period, 1900–1917, in which water supply companies established and stabilised themselves. Then came the years of maximum expansion and the highest levels of profit, between 1918 and 1936. From a more general perspective, Tafunell (1996) speaks of another major disruption that occurred during the years of the First World War. From 1915 to 1918, there was an explosion in profits, which to a large extent was to be rolled back by inflation.

The growth of the sector in the 1920s shows that there was no lag between investment and profits. Moreover, the rise in investment was significantly stronger than the rise in profits. A hypothetical explanation for such a peculiar phenomenon may be that the sensational investment boom of those years was financed in part by profits accumulated during the First World War (Tafunell 1996, pp. 46–47). After the hiatus of the Spanish Civil War, between 1940 and 1955, almost all companies experienced a downward trend in profitability, which led to the municipalisation of many of them. From that moment on, the surviving companies experienced a clear recovery in their performance, thanks to Spain's economic development and increased demand. This sparked a strategy of business takeovers led mainly by *Aigües de Barcelona*, which over these forty years had become the representative figure of the private sector: "He who resists, wins".

Conclusions

Private water supply companies played an important role in the late nineteenth and early twentieth centuries. Their establishment in the different regions coincided with the urban and industrial map existing in those years in Spain. The relationship between regions with strong urban or industrial growth and the establishment of drinking water supply companies is evident.

Catalonia, Andalusia, Valencia, and Murcia were the regions with the highest concentration of companies, both in terms of the number of companies and the amount of capital invested. The majority of their employees were located in three areas: Barcelona, Alicante, and Valencia, which accounted for the largest number of companies, while in Andalusia they were more spread out due to the region's urban structure. The most industrialised areas, such as Catalonia, which experienced strong demographic growth, received a large proportion of the investment initiative. A similar story played out in Basque Country, although to a lesser extent, given that the scale of the investment in Barcelona frustrates any attempt at comparison.

Andalusia represented a region with strong urban roots and a great need for water, and this was one of the important areas where a significant number of companies took root. Above all, they were seeking the demographic market offered by the agro-towns and the mining areas, both very important in this zone. This region did not cling to a model in which private enterprise predominated and by 1950 the existence of municipalised services was already detected. The localities that still had private water companies at that time were small and rather inconsequential. On other occasions, the municipalised service and the concession to a private company coexisted in the same city, which over time ended up being absorbed by the municipality.

Overall, the capital invested in Catalonia and Andalusia stands out from that disbursed in other areas of the country. The Valencia region benefitted from its dual nature, on the one hand as an enclave of important agricultural cities, and on the other, for being the third most industrialised region of the country. In addition, the coordination of the domestic water supply with the search for water for irrigation played an important role in the development of this sector in this area of the Mediterranean.

In the rest of the regions – Aragon, Asturias, Balearic Islands, Extremadura, and La Rioja – the entrepreneurial initiatives were characterized by being small entities that emerged between 1870 and 1900, that is, in the early stages of the sector. All of them began with minimal capital, had the attraction of belonging to a virtually uncharted sector, and were the result of the dynamism of small entrepreneurs willing to embark on projects that were novel in the late nineteenth century.

The business of supplying drinking water had its own characteristics that distinguished it from other economic activities: a regulated sector, a natural monopoly, and the establishment of tariffs by the town councils. These particularities determined the way in which the private water companies operated in the late nineteenth and early twentieth centuries. For example, the companies were faced with excessive market control and displayed a certain diffidence in the face of competition. As time went by, the predominance of large companies was the rule. At the same time, small companies gradually disappeared, sometimes because of the successive takeover processes they underwent and, on other occasions, because of the municipalisation policies of local councils.

Small-, medium-, and large-sized companies were the result of the investment actions of foreign companies in Spain, but we cannot ignore the role played by a good number of entrepreneurs, developers, and local community leaders who saw the water business as an important market niche. Despite the economic crises and political ups and downs, some of these companies have endured over time, a fact that shows that they had relatively secure profitability and stability.

Sources

Anuario de Sociedades Anónimas (GARCEB) 1918–1923. *Estudio económico financiero de las existentes en España*. Madrid: Ed. de José García Ceballos, Suc. de Rivadeneyra.

Anuario Financiero de Bilbao which includes the Historial de los Valores Públicos y de Sociedades Anónimas de España [AFB]. (1915–1972). *Aguas*. Bilbao: Banco de Vizcaya.

Anuario Financiero de Valores Mobiliarios (AFVM) 1916–1918. *Sociedades de aguas*. Madrid.

Anuario Financiero y de Sociedades Anónimas de España [AFSAE]. 1916–1977. *Sociedades de Aguas Potables y de Riegos*. Madrid.

Anuario Técnico e Industrial de España [ATIE]. 1913. *Empresas y sociedades de abastecimiento de aguas*. Madrid.

Dirección General de Contribuciones. 1901–1933. *Estadística de la Contribución de Utilidades de la Riqueza Mobiliaria*. Madrid.

Estadística de Obras Públicas. 1895–1900. *Compañías concesionarias de abastecimientos de aguas*. Madrid: Ministerio de Fomento.

Reseña Geográfica y Estadística de España 1888. *Obras de abastecimiento*. Madrid.

Revista de Obras Públicas. 1851–1990. Madrid: Colegio de Ingenieros de Caminos, Canales, y Puertos.

References

Bartolomé, I. 2007. *La industria eléctrica en España (1890–1936)*. Madrid: Banco de España.

Bel, G. 2006. *Economía y política de la privatización local*, Madrid, Marcial Pons.

Carreras, A. & X. Tafunell. 1994: Notas sobre la evolución de la gran empresa en España. In *Introducción a la Historia de la Empresa en España*, eds. G. Núñez & L. Segretto, 89–114. Madrid: Abacus.

Castro-Valdivia, M., M. Fernández-Paradas, & J. M. Matés-Barco. 2019. Las empresas extranjeras de agua y gas en España (circa 1900–1921). In *Los servicios públicos en España y México*, coord. J. M. Matés-Barco & A. Torres-Rodríguez, 51–74. Madrid: Sílex.

Castro-Valdivia, M. & J. M. Matés-Barco. 2020. Los servicios públicos y la inversión extranjera en España (1850–1936): Las empresas de agua y gas. *História Unisinos* 24 (2): 221–239. Unisinos – doi: 10.413/hist.2020.242.05 revistas.unisinos.br/index.php/historia/article/view/hist.2020.242.05

Fernández, A. 2007. Compagnies privées et municipalités. Enjeux de pouvoir autour de l'installation des réseaux téchniques dans les villes espagnoles. In *Réseaux téchniques et conflits de pouvoir. Les dynamiques historiques des villes contemporaines*, D. Bocquet & S. Fettah, 291–309. Rome : École Française de Rome.

Fernández, A. 2009. *Un progessisme urbain en Espagne. Eau, gaz, électricité à Bilbao et dans les villes cantanbriques, 1840–1930*. Bordeaux: Presses Universitaries de Bordeaux.

Fernández-Paradas, M. 2009. Empresas y servicio de alumbrado público por gas en España (1842–1935). *TST. Transportes, Servicios y Telecomunicaciones* 16: 108–131.

Ferreira da Silva, Á. & A. Cardoso de Matos. 2004. The Networked City: Managing Power and Water Utilities in Portugal, 1850s-1920s. *Business and Economic History On-line*, 2.

Garrido-González, L. 2015. El desarrollo en España desde finales del siglo XIX hasta mediados del siglo XX. In *Cambio y crecimiento económico*, ed. L. Caruana, 269–316. Madrid: Pirámide.

González, L. & G. Núñez. 2008. Crecimiento urbano y desarrollo empresarial: notas sobre los servicios urbanos y la actividad financiera en Andalucía a principios del siglo XX. In *La modernización económica de los Ayuntamientos: servicios públicos, finanzas y gobiernos municipales*, eds. L. González-Ruiz & J. M. Matés-Barco, 299–312. Jaén: Universidad de Jaén.

González-Gómez, F. 2006. ¿Está justificada la privatización de la gestión del agua en las ciudades? Teoría y evidencia a partir del criterio de eficiencia. *Ciudad y Territorio / Estudios Territoriales* 38(147): 139–157

González-Ruiz, L. (2013): La economía en la crisis finisecular (1880–1913). In *Historia Económica de España*, eds. A. González-Enciso & J. M. Matés, 463–484. Barcelona: Ariel.

Knight, F. H. 1921. *Risk, Uncertainty and Profit*. Boston: Schaffner & Houghton.

Larrinaga, C. 2008. Modernización y servicios urbanos en San Sebastián en el primer tercio del siglo XX. In *La modernización económica de los Ayuntamientos: servicios públicos, finanzas y gobiernos municipales*, eds. L. González-Ruiz & J. M. Matés-Barco, 81–116. Jaén: Universidad de Jaén.

Martínez, A. 2020. Inversión extranjera y abastecimiento de agua: Algeciras, 1895–1952. *História Unisinos* 24-2: 209–220.

Matés-Barco, J. M. 1997. Las empresas de abastecimiento de agua en España (1840–1970). Catálogo Sociedades, 2 vols. PhD diss. University of Granada.

Matés-Barco, J. M. 2002. Strategies of foreign firms in the sector of water supply in Spain (1850–1990). In *Transnational Companies, 19th-20th Centuries*, coord. H. Bonin, 301–316. Paris: Pláge.

Matés-Barco, J. M. 2004. The development of water Supplies in Spain: 19th and 20th Centuries. In *Urban Growth on Two Continents in the 19th and 20th Centuries: Technology, Networks, Finance and Public Regulation*, eds. A. Giuntini, P. Hertner, G. Núñez, 165–177. Granada: Comares.

Matés-Barco, J. M. 2009. Las sociedades anónimas de abastecimiento de agua potable en España (1840–1960). *Revista de la Historia de la Economía y de la Empresa* 3: 177–218.

Matés-Barco, J. M. 2013. La conquista del agua en Europa: los modelos de gestión (siglos XIX y XX). *Agua y Territorio* 1: 21–29. revistaselectronicas.ujaen.es/index.php/atma/article/view/1030/868

Matés-Barco, J. M. 2014. Las empresas concesionarias de servicios de abastecimiento de aguas potables en España (1840–1940). *Transportes, Servicios y Telecomunicaciones* 26: 58–89. www.tstrevista.com/sumarios/sum26/sumario_26_002_es.asp

Matés-Barco, J. M. 2018a. La distribution de l'eau dans les villes d'Espagne (1840–1936): Le rôle des compagnies privées. *Histoire, Économie & Société* 3: 14–29. www.revues.armand-colin.com/histoire/histoire-economie-societe/histoire-economie-societe-32018/distribution-leau-villes-despagne-1840-1936-role-compagnies-privees

Matés-Barco, J. M. 2018b. De la Regulación a la Privatización y viceversa: la gestión del agua en España y Gran Bretaña. In *Agua y Servicios Públicos en España y México*, coord. J. M. Matés-Barco & José Juan Pablo Rojas-Ramírez, 29–68. Jaén: University of Jaén and University of Guadalajara.

Matés-Barco, J. M. 2019a. El abastecimiento de agua a Barcelona (1850–1939): Origen y desarrollo de las compañías privadas. *Historia Contemporánea* 59-1: 165–194. doi.org/10.1387/hc.19434 www.ehu.eus/ojs/index.php/HC/article/view/19434

Matés-Barco, J. M. 2019b. Estrategia empresarial y control del mercado: la gestión del abastecimiento de agua potable. In *Empresas y empresarios en España: de mercaderes a industriales*, coord. J. M. Matés-Barco, 223–240. Madrid: Pirámide.

Mirás, J. 2003. Intervención y regulación del abastecimiento de agua en el franquismo. *Revista de História Económica e Social* 5: 35–62.

Mirás, J. 2004. Shifts in the economic structure of a medium-sized Spanish town during the post-war period: La Coruña, 1939–1960. *Urban History* 31–3: 357–354.

Mirás, J. 2006. Evoluzione del settore terciario in una cittá spagnola: La Coruña, 1914–1935. *Storia Urbana* 110: 47–67.

Núñez, G. 2000. Le infrastrutture urbane nella storia. Note per un'analisi. *Richerche Storiche* 30–3: 439–447.

Núñez, G. 2004. La municipalisation des services locaux et les entreprises municipales en Espagne dans la première moitié du XXe siècle. In *L'entreprise publique en France et en Espagne*, eds. Ch. Bouneau & A. Fernández, 209–223. Pessac Cedex: Centre Aquitain d'Histoire Moderne et Contemporaine, Maison des Sciences de L'homme d'Aquitaine.

Núñez, G. & L. Segreto. (eds.) 1994. *Introducción a la Historia de la Empresa en España*. Madrid: Abacus.

Ruiz-Villaverde, A. 2013. Reflexiones sobre la gestión de los servicios urbanos del agua: un recorrido histórico del caso español. *Agua y Territorio* 1: 31–39. doi.org/10.17561/at.v1i1.1031

Tafunell, X. 1996. *Los beneficios empresariales en España (1880–1981): Elaboración de una serie anual*. Madrid: Fundación Empresa Pública, DT 9601.

Villar-Chamorro, F., M. Castro-Valdivia, & J. M. Matés-Barco. 2019. Crecimiento urbano y abastecimiento de agua potable en España: el protagonismo de las empresas privadas (1840–1950). *Posición* 1: 1–21. 716132a6-9cf5-45de-baee-6a15e46210f7.filesusr.com/ugd/df634b_947ca999aea740a9b61a2f4fd04be233.pdf

7 Credit Companies, Merchant-Bankers and Large National Banks. The Case of Andalusia (1800–1936)

María José Vargas-Machuca

Introduction

Over the years, covering the financial needs of the population has suffered a special development. Although loaning and savings funds have existed since ancient times, it can be said that its systematisation started as a result of the expansion experienced in the Modern Age. Beyond the lending activity between individuals that has always been a common activity, beginning in that era agents began to emerge that were formally dedicated to granting loans and accepting deposits.

During the nineteenth century, private banking activity in Spain was carried out by other two types of agents. On the one hand, those constituted as stock companies, such is the case with banks of issue and credit companies, and on the other hand, bankers and private banking houses. In the latter group, some merchants, parallel to their commercial operations, began to start lending money to customers in the same way traditional money-lenders did. As time went by, the development of many of these small merchant-bankers became common. Commercial activity started to give ground to financial activity, and eventually they turned into companies and, in the twentieth century, the next generation turned the business into a limited company that, in many cases, ended up being sold to a large bank that used it as an expansion strategy. (Titos Martínez 2003, p. 109). Together with them, the first savings banks started to operate, in many cases linked to pawnshops that had already been working in some Spanish towns for a long time.

The aim of this chapter is to study how this banking private sector structure was articulated in Andalusia in the nineteenth century and in the first third of the twentieth century. This analysis distinguishes two chronological phases: the nineteenth century and the years prior to the Spanish Civil War. For each of them, the activity considered as private banking will be discussed, that is to say, the activity carried out by agents that had such consideration, but that, over time, has had different legal forms: from banks of issue and credit companies, including bankers and private banking houses, to modern banks that were a characteristic of the Spanish financial system until the end of the twentieth century.

Private Banking in the Nineteenth Century: Banks of Issue, Credit Companies and Merchant-Bankers

The nineteenth century was a time period of intense transformation in the Spanish financial system due to the appearance of successive regulations that affected banking activity essentially through the regulation of the entities that could carry it out. Activities that, until then, did not have any regulations and depended on – sometimes arbitrary – concessions of the administration, began to be regulated.

To this effect, in 1829, the first Commerce Code of Spain appeared, and in 1931 the Stock Market was founded as the essential element to develop a new way of corporate organisation: public limited companies (Titos Martínez 2003, p. 96). These companies were originally regulated by the Commerce Code together with partnerships and limited partnerships. These last two could be constituted by simple registration, whereas the public limited companies needed approval from the Provincial Court of Commerce and, in case of any privilege, as it happened with banks, royal approval. Nevertheless, public limited companies suffered subsequent modifications by the Law of Stock Corporations of 1848, which was very demanding as it established the need of a Law or Royal Decree to create those entities. The Law of 1870 was more liberalising and it repealed the previous one.

The Banks of Issue and Credit Companies Laws (Spanish law) of 1856 were of high importance, and, thanks to them, there was a certain specialisation in the Spanish financial system. On the one hand, some "banks of issue" were created, closely linked to the government and which, in addition to issuing money, worked by granting credits and discounts. On the other hand, there are the so-called "credit companies" that started to develop a wide range of activities, mainly oriented to the industrial promotion linked to the railway sector, but with no investment privileges (Pons 1999, p. 84). Then began a phase of strong bank expansion linked to two circumstances: a permissive legislation and a favourable economic situation, which was driven by the State and which was tightly linked to the construction of the railway network. Nevertheless, between 1864 and 1868, some railway companies went into receivership, so many credit institutions saw their investments compromised, which led to bankruptcy and disappearance.

After the credit companies, difficulties reached the banks of issue. The Law of 1874 (known as the Echegaray Decree) gave the Banco de España (Bank of Spain) the unique right of investment and obliged the rest of the banks of issue to annex their branches or to modify their statutes to turn into loan and discount banks. For several of those banks, the opportunity to join together with the Banco de España (Bank of Spain) was a great opportunity, providing the difficulties that they have had since the crisis of 1866 (Titos Martínez 2003, p. 97).

Therefore, the crisis of 1866 and the Law of 1874 were important for restructuring the Spanish financial system, bringing about a reduction in the total number of private banks and setting up an investment monopoly from the Banco de España (Bank of Spain).

On the other hand, in the financial system, aside from these unions, the individual bankers kept providing their services (Tedde de Lorca 1974, p. 254). Most likely the absence of banks and credit companies in a lot of provinces and their disappearance between 1864 and 1866 contributed to the creation of a vacuum that was filled with private bankers, savings banks, and other minor money-lenders.

The Commerce Code of 1829, for the first time in nineteenth-century Spain, regulated the bankers' performance, including that of merchants. To be allowed to practice banking activity, they were required to register an enrolment as merchants to carry out the so called "trade activity". Additionally, the enrolment in the merchants registry forced them into a certain type of taxation (business subsidy, industrial and business subsidy, or industrial property tax, depending on the era) (Titos Martínez 1999, p. 108).

The regulation of private bankers was kept stable during the nineteenth century, in particular, until the banking changes of 1921 were approved. They were not involved in the successive regulating rules that appeared during these years about public limited companies, banks of issue, and credit companies. However, they were involved in the successive tax changes that modified the formula and amount of fiscal contributions that these bankers needed to make.

The activity of these bankers has been categorised for the first years of the nineteenth century: they acted as money-lenders, discounted, acted as guarantors, transferred short-terms drafts, and traded with currency from several countries, and, at the same time, a lot of them sold lingerie merchandise or imported goods (Tedde de Lorca 1983, p. 303). In such way, a lot of them could actually be considered "merchant-bankers", that is to say, agents that started their activity as retail traders, then started to carry out, on a small scale, the main banking operations (transfers, negotiations, loans, etc.) first to fulfil their own needs and, gradually, for a higher number of clients, until ending up specialising in this activity and even leaving their original business occupations (García-López 1989, p. 115). Such transformation was generally a slow process and, in some occasions, imperceptible. Probably, the only recognisable fact in such process was the registration of the tax enrolment, which was the exterior official appreciation.

In some way or another, in the first half of the nineteenth century and, to a large extent later, private bankers were the capitalist substitutes of the larger public limited companies dedicated to credits, which were almost non-existent during the first half of the century and were very limited after that (Titos Martínez 1999, p. 115).

However, in their future development, many of these individual bankers ended up turning into companies. The history of each of them is similar: they started their banking activity linked to any commercial profession and they practised it strictly personally. Later on, in a second generation, they turned into partnerships and the banking activity displaced the other commercial activities. Successive generations, in the second third of the twentieth century, turned the company into a limited company and ended up selling the banking business to any large national bank that, before difficulties of expansion and access to the banking activity, made the most of the situation to get established in the locality over the prestige basis of the local banks and strengthened customers (Titos Martínez 2003, p. 109).

In summary, in the nineteenth century, the private banking activity in Spain was carried out by three types of agents: banks of issue, credit companies and private bankers. That is why the study of the financial activity of these agents in Andalusia will be done separately.

Credit Companies in Andalusia (Nineteenth Century)

The 1856 ordinance established the differences between banks of issue and credit companies, reserving investment privilege for the former. Credit companies, and also public limited companies, were originally oriented to direct industrial promotion and performed the ordinary duties of commercial banks. They lacked the fiduciary issue power, although they could issue short-term bonds that, in practice, worked as bank notes (Sánchez-Albornoz 1975, p.26).

In these central years of the nineteenth century, Andalusia is involved in the movement creating financial institutions that the whole country utilised. Since the final constitution of the Banco de Málaga (Bank of Málaga) took place in 1856, a proliferation of credit institutions was noted in the region, becoming one of the areas in Spain with the most business activity. In this case, the banking peak was accompanied by, and in many cases preceded by, an industrial and miner movement and infrastructure development at a level that has not happened again in the region (Titos Martínez 1976, p. 195).

In Spain, in addition to the three large credit companies of foreign capital and national scope, a series of little local companies proliferated, of which Andalusia saw the birth of five of them (Titos Martínez 2003, pp. 105–107):

a) The Crédito Comercial de Cádiz (Trading Credits of Cadiz) (1860–1866). It has its origin in the limited partnership of Conte y Cia (Conte and Company), which had been working in the Cadiz capital for many years and that, in 1860, under the protection of the 1856 legislation, requested to be constituted as a credit limited company with the involvement of some traders from Cadiz. Probably, it is the most important Andalusian credit company from a quantitative point of view. The company, deeply affected by the crisis of 1866, became bankrupt by the end of that year.

b) The Compañía Gaditana de Crédito (Credit Company of Cádiz) (1861–1867) This company was constituted some months after the previous one. Among its founders, there were people that had participated in the constitution of the Banco de Cádiz (Bank of Cadiz) and other companies. Like the previous one, it was gravely affected by the crisis of 1866 and became bankrupt at the end of 1867.

c) The Crédito Comercial de Jerez (Trading Credits of Jerez) (1862–1866). Authorised in September 1862, this company was not able to face the problems derived from the 1866's crisis either, and the stockholders decided to liquidate the company in December of the same year.
d) The Crédito Comercial de Sevilla (Trading Credits of Seville) (1862–1868). This company was founded in May 1862 on the basis of the old Le-Roy y Cia (Le-Roy and Company) limited partnership. Five of the seven founding partners had also founded the Banco de Sevilla (Bank of Seville). Regarding its financial activity, it is worth mentioning the close relations with the Banco de Sevilla (Bank of Seville) to which it asked for many loans. The 1866 crisis left the company practically out of activity, although it was able to continue in this precarious situation until 1868.
e) The Crédito Comercial y Agrícola de Córdoba (Trading and Agricultural Credits of Cordoba) (1864–1867). This was the last Andalusian credit company. Its history comes from a limited partnership founded in 1863 named Lopez y Cia (Lopez and Company), but it was commercially called "Crédito Comercial y Agrícola de Córdoba (Trading and Agricultural Credits of Cordoba)". It was constituted with capital that came from Cadiz and Seville, where all the possibilities of new constitutions had disappeared. This company, authorised in November 1864, worked more as a deposits and discounting bank than as a trading or agricultural investment or promotion bank, which was the original aspiration. Nevertheless, during its existence it did always get profits from its operations, and it was able to open a branch office in Granada. The 1866 problems specially affected the Trading Credits of Cadiz, with whom they had partners in common. The bankruptcy of the company in Cadiz alarmed the clients in Cordoba, and their distrust caused a decrease in the demand of banking services. In this situation, the partners, to avoid more serious events, decided to liquidate the company at the beginning of 1867.

It is worth referencing a foreign company, the Sociedad General Española de Descuentos (Spanish General Discounts Society) (1859–1866), because of the high interest in opening branch offices in Andalusia. The entity was founded in March 1859 as an initiative of the Compañía General de Crédito en España (General Credit Company in Spain) and the founders decided to create Discount Banks in many other provinces. Actually, according to the general plans of its mother company, the aim was to direct to Madrid the money of those areas and invest it from there. They were able to create three branch offices in Andalusia: Granada (1859), Málaga (1859), and Seville (1861). Due to the payment problems that they had had since 1864, it ended up being liquidated in 1866 (Titos Martínez 1980, pp. 90–94).

Banks of Issue in Andalusia

In Andalusia, among the financial institutions constituted as societies, there are four banks of issue (Titos Martínez 2003, pp. 97–105).

The Banco de Cádiz (Bank of Cadiz) was created in December 1846. In this city, since some months earlier, a branch office of the Banco de Isabel II (Bank of Isabella II) has been working with the name Banco Español de Cádiz (Spanish Bank of Cadiz). Almost a year later, in November of 1847, a merger of the two was agreed upon in order to create a new entity that would keep working under the name of the first. The crisis of this bank began in 1860 with the decrease of current accounts and the important volume of their own notes in till and this was emphasised in the next several years. At the end of the 1860s, the situation was critical. Almost all the loans, advances, and cash having disappeared, it took the Ministry (of Spain) to introduce a Bill in 1870 to the Congress (of Spain) for its dissolution and liquidation.

The rest of the banks of issue arose under the Banks of Issue Law of 1856 (Spanish Law), although the one in Jerez was slightly delayed. Their existence ended as a result of the (Spanish) Echegaray Decree of 1874, which merged them with the Banco de España (Bank of Spain) as its branch offices, their autonomous entities disappearing. Nevertheless, the circumstances of this merging were different. Although the banks of Málaga (1856–1874) and Jerez de la Frontera (1859–1874) were kept active, mainly the first one, the one in Seville (1857–1874) only existed documentarily as its activity was completely paralysed several years earlier due to the serious difficulties derived from its management and the crisis (Titos Martínez 2003, p. 196).

In the other provinces of Andalusia, either there was no bank of issue founded or there were some attempts that were not successful. There is no evidence that there was any project presented to constitute any banks of issue in Huelva, Cordoba, or Jaen during the nineteenth century, although there is of other types of credit institutions. In Granada, there are three registered attempts, all of them failed, due to the fact that, basically, local banking services were successfully covered by the Banca Rodriguez-Acosta (Rodriguez-Acosta Bank). In Almería, in the middle of the 1866 crisis, a group of traders requested the government and authorisation to find a bank of issue, which did not work due to the difficulties that affected the banking system those years.

Regardless, the size of the banks of issue was reduced for what was expected. It is worth mentioning that the functioning problems that they had (especially the one in Seville), the short time period that they were working, and the fact that, only in the Banco de Jerez (Bank of Jerez), the capital was completely paid. In general, these banks did not fully use their investment capacity nor the local savings creation, showing, in most cases, a limited capacity of resources raised from third parties. Regarding the investment orientation, loans were not that important. Thus, the role as direct industrial promoter was non-existent, the preferential orientation was commercial, and they only supported the downstream industry through discounts that were the most representative part of their assets (Titos Martínez 2003, p. 108).

In conclusion, the disappearance of credit companies as a consequence of the 1866 crisis and of banks of issue as a result of the Echegaray Decree (in Spain) (1874) practically entailed the disappearance of the banking system in this region of the Spanish financial map. This emptiness of native entities would

The Case of Andalusia (1800–1936)

be long. Until in 1900, when the Banco de Andalucía (Bank of Andalusia) was created, this territory did not have its own banking company and even this one did not last long. There were no companies like that in Andalusia until a long time after the Spanish Civil War. Instead, the role was filled by private bankers.

Private Bankers in Andalusia in the Nineteenth Century

In general, the banking institutions constituted as companies in the nineteenth century in Spain were scarce, and in many cases, they were of small size and irregularly distributed in the territory. It makes you think that, since the business activity in the country was increasing, the money mediation business had to be carried out by other agents. These agents were private bankers, whose activity was relatively important during this century (García López 1989, p. 114). In the case of Andalusia, the banks and credit companies' absence in many provinces and their disappearance in the rest between 1866 and 1874 increased the banking companies emptiness that was replenished mainly by these private bankers. The scale of individuals who mainly operated with their own capital or credit extends from the local lender to the great banker of the court.

The Spanish legislation provided a wide freedom of action for private bankers from the promulgation of the Commerce Code of 1829 to the Banking Organisation Law of 1921 (both in Spain). This provided those intermediaries a ruling stability that contrasted with the continuous regulating reforms that affected banking companies.

The data available for the end of the nineteenth century (1985–1986) shows a total of 30 merchant-bankers enrolled in the Industry Contribution. The distribution per provinces is: 13 in Cadiz; 6 in Jaen; 3 in Granada and 2 in Cordoba, Huelva, Malaga, and Seville, respectively. This data exposes, first, that Andalusia was reasonably represented in regards to bankers enrolled in the Industry Contribution in relation to the total of Spain –16 percent, an amount that exceeds the demographic weight that the region had back then (Titos Martínez 2003, p. 118).

However, the number of bankers registered in the Bailly-Baillière Annual Directory[1] in 1897 amounts to 132, with the following distribution per province: 24 in Almeria; 21 in Cadiz; 20 in Malaga 2; 19 in Huelva; 15 in Jaen; 14 in Cordoba; 13 in Seville, and 6 in Granada (García-López 1989, pp. 122–123).

The figures provided by the Industrial Contribution and the Bailly-Baillière Annual Directory were remarkably different. This difference was probably derived from the fact that many small merchant-bankers, especially those established in small towns, opposed registering in the tax enrolment as bankers as it meant a payment of an additional contribution to what they already paid. This new requirement was excessively onerous for them compared to the profits generated by many banking operations. Probably, the more important houses actually were enrolled, as due to their business volume, it was not possible for them to hide from the Spanish Tax Office and the rest of the sector.

In the case of Granada, such difference was not very significant. This could be due to the presence of the Banca Rodriguez-Acosta (Rodriguez-Acosta

Banking), as it achieved enough dimensions to cover a great part of the financial needs of the area. Hence, the limited number of bankers in the province. This house started its activity in 1831 and kept it until 1946, the date when it was absorbed by the Banco Central[2] (Central Bank).

In most cases, the business consisted of a sole office, probably because of the direct management of the activity by the owners. Nevertheless, the case of the banker from Cordoba, Pedro Lopez, is an exception, as he kept a branch office in Granada between 1868 and 1870. Just as with the banks that were constituted as public limited companies, the size was not large enough to firmly support the industrial development in the region. In most cases, the investment in local values or direct industrial business was practically absent, except in the case of the Banca Rodriguez-Acosta (Rodriguez-Acosta Banking), which offered a different investing model, especially during the twentieth century. Additionally, even though they did not have investment privileges, they started to work with promissory notes and bearer responsibilities that worked practically the same as the bank notes, at least until 1874 (Titos Martínez 2003, p. 119).

This was the model instituted by private banking in Andalusia in this first phase, which would be prolonged until the third decade of the twentieth century.

The Private Banking (1900–1936): Local Bankers and Large National Banks

The most important legal regulation related to the banking system during the Spanish Restoration period was the Banking Organisation Law (Spanish law) of the 19th of December of 1921, known as the Cambo Law. This law affected the Banco de España (Bank of Spain) as well as private banking. Regarding the former, it regulated basic aspects such as its abilities and its organisation. Regarding the latter, it established the regulation basis for its activity and created the Camaras de Compensacion (Clearing Houses), the Consejo Superior Bancario (Banking Control Council), and the Comisaria de la Banca (Banking Commission). New banks were obliged to register in this last one if they wanted to have the privileges and benefits provided by the law, that is to say, the recognition of bonus for the operations with the Banco de España (Bank of Spain), the ability to create with the State a special regime for certain operations, and the formalisation of agreements regarding some taxes.

Even though after the passing of this law the intervention on the banking system was strengthened, these entities continued initially enjoying a high freedom of action, which was slightly limited in 1926 with the reform of some articles of this regulation.

Some years later, the republican regime proclaimed on the 25th of November of 1931 that the provisional government had approved the text of a new Banking Organisation Law (for Spain), more focused on monetary aspects than on the organisation or the credit. Even though the scope of this new law does not allow space to talk about reform, it is this law that begins the process of the reduction of the Banco de España's (Bank of Spain) autonomy with regard to the government that culminated with its nationalisation.

Regarding private banking, the scene outlined by the Cambo Law in 1921, with all the expansion limitations, was kept in force during the whole of the 1920s and was strengthened in the following decades (Titos Martínez 2003, p. 123).

The Territorial Expansion of the National Banking in Andalusia in the First Third of the Twentieth Century

The first years of the twentieth century represent the start of a period of strong expansion of banking at a national level characterised by two aspects. On the one hand, the creation of new entities, some of them transforming the old banking houses or credit companies. On the other hand, a strong expansion of the activity of those entities through the establishment of new branch offices beyond their initial operational areas.

In Andalusia, as it has been mentioned, the 1866 crisis and the Echegaray Decree of 1874 caused the native bank's presence during the last quarter of the century to be nonexistent. In fact, there is no company registered in the region until 1900 and the presence of branch offices or agencies of foreign banks was still very weak. Other than the branch offices of the Banco de España (Bank of Spain) and the Mortgage Bank, in 1884 only the Banco de Castilla (Bank of Castile) had an agency in Cadiz and a foreign bank, The Union Bank of Spain and England, had opened a branch office in Seville (Titos Martínez 2003, p. 120). While all of this was happening, as it was mentioned, a wide range of private bankers rose up to cover the financial needs of the region during this time.

Under the protection of the expansion phase of the banking institutions in Spain, Andalusia, which, at that time, did not have its own banking system, the initiatives were not lacking, the most esteemed one being the Banco de Andalucía (Bank of Andalusia) (Martín-Aceña 2011, p. 121). Created in 1900 in Seville, under the protection of the interest of people in Asturias, it had few impacts, and a short life that finished with its liquidation in 1907 when it was absorbed by the Banco de Cartagena (Bank of Cartagena), which was in the process of expanding throughout the region of Andalusia.

During this time, foreign entities found favourable conditions for the expansion of their activities in Andalusia due to the lack of an organised regional banking under the limited company system, especially during the second and third decades of the century. Large banking companies with goals of expansion gradually occupied the Andalusia region, evolving from two entities in 1907 to six in 1928. The increase in the branch office network in this territory was equally significant, with 121 offices open by 1928 (Titos Martínez 2003, p. 167).

The great protagonist of the office-opening process in this region is the Banco Español de Crédito (Spanish Credit Bank). Although in 1913 it had branch offices in five squares (Cordoba, Linares, Almería, Ubeda, and La

Carolina), since that date it had started becoming established, step-by-step, in new localities until in 1920 its network was made up of 20 offices[3]. The process continued, growing more accelerated at the end of the decade, until reaching a total of 70 offices in 1928.

The Banco Hispano Americano (American Hispanic Bank) was born in 1901 from the investment initiative of some Spanish business owners located in America with capital that they had repatriated (Martín-Aceña 2011, p. 120). It started its expansion in Andalusia between 1910 and 1913, opening the three first branch offices in Granada, Malaga, and Seville. In 1922, this number had increased to 11, including those of Antequera, Cabra, Cadiz, Cordoba, Huelva, Jaen, Jerez, and Linares. Subsequently, more would be added until the 19 that were created by 1928.

The Banco de Cartagena (Bank of Cartagena) was an entity that, shortly after being founded, had set in motion an important expansion plan. In 1907-1908, it took over the Banco de Andalucía (Bank of Andalusia) that had been created in 1900 in Seville. Since that moment, the Banco de Cartagena (Bank of Cartagena) began to leave its original territory towards close markets such as the one in Valencia, La Mancha and the rest of Andalusia. In the latter, it opened three branch offices in Seville, Cadiz and Huelva, where it maintained delegations in Ayamonte and Isla Cristina. For this bank, the possibilities of good businesses that the West of Andalusia offered compensated the closeness advantage of the East zone of this region (Titos Martínez 1980, p. 113). In 1924, it became the Banco Internacional de Industria y Comercio (Industry and Trade International Bank), increasing its three branch offices in Andalusia to seven.

In 1921, the Banco Central (Central Bank) absorbed the Banco de Albacete (Bank of Albacete) that already had two branch offices in Andalusia: Cordoba and Andujar. Shortly, these were joined by offices in Lucena and Malaga, and, just a few years later, three more, bringing the total number of offices in 1928 to seven.

The Banco de Bilbao (Bank of Bilbao) started its course in Andalusia in 1921, opening the first branch office in Seville, which, in 1926, was joined by one in Cordoba.

In 1926, the Banco Urquijo (Urquijo Bank) opened the first office in Andalusia, specifically in Seville, adding one in Granada the next year, as it absorbed the local bank Hijos de Enrique Santos (Enrique Santos' Children).

Besides the already mentioned banks, there is evidence that other banks worked in Andalusia under branch offices or correspondent's offices. Titos Martínez (2003, p. 167) includes a global synopsis of "other banks", not specifying their names. It is likely that these are some of the banks that were open in 1922 alongside the ones already mentioned: Banco Rural (Rural Bank), Banco Peninsular Hipotecario (Peninsular Mortgage Bank), Banco Vasco (Basque Bank), El Hogar Español (The Spanish Home), Banco Español del Río de la Plata (Rio de la Plata Spanish Bank), Anglo South American Bank, Crédit Lyonnais, Bank of British West Africa and Comptoir Foncier d´Algerie et Tunnisie (Arroyo Martin 2000, p. 18). According to the information by this author, all the banks back then would have an office in Andalusia except for the Banco Rural (Rural Bank), which had two. To these should be added some brief local projects, such as the Banco Hispano Comercial (Hispanic Commercial Bank), which had the corporate headquarters in Seville.

The Banco Matritense (Bank of Madrid) has to be mentioned separately, founded in Madrid in 1911 and which, when it was liquidated in 1922, worked in 26 squares of Andalusia. However, the fact that those branch offices are not included in most of the consulted sources, may mean that the bank actually worked through other agents that behaved as correspondents. The case is similar with the Banco Popular de los Previsores del Porvenir (Popular Bank of the Future Fore Sighting), which had offices in Cadiz, Jerez de la Frontera, Seville, and Jaen (Titos Martínez 2003, o. 121).

In 1930, the presence of national banking had become widespread in Andalusia, where it had spread to 147 localities. Very few bankers of Andalusia opened branch offices outside of the capitals, so it was the large banks who reached those destinations. The Banco Español de Crédito (Spanish Credit Bank) was still in the lead, with predilection for the Cordoba, Jaen, and Seville provinces. Some national banks that progressed more slowly in their expansion in Andalusia completed it at the beginning of the 1930s: the Banco de Bilbao (Bank of Bilbao) opened another 4 branch offices between 1930 and 1935 and the Banco de Vizcaya (Bank of Vizcaya) opened an office in Cordoba in 1931.

If we keep in mind the provincial distribution of these offices, we can see an obvious disparity within the region: Cordoba was by far the most attractive province to establish branch offices. This banking power will later be confirmed by the abundant presence of local bankers. Cordoba is followed by Seville and Jaen. This last one, with a traditionally low financial level, is similar to Cordoba regarding the agricultural and mining wealth, which was an attractive factor for national banks.

Local Bankers' Behaviour until 1936

At the beginning of the twentieth century, the number of private bankers working in Andalusia was very imprecise. On the one hand, we have the information of the bankers registered in the Industry Contribution which, as it was already mentioned, probably only included a part of the agents working on this activity because of the reticence of some of them to get registered in order to avoid paying an additional contribution, which was excessively expensive for their businesses. On the other hand, we can also count on the information gathered in the economic annual directories and the financial press of the era. However, the data disparity is great in this case as well.

Table 7.1 shows the number of bankers operating in Andalusia around 1922 according to two different sources. The first column reflects the data obtained by Arroyo Martin from the Banking Directory, and the second, the information that Patxot and Giménez Arnau (2001) deduced from other annual directories and the economic press of the era.

Table 7.1 Number of Bankers in Andalusia (1922)

Province	Banking Directory	Other annual directories
Almeria	42	46
Cadiz	33	41
Cordoba	40	52
Granada	33	33
Huelva	22	20
Jaen	62	65
Malaga	37	44
Seville	51	53
TOTAL	320	354

Source: author, based on Arroyo Martín (2000, p. 15) and Patxot and Giménez-Arnau (2001, pp. 293–342).

From that information, two matters stand out. In the first place, the figures disparity, which can make us think that, whereas the information of the Banking Directory may be a little more tight, the information presented by the economic banking annual directories probably included agents with different activities aside from strictly banking (Titos Martínez 2003, p. 124). In the second place, it is worth mentioning that, having in mind both sources of information, the Jaen province, with a traditionally low financial level but with important agricultural and mining activity, is the one with a higher volume of agents working in the banking. For the rest of Andalusia, we can say that the merchant-bankers were a little bit more uniformly distributed than the branch offices of the large national banks (Arroyo Martin 2000, p. 16).

Either way, before 1922, the data availability regarding the activity of these bankers was very limited. For some specific bankers, the whole series of their activities can be reconstructed – such is the case of Rodriguez-Acosta in Granada, or partially the case of Pedro Lopez in Cordoba (Titos Martínez 2003, p. 123). However, for most of the bankers, the information gathered is limited to what has been obtained from annual directories and business agencies, and is not entirely precise. Thus, when the Spanish Banking Organisation Law (Cambo Law), which had been approved the previous year, came into force in 1922, the number of private bankers working in Andalusia was as extensive as it was imprecise.

Thenceforward, the voluntary registration procedure in the banks and bankers registry of the Private Banking Ordering Commission (Spanish Organisation), established by the new law, and the privileges derived from such registration, would contribute to regulate the situation and ensure the professional activity of those who were actually considered bankers.

The number of bankers considered as such by the Consejo Superior Bancario (Banking Control Council) and the Comisaria de la Banca (Banking Commission) with headquarters in Andalusia, increased after the creation of those bodies in 1932, when it reached its highest number with a total of 19

The Case of Andalusia (1800–1936) 111

banks. Among them, the highest number appeared in the Cordoba province, which had 8 banks in 1931 and 1932.

Since then and through a slow process of liquidations, moving of the corporate headquarters to areas outside of Andalusia, mergers and absorptions, the number of Andalusian banks was reduced, not only until the years prior to the Spanish Civil War, but also in the years after. This continued until, when the twentieth century ended, there were no more banking groups with headquarters in this autonomous community.

Between 1922 and 1936, 22 banking houses from Andalusia were registered or provided information about their activity to the Consejo Superior Bancario (CSB) (Banking Control Council). All of them grouped together are shown in Table 7.2.

Finally, as some of them later abandoned the activity, in 1936 there was a total of 14 Andalusian banks and bankers registered in the CSB. Only half of them were still active (Titos Martínez 2003, pp. 124–126).

Table 7.2 Bankers and Banking Houses with Activity in Andalusia (1922–1936)

Province	Banker or banking house	Locality
Almeria	Antonio Gonzalez Egea	Almeria
Cadiz	Aramburu Hermanos (Aramburu Brothers)	Cadiz
	Diez Vergara y Cia (Diez Vergara and Company)	Jerez de la Frontera
	Herederos de Antonio Ridruejo (Antonio Ridruejo's Inheritors)	Sanlucar de Barrameda
Cordoba	Pedro Lopez e Hijos (Pedro Lopez and Children).	Cordoba
	Carbonell y Cia (Carbonell and Company)	Cordoba
	Banco de Andalucía, S.A. (Bank of Andalusia)	Cordoba
	Leopoldo Villen Cruz	Rute
	Valeriano Perez Gimenez	Rute
	Jose Maria Naranjo	Montilla
	Miguel Garcia Juan	La Rambla
	Gimenez y Cia (Gimenez and Company)	Fernan Nuñez
	Protectora Montoreña (The Montoro Protector)	Montoro
	Emiliano Redondo Fernandez	Pueblo Nuevo del Terrible
Granada	Hijos de Rodriguez-Acosta (Rodriguez-Acosta's Children)	Granada
	Enrique Santos Guillen	Granada
	Hilario Rodriguez	Baza
Jaen	Hijo de Dionisio Puche (Dionisio Puche's Son)	Baeza
	Miñon Hermanos (Miñon Brothers)	Andujar
Malaga	Francisco Lopez	Malaga
Seville	Mariano Borrero Blanco	Seville
	Viuda de Matias Valdecantos (Matias Valdecantos' Widow)	Constantina

Source: author, based on Titos Martínez (2003, pp. 124–126).

Regarding the dimensions of these banks and bankers, the figures of their total actives show the total supremacy that, during that time, had Rodriguez-Acosta from Granada, followed by Pedro Lopez from Cordoba, and, a little bit after, Mariano Borrero Blanco in Seville.

Conclusions

In the nineteenth century, the banking activity, in the private aspect, was developed in Spain by two types of agents. On the one hand, the banks constituted individually, in some occasions, as partnerships or limited partnerships, as was the case of the bankers, merchant-bankers, and banking houses. On the other hand, were those organised as public limited companies, as banks and credit companies.

During the central years of the nineteenth century, Andalusia was involved in creating the movement of financial institutions that the whole country experienced, sponsored by the approval of the Banks of Issue and Credit Companies Laws of 1856.

Nevertheless, the crisis of 1866 led to the disappearance of the credit societies and the Echegaray Decree of 1874 involved the liquidation of the issuing banks. In this way, the network of Andalusian banking entities disappeared. This situation lasted until 1900 when the Bank of Andalusia was established in Seville. However, this bank had a really short-lived life. Consequently, until long after the Spanish Civil War, entities of this type did not appear again in Andalusia.

This role was filled by the private bankers that covered the financial needs of the population in the absence of the banking companies. During the nineteenth century, the number of these agents working in Andalusia was as extensive as it is imprecise. And some of them actually were merchant-bankers. Given that the recognition of their double-activity meant a higher payment to the contribution, it is not surprising that a lot of them (especially the littlest ones) decided not to register their financial activity, and that they kept working illegally tax-wise.

As time goes by, the business delimitation became specific and bankers needed to regularise their activity by registering in official registries. At that point, in 1922, there was a total of 320 Andalusian bankers registered in the Banking Directory. Between that year and 1936, 22 banking houses from Andalusia were registered or provided information about their activity to the Consejo Superior Bancario (CSB) (Banking Control Council). And after several adjustments, in 1936 there was a total of 14 Andalusian banks and bankers registered in the CSB, of which half of them were active, there not being any evidence of the activity of the other ones.

At the same time, in the second and third decades of the new century, an important consolidation process of the large Spanish banks implemented a great expansion over the whole national territory. In Andalusia, a total of 6 foreign banks came to develop a network of 121 branch offices in 1928.

In this way, in the mid-thirties, the private banking sector, with official acknowledgement in Andalusia, was composed by 14 local firms (half of them registered in the Consejo Superior Bancario (Banking Control Council) but without apparent activity) and a great number of offices belonging to 8 foreign banks located in 147 municipalities in the region. Several years later, well into the 20th century, the local banking houses ended up disappearing from the regional banking outlook because of their dissolution or their absorption by the large national banks.

Notes

1 The Annual Directory and Almanac of Commerce, Industry, Magistrature, and Administration (Bailly-Baillière Annual Directory) was first published in 1879. It was a guide that included hundreds of thousands of pieces of information about the people forming the state and provincial institutions in every sector (political, educational, military, religious, judicial, etc.) besides the professionals and professions, shops, businesses, factories, and industries in Spain as well as in the overseas countries and Latin America (and since 1881, also in Portugal).
2 In Titos-Martínez (1978) can be seen a detailed study of the history of this banking house.
3 Besides the three initial ones, it opened offices in: Jaen and Puente Genil (1916); Berja (1917); Malaga and Ronda (1918); Granada, Guadix, Algeciras, La Linea, Seville, and Jerez (1919) and Huelva, Ecija, Moron, and Carmona (1920).

References

Arroyo Martín, J. V. 2000. *La banca privada en Andalucía entre 1920 y 1935*. Bilbao: Archivo Histórico del Banco Bilbao Vizcaya Argentaria.

García López, J. R. 1989. El sistema bancario español del siglo XIX. ¿Una estructura dual? Nuevos planteamientos y nuevas propuestas. *Revista de Historia Económica* VII (1): 116–119.

Martín Aceña, P. 2011. La banca en España entre 1900 y 1975. In *Un siglo de historia del sistema financiero español*, ed. J.L. Malo de Molina and P. Martín Aceña, 117–161. Madrid: Alianza.

Patxot, V. & E. Giménez-Arnau. 2001. *Banqueros y bancos durante la vigencia de la Ley Cambó (1922–1946)*. Madrid: Banco de España.

Pons, M. Á. 1999. Las grandes sociedades anónimas bancarias 1860–1960. In *El sistema financiero en España. Una síntesis histórica*, ed. P. Martín Aceña and M. Titos Martínez, 83–103. Granada: Universidad de Granada.

Sánchez-Albornoz, N. 1975. *Jalones de la modernización de España*. Barcelona: Ariel.

Tedde de Lorca, P. 1974. La banca privada española durante la Restauración 1874–1914. In *La banca española en la Restauración. Tomo I Política y Finanzas,* ed. Servicio de Estudios del Banco de España, 217–455. Madrid: Banco de España.

Tedde de Lorca, P. 1983. Comerciantes y banqueros madrileños al final del Antiguo Régimen. In *Historia económica y pensamiento social*, ed. G. Anes, L.A. Rojo and P. Tedde de Lorca, 301–334. Madrid: Alianza Editorial.

Titos Martínez, M. 1976. Panorama general de la banca en Andalucía en el siglo XIX. In *Actas del I Congreso de Historia de Andalucía. Andalucía contemporánea (s. XIX y XX),* 195–208. Córdoba: Monte de Piedad y Caja de Ahorros de Córdoba.

Titos Martínez, M. 1978. La banca Rodríguez-Acosta (1831–1904), un estudio modelo sobre la actuación de los banqueros del XIX. In *Crédito y ahorro en Granada en el siglo XIX*, ed. M. Titos Martínez, 377–582. Granada: Banco de Granada.

Titos Martínez, M. 1980. *Bancos y banqueros en la historiografía andaluza*. Granada: Universidad de Granada e Instituto de Desarrollo Regional.

Titos Martínez, M. 1999. Banca y banqueros privados. In *El sistema financiero en España. Una síntesis histórica,* ed. P. Martín Aceña and M. Titos Martínez, 105–133. Granada: Universidad de Granada.

Titos Martínez, M. 2003. *El sistema financiero en Andalucía: tres siglos de historia (1740–2000)*. Seville: Instituto de Estadística de Andalucía.

8 The Private Period of Spanish Railways 1848–1941

A Liberal Project to Modernise Spain

*Miguel Muñoz Rubio and
Pedro Pablo Ortúñez Goicolea*

The Early Steps of the Spanish Railway System: The National Way and the Foreign Way

Once the reign of Fernando VII had come to an end, Spanish liberals, whether moderates, progressivists, or revolutionaries, applied an economic policy whose main objective was to achieve industrialisation. Between 1840 and 1914, the secondary sector did indeed make significant progress, as evidenced by its relative weight in GDP which, between 1850 and 1914, rose from 17.19% to 30.01%. Nevertheless, this growth came to a halt before it increased on a scale large enough to bring about the structural change through which the process could be culminated (Carreras & Tafunell 2003). Yet there was indeed substantial modernisation, with one major accomplishment being the widespread construction of a railway network (Comín et al. 1998).

In 1840, conventional existing transport, which had been making significant strides since the eighteenth century thanks to the reforms of the enlightened Bourbons, was more than capable of catering to the mobility needs of an agricultural sector which, in turn, had been undergoing substantial growth since 1815 thanks to the increased amount of available cropland, and which at the same time enabled considerable demographic and, in particular, urban expansion (Madrazo 1984).

Although productivity understandably remained unchanged, the commercialisation of agricultural products did increase, which was why José Díez Imbrechts, a winemaker from Cádiz, received government authorisation in 1830 to look into the possibility of constructing a railway line between Jerez and El Portal. This early initiative was followed by others until the State decided to take a hand in the matter, since each concession was being granted under different conditions. The liberal government of Narváez requested a report from the Highways, Canals, and Ports Office as to how to manage this new phenomenon. In turn, this office commissioned the engineers Juan Subercase, his son José, and Calixto Santa Cruz to undertake the task. These engineers drew up the so-called "Subercase Report" which, signed on 2 November 1844, came to provide the basis for the first Spanish legislative measures taken on the matter of railways: the Royal Order of 31 December 1844.

This Royal Order merely served to set out a series of general conditions through which individuals were granted the right to build railway lines, taking into account the fact that the new transport system was of public interest, given the enormous influence it would have on the economy. There was therefore no doubt that construction and exploitation should be undertaken by private entrepreneurs. Yet due to the enormous mistrust which the latter sparked amongst the authorities, and in particular the tremendous fear that private entrepreneurs might create a monopoly, it was also made abundantly clear that responsibility for funding rested solely on their shoulders. As a result, a series of conditions were laid out to safeguard public interest. However, it was also left to the discretion of *ad hoc* negotiation between concessionaires and the State to establish certain concessions or privileges. This led to speculation rather than the search for any real business and the construction of the lines. All of this turned the *primarii lapidis* of Spanish railway legislation into a straightjacket that in practice made it impossible to develop the new means of transport[1].

As a legislative measure, the Royal Order pushed forward the institutional framework which was to govern this period, as well as its principal technical characteristics. Prominent amongst the latter was the decision to opt for a different gauge to the one being introduced in the rest of Europe given that, based on the report issued by the Royal Commission on Railway Gauges, this was felt to be the best. This decision may have been open to question, but it was one of many that had to be taken at the time. No credit whatsoever should be given to speculation that the decision was designed to prevent a possible French invasion (Moreno Fernández 1996).

Many have been insisted upon the fact that the railways came to Spain late, yet in 1844 there were barely ten countries that could boast a railway system. One of these had been in operation since 19 November 1837, in Cuba – La Habana-Bejucal – which at the time was under Spanish rule. The problem was rather that the first institutional framework set up to channel its development only made it possible to install 7.4% of the 6,000 kilometres that had been applied for between 1844 and 1855: Barcelona-Mataró (28.1 km.), Barcelona-Granollers (28.7), Barcelona-Molins de Rey (17.7), Játiva-Grao de Valencia (60.7), Madrid-Albacete (279.7), Jerez-Puerto de Santa María (14.7), and Sabadell-Montcada (13.7) (Muñoz Rubio & Ortúñez 2013a).

There is therefore no question that this first initiative of the moderate governments proved to be a failure, although those who did manage to achieve their goal, most of whom were local entrepreneurs, did have a hand in creating a "*national way*" in railways.

This situation reached a turning point in 1854 when the progressive liberals came to power since they removed all the obstacles that, during the "moderate decade", had prevented economic modernisation from taking a decisive step forward. On 3 June 1855 Francisco de Luxán, Infrastructure Minister, signed the first General Law on Railways. Its main contributions were, first, that the State would assume the power to set up a national network, second, in contrast to the many limits imposed under previous legislation concerning private capital, it established a universal condition to allow the entry of private capital through concessionaires that was backed up by public funding; and third, the "national safeguard" established to protect any foreign capital that might be invested in the business.

Aided by the various financing laws that helped channel capital towards the sector, these changes soon had a decided effect. In fact, between 1855 and 1865, some 4,756 km of track, 68.7% of the total granted, went into operation. This period not only witnessed the fastest growth ever but also allowed the Spanish railway network to reduce the gap with other European networks, since total track length between 1850 and 1870 went from being 209.1 times less to 3.6 times less than that of Germany's, 349.8 to 4.1 times less than that of Great Britain's, 104.1 to 2.9 times less than that of France's, and 22.1 to 1.2 times less than that of Italy's.

The law also pursued another goal: to allow the French companies Pereire and Rothschild to gain a stake in Spanish railways. To do this, progressive governments set up a solid institutional apparatus which they placed at the service of these financing houses so as to favour them through the direct influx of capital and subsidies from a significant part of public debt. This opened up the path to a *"foreign way"* in railways, which led to the setting up of two major Spanish companies – Norte and Madrid Zaragoza Alicante (MZA) (Tedde de Lorca 1978). Driven by a desire to gain control of the main line of communication with France, these companies established their main axes during the second stage on the original concessions awarded – Madrid-Irun in the former case; and Madrid-Alicante, Madrid-Cordoba, and Madrid-Zaragoza in the latter.

The Test of the Financial Crisis for the Companies

When the crisis hit in 1866, the business scene for Spanish railways displayed a two-fold appearance since there was an "apparent" climate of peaceful coexistence between regional companies, funded through local capital, and Norte and MZA, which were financed equally between French and Spanish capital – although it was really the former that was in control. Yet once these early lines had been built, the concessionaires found that the volume of traffic was not enough to meet their debt payments. The situation became even worse with the crisis the Spanish economy went through during the 1860s, given that demand stemmed mainly from the primary sector. Financial years were closing at an operating loss, which meant that Norte and MZA were unable to respond by securing further capital since they had reached the legally allowed maximum debt limit. Nor could the State help them out as it was immersed in its own treasury crisis. Moreover, the Paris and London stock exchanges closed the door on the Spanish economy, given the latter's renowned failure to pay, added to which there were the effects of the international crisis (Tortella Casares 1973).

Railway share prices and bond values immediately began to tumble and, as a result, dragged much of the Spanish financial system down with them.

While local projects were barely able to survive, Norte and MZA, thanks to the financial support provided by their parent companies, were in a position to weather the storm – yet not without getting Spain to foot the bill. As a result, after the frustration of the failed government loan in July 1867, Norte and MZA came to the conclusion that the approaching revolution would provide the effective solution to their financial problems. They therefore had no qualms about playing an active role in the conspiracy. Their leader, Francisco Serrano, went from being president of Norte to being president of the first revolutionary government. Yet he was not the only one. Other leaders of courtesan politics, such as Sagasta, Rivero, Cánovas, and Montero Ríos, amongst others, were linked to the railway concessionaires.

It therefore comes as no surprise that one of the very first measures taken by the revolutionary government was to set up a fund to rescue the railways. Nor did the government waste any time in amending the institutional framework that regulated the public works to support their objective since Manuel Ruiz Zorrilla, Infrastructure Minister, signed the "Decree Bases for Legislating Public Works"[2] on 14 November 1868.

Eventually, the crisis of 1866 put paid to the savings of the local bourgeoisie and, as these formed the basis of the so-called "*national way*", this led to the Spanish railway system becoming a duopoly of the Rothschilds and the Pereires. Even so, this was the result of a violent process, because MZA and Norte were forced to collude in order to achieve it. It was also gradual, not concluding until 1900, and it was imperfect because two regional companies would survive: Andaluces and Oeste. In any event, at the turn of the twentieth century, the Spanish railway network was complete, and the two leading companies held 75% of the total.

The Modernising Impact of the Railway

Despite these ups and downs, the railway's impact on the economy and on society immediately became clear. The virtues of the new transport system amazed contemporaries who saw how it cut journey times by 70% while costing about half of the price. Given these advantages, it came as no surprise to see demand grow consistently and spectacularly, since the number of passengers carried by Norte and MZA multiplied by almost tenfold between 1864 and 1914, whilst the volume in tonnage of freight increased sevenfold. The 30 million passengers and the 15.5 million tonnes amassed by these two companies in 1914 confirmed, without any doubt, that the railway had become a dominant and irreplaceable form of transport.

The mercantile traffic of the concessionaires covered almost all areas of production. In MZA, the freight that represented the greatest percentage included crops, wines, wools, cotton and leather, mineral coal, fabric and footwear, iron, steel, and machinery, as well as lead and minerals. Although manufactured products, machinery, and steel products gradually came to play a part, the company continued to specialise in the agri-mining sector, since in the second half of the nineteenth century, the economic structure of the southern part of the peninsula barely changed.

Norte had laid track in areas – the Basque Country, Galicia, Catalonia, Aragón, Castile, and Valencia – which specialised in a wide variety of economic sectors. This enabled the company to diversify its traffic far more than MZA was able to do, although it was agricultural products that made up the bulk of its commercial portfolio. The Castilian plateau provided crops – mainly wheat and flour – as a by-product. Together with wines, spirits, and coal, these accounted for most of Norte's revenue from freight transport. The continual annexing of lines allowed the company to include new goods, such as mining products, destined to supply Madrid and the industrial Basque Country, as well as metal finishings.

This traffic clearly shows how the most decisive contribution made by the railway was to act as the main driver that converted regional markets into a single national market because, although this process had been occurring since the mid-eighteenth century, it was only able to establish itself thanks to the introduction of the railway. Empirical evidence shows how there was a gradual convergence of prices between the different regions, which was to conclude around 1880 when the railway network achieved national scale, triggering the process of regional production specialisation.

The agricultural sector, in particular the wheat sector, remained a basic subsistence product in nineteenth century Spain. Thanks to the institutional reforms which accompanied the expansion of the railway, the sector organised itself around the market. In other words, it submitted itself to the discipline of competition between various peninsular regions and, therefore, witnessed moderate progress in terms of its specialisation.

Livestock, both settled and transhumance, another backbone of the Spanish economy, underwent a similar process of regional specialisation. This process proved decisive in making urban expansion possible by being able to supply live meat, which was becoming an increasingly important part of the Spanish diet (Muñoz Rubio 2015). In fact, it was common for city abattoirs to be supplied with live animals that had been shipped in railway carriages. This also helped to offset the strangulation which certain regional agricultures had been suffering since the second half of the nineteenth century due to the shortage of draught animals by returning these animals to agricultural tasks as they were no longer required to haul over land.

After the second half of the nineteenth century the railway also became a key element for metal mining (iron, lead), exports of which to British factories provided many of the financial resources used to import the machinery that helped to modernise Spanish industry. In the case of energy mining, coal was also determinant since it was a sizeable good but of little unitary value, yet essential for manufacturers. It was only thanks to the railway that it could be shipped at a competitive price and, as a result, that the secondary sector could cut its production costs and improve the distribution of products in markets.

One example of the benefits to manufacturers can be found in the wool industry in Catalonia which, having been replaced by cotton, managed to recover and conquer new markets in the Spanish hinterland. It now proved possible to obtain a regular supply of the raw material at a relatively low price due to the cheaper transport costs in Extremadura or Castilla and to process it in factories in Catalonia. Yet if there is one paradigmatic case, it is undoubtedly Catalonian cotton. The railway opened the door to Spanish markets inland and led to some Catalonian areas specialising in yarn whilst others did so in weaving.

On the demand side, the railways also made a substantial contribution. They boosted the construction of public works since the previously unknown scale of railway infrastructure led to the emergence of new companies who needed greater financial and management capacity than had hitherto existed. These companies engaged in bigger deals, acquired greater business and technical skills, and expanded beyond the scope of the smaller works that were typical of rural areas.

As pointed out, improvements in transport help to explain the growth of urban nuclei after 1857. Urbanisation in the second half of the nineteenth century received a boost since larger populations needed to expand the radius of their supply markets, and railways helped to provide transport not only for food but also for larger and heavier construction material.

The railways also obviously had a positive effect on employment. During the construction phase, it offset the chronic underemployment of inland Spanish agriculture and it improved, through the salaries offered, workers' pay and as a result increased demand for consumption. During the exploitation and consolidation period, the sector provided stable employment. It should also be highlighted that the demand for technical jobs made the railway concessionaires one of the favoured destinations for highways and industrial engineers. At the turn of the century, many of these joined the management and technical teams.

However, the possibilities of providing additional demand to the steel and equipment sector were hampered by the approval of a tariff franchise. This allowed the main production equipment – engines, carriages, and tracks – required to build and operate the lines to be introduced freely into the Spanish market. As a result, most of the materials the companies needed were imported.

Although it is true that these sectors lacked the production capacity to meet the needs of the railways, they began to acquire it towards the end of the nineteenth century. Spanish industry participation was ultimately reduced to assembling equipment and parts, all of which were imported, and to constructing a few low-added value and low-tech auxiliary parts. The most notable contribution was the partial construction of the first carriages by *Herrería Barcelonesa* in 1860 and the finishings of the first steam engines by *La Maquinista Terrestre y Marítima* in 1884. In any case, national production of more complex railway material, the rolling stock, was purely anecdotal throughout the nineteenth century: 21 steam engines, 242 coaches, 52 vans, and 1,976 carriages.

The railway emerges as a trigger or necessary factor in most of the progress made during the first stage of Spanish capitalism.

Spanish Railway Companies at the Beginning of their Decline: Circa 1900–1913

An economy like Spain's which was unable to make that final transition towards an industrialised economy, which lacked a productive agricultural sector, and which had seen the demographic development of its urban population, explains why not all privately-owned railway companies were profitable. Fixed costs were high, which was a problem that affected both private as well as national capital since the latter was still insufficiently organised from the administrative and fiscal standpoint to be able to help or replace companies in providing such a service.

The system of concessions approved under the 1855 law meant that companies had limited scope for decision making, particularly when revenue proved insufficient even to cover operating costs. The first to be hit by difficulties were the smaller companies who had small-scale railway networks operating in more economically depressed areas. Business concentration sought to offset these limitations, yet these solutions could only delay the inevitable change in the operating model. There were four railway companies sharing the Spanish railway network, and they had little desire to compete with one another: Norte, MZA, Andaluces, and Oeste. Once the difficult period at the end of the century had concluded only the first two of these companies experienced a situation of relative comfort until the First World War. Even so, any profits that would allow for dividends to be paid to shareholders and for reserve funds to be set up were few and far between. Moreover, the State's limited capacity to act was closely linked to the companies' fragility since there were no efficient mechanisms for acting or intervening.

The concentration of networks generated economies of scale, yet the money invested in this whole business adventure, which had been particularly bold on the part of Norte, was reflected in the balance sheets. Norte's acquisitions were mainly concentrated between 1878 and 1893, with the procedure in all the cases being very similar: waiting until the targeted company was in difficulty, which would reduce their bargaining power and their price, and then subrogating payment of their bonds and converting the company's shares into Norte bonds. The tactic was similar to that used by MZA, where this process was mainly carried out between 1875 and 1898.

For MZA, acquisition of the Tarragona to Barcelona and France Railway Company (721 kilometres) in 1898 proved to be highly profitable: revenue soared, and the deal provided them with a line to France in addition to endowing their old network with a key complement by being able to run traffic to Zaragoza. It also gave them a substantial slice of coastal traffic in the Mediterranean. After 1906 and until 1916–1917, results were good and allowed them to pay their shareholders dividends, something which the shareholders were not very accustomed to.

The economic situation of the country and the policy of the company are the key factors to be considered when evaluating railway companies' financial performance: the late nineteenth century crisis or the weight of the bonds lie behind the bad results obtained until 1906. Between 1891 and 1914, GDP *per capita* grew at an average interannual rate of 0.98%, whereas between 1851 and 1890 the figure had been 1.13%. This difference slowed down the modernising push of the Spanish economy since the relative weight of the secondary sector, which peaked in 1891 at 29 points, remained unchanged until 1914 at a mean figure of 29.08. Industrial product went from an average interannual rate of 0.71% between 1851 and 1890 to 0.85% between 1891 and 1914, which meant that while during the first stage it had grown by 28.4 points, in the second it did so by only 20.3 points.

Protectionism and public support for the national industrial sector became the axes of the new economic policy, as it did in other more advanced economies, although protectionism was more radical in Spain. The outcome could not have been worse, since Spanish GDP *per capita* fell by 19 points between 1891 and 1913 compared to the European average, and levels of well-being among the population were lower (Maluquer de Motes 2002). In addition, farming of marginal land grew and Spanish migration reached 3.4 million people between 1881 and 1910, whereas between 1851 and 1880 it had only stood at 0.2 million. Nevertheless, the arrival of capital resulting from the loss of territories overseas, and equivalent to one quarter of annual national rent, enabled the creation of large modern businesses, particularly in the banking sector, as well as the spread of technologies linked to the second technological revolution, such as electricity, and which allowed the burden of energy costs to be overcome.

During the period leading up to the start of the Great War, the moderate growth in the Spanish economy did not enable any headway to be made in production convergence and modernisation as it had done during the previous period. Some progress was made, yet this was soon to evidence all its weaknesses in the face of such a monumentally adverse event as the First World War.

Yet it was precisely during some years of this pre-war period, after 1907, when Norte and MZA were to have their finest hour, if we consider the stability they enjoyed and the dividends they paid out to their shareholders. It proved to be a kind of swan song before the great crisis triggered by the war. The leading companies were finally enjoying what they had set out to achieve: sharing traffic in their areas of influence. Norte and MZA in fact represented a duopoly, while Andaluces and Oeste, in serious difficulties because of their poor results, controlled regional traffic in the south and west of the peninsula (Cuéllar & Sánchez 2008).

Norte experienced greater difficulties than MZA during this pre-war period, as is reflected by the number of years at which they ran at a loss (Norte was making a loss between 1893–1897 and again between 1904–1906). This meant fewer dividends being paid out to its shareholders. Specifically, in ten of the twenty years between 1900 and 1920, Norte's shareholders failed to receive any dividend, while the average for the period as a whole only came to 7.78 pesetas after tax. In contrast, MZA shareholders received dividends every year at an average of 14.28 pesetas per share. Only in 1912 and in 1913 did the two companies manage to get the market value of their shares to rise above the nominal value.

Norte enjoyed a good run in the early 1880s thanks to wine exports to France, despite the agribusiness crisis which Spain was experiencing. However, in the 1890s and early years of the twentieth century, losses once again appeared. This was because there was no increase in revenue as a result of the reduction in traffic and the end of exports to France, and due to the higher costs – particularly financial costs – resulting from the debt taken on when the company had expanded, coupled with a depreciation of the peseta vis-à-vis the franc, the currency in which interest payments were indexed. These circumstances led to heavy losses for Norte. After 1895, the company was forced to seek agreements with its shareholders and bondholders in order to alleviate, in the short term, the burden of its commitments. The reduction in operating costs, a stronger peseta compared to the franc and the gradually paying off of the bonds that were fixed in francs led to an improvement in performance until the economic and social upheavals that triggered the First World War, which once again gave rise to losses.

Amongst the larger companies, Andaluces was one of the last to be set up. This meant they were able to avoid the financing costs which others had incurred when forced to face the crisis of the late 1860s: the burden of bonds was not as heavy for them as it proved to be for other companies. Yet this late entry came at a price – its lines did not run to Madrid. Moreover, it was hit by the crisis of the late nineteenth century after 1894, which forced it, as occurred with Norte, to suspend regular payment of interest and amortisation of bonds. During the first decades of the twentieth century it had pursued its policy of annexing small companies, which led to a gradual increase in kilometres of operating track from 1,261 in 1913 to the 1,646 it had when it was taken over in 1936. More than annexations or take-overs, it was a "reunification of provincial or district lines into a regional size company" (Tedde de Lorca 1980). This policy failed to have any positive effects for Andaluces's operation since it put paid to the founders' initial idea which was based on limiting their own investment and keeping down levels of debt, added to which it also reduced the chance of making any profit. This was reflected in the results, with losses that persisted over time as a result of the war. Moreover, between 1900 and 1920, its shareholders received nothing in nine of the years and the average was a mere 4.98 pesetas.

The Change of Model: From the System of Concessions to Intervention, 1914–1931

In the major railway companies, financing through outside resources had grown much more than through their own resources. Up until that point, attempts to solve any problems which emerged had involved extending the networks. Yet once the companies had expanded all they could, and with few resources available and no other interesting companies left to take over, where would the solutions to new problems come from now? Any possible agreements between the companies who controlled the railway oligopoly were bound to prove tricky, with each jealously guarding both the network it ran as well as its own particular style of management.

Yet there were fresh difficulties to come. These were of an intensity and were on a scale with such devastating repercussions that had been unimaginable up until that point: the First World War. This had an impact on absolutely everything, both in the countries that were actually fighting as well as in neutral countries, and indeed right up until at least the crisis and depression of the 1930s. Spain was no stranger to all of these circumstances, and the war's effect on the railways, a sector regulated by the State, was enormous. The problems of regulation through concessions became evident and indeed were aggravated since these were about to expire. Economic difficulties increased, and companies lacked the freedom to establish prices. Problems were exacerbated by the inflation triggered as a result of the 1914–18 conflict. Companies lost control over running costs. It should be remembered that between 1913 and 1920 these increased for Norte at an annual rate of 14.0%, whilst in the case of MZA they did so at an annual rate of 17.7% and in Andaluces at 14.2%. Meanwhile, revenue from freight and passenger traffic only grew by 8.7% in Norte, by 8.9% in MZA and by 8.1% in Andaluces.

The lack of control over costs and inflation and with revenue being regulated, the sector plunged into a crisis which the railways would not be able to overcome, if we consider the issue from an economic perspective. With the exception of MZA, all of the other Spanish railway companies ran at a loss for at least one year or were unable to overturn their losses.

This accumulation of circumstances forced the State, which up until that point had taken a back seat, to intervene more directly in the sector. Its economic importance and the labour conflict sparked by railway workers, in particular after the demonstrations of 1916 and 1917, coupled with social demand for an inexpensive and efficient system of transport brought things to a head. What had been a regulating State was now to become, because of the conflict, an intervening State. There were calls for a change to the operating system. Although there was still no talk of nationalisation, in the sense that the State would exercise its right to rescue the concessions and directly run the railways itself, the issue – the "railway problem" – was being discussed in any number of forums: parliament, specialised press, and newspapers. The problem was that although positions were not clear, the manifestations made both during and after the war left no room for doubt: there were delays and disorder in operating, the decapitalisation of assets, an impending reversion to the State of the first concessions that had been granted, difficulties securing funding in the market, and each company was incapable on their own to assume the increased running costs and rising labour costs imposed by the need to match salaries to inflation and to adapt the workforce to the legislation imposed by the eight-hour day.

For the infrastructure ministers of the period, the issue of what was to be done with the railways was at the top of their agenda. All other investments were conditional upon the "railway problem" being solved. The solution preferred by the railway companies themselves involved the State authorising them to increase the maximum charges as much as possible so as to guarantee financial independence: they would thus regain control over revenue and would obtain the flexibility to adapt charges to business criteria. For its part, the State was in doubt about what to do, fearing, as it did, a social backlash to any hike in prices coupled with its limited scope for action given the institutional instability of the moment. There were ministers who barely had time to gather together the necessary information given how little time they were actually in office.

Minister Cambó agreed to an increase in prices in December 1918, although not in the terms the companies wanted, since the percentage rise was lower than requested and was applied to existing charges and not to the maximum prices, which meant a difference of many millions. In 1920, one of his successors instigated the system of refundable advance payments, an intermediate solution which failed to satisfy almost anybody since, in sum, it recognised the need to boost the companies' revenue yet made them dependent upon the resources which the State could acquire. Through these advance payments, the companies were able to finance labour costs and to purchase material. This measure heralded a decisive landmark in State–company relations, as from that moment onwards intervention can be said to have begun. The State set out that all of these amounts should be clearly distinguished in the companies' accounts and, drawing on the need to ensure control over what was being done with the funds provided, organised administrative intervention systems: the Higher Railways Council.

Parliament discussed the issue of recouping the concessions through various projects, yet in all the cases in question they were faced with what was an insurmountable obstacle for the prevailing liberal mentality: the need to compensate the companies in accordance with the stipulations laid down by law. The problem was that the State lacked the necessary resources to do so. There was also the problem of what to do later as regards running the railways once they came under state control.

Most of the concessions were for 99 years, although some lines had been granted on a perpetual basis. This meant that there were many different dates on which lines would revert to the State. As the collateral of the bonds were the operating results of the lines over a long period of time, the impending expiry date of the concessions reduced the time to pay back the debt and made debt issuance with shorter maturity harder. All of this meant that it was impossible for the companies to self-finance and explains why, given the objective need for financial resources, the State would resort to subsidising the railway companies.

The declaration made by General Primo de Rivera in September 1923 came when the intermediate solution had already been put into effect: advance payments and the creation of the Higher Council. These measures enabled the major companies, who would later be followed by Andaluces, to recover in terms of financial performance and as regards volume of transport, and this allowed them to almost reach pre-war levels. However, no progress had been made vis-à-vis the underlying issue: what role the State was to play.

For public opinion, the solutions were slow in coming. This encouraged the dictator to make the railway problem the star project among the issues which the dictatorship would deal with and which the previous political system of the "Restoration" had shown itself incapable of solving. The measures they adopted in this matter were also doomed to failure because their project, which was over ambitious and even unrealistic in some cases, was left unfinished due to the lack of sufficient financial resources. Moreover, the problem was inherited by the Second Republic, who were only able to worsen the situation.

This was the time of the Railway Statute, which, after 1926, was able to draw on funding from the State Railway Fund. The Fund was fed by issuing public debt and substantially increased the resources obtained through the advance payment system. Without these financial resources, the companies would have collapsed after 1926 under the weight of their debt. Specifically, between 1926 and 1935, companies' property, plants, and equipment barley increased, while the State's did so in Norte by 18.6% and in MZA by 29.4% – that is to say, it was the State that was keeping the companies afloat. During this period, revenue went up but at a slower rate than during the war. Although financial expenses were greater, operating costs rose less than they had during the previous cycle and profits were channelled to shareholders. In this regard, it was Andaluces who came off worst, since although their revenue increased between 1921 and 1930, their operating costs did so even more. The company's best results were obtained in 1924, after which the firm went into decline and it would eventually run at a loss after 1928.

The Railway Fund provided the companies with money which they would never have been able to obtain through revenue from traffic. Thanks to the funds made available, the companies were able to invest in purchasing machinery and in renewing fixed material and stations, which had remained greatly outdated as a result of the difficulties caused by the war. The differences in results between one company and another are largely due to the favourable treatment received by Norte and MZA. By way of an example, it should be remembered that the support given to Norte in 1928 by the Railway Fund was equivalent to 27.6% of its operating revenue. Not surprisingly, all of these amounts came to swell the State's property, plants, and equipment.

The aim of the Fund's statute was to endow the companies with the resources that would enable them to return to operating normally and place their house in order. Nevertheless, the formula applied proved to be the wrong one. Firstly, the investments failed to reach the whole of the network, which would have been impossible in any case. Secondly, the pace of the investments would have needed to have been maintained over time, which was also impossible for the State, and thirdly because it left the companies unable to secure resources through the financial markets or by raising prices. The resources obtained by the Fund were also devoted to other investments, some of which proved to be preposterous even before the works had concluded. The weight of the works that had already been started but that were not finished coupled with projects that were running at a loss from day one, was later to fall on the shoulders of the republican governments, making their stability even more difficult.

The End of the Concession System: 1931–1941

The final stage in chronological terms corresponds to the 1930s, when companies were hit particularly hard by the international economic crisis, competition from the roads, and republican legislation, which the companies felt was hostile to their interests. MZA's decline in terms of results preceded that of Norte. The companies sought to adopt measures to cut costs, which they managed to achieve between 1931 and 1932, but which they were subsequently unable to maintain. Between 1931 and 1935, revenue from traffic for Norte and MZA fell. Not even the increase in prices approved in May 1934 was able to help the companies' revenue recover. Once again, a deeper analysis, through a study of how freight transport evolved, reflects a continued decline after 1929 in MZA and after 1930 in Norte. The rise in prices did at least help to contain the slump in revenue, even though the volume of traffic dropped. In sum, the companies' final crisis to a large extent reflected the more general crisis which the Spanish economy was experiencing.

The amount of rail traffic during this period of the twentieth century can be divided into four stages which very closely reflect the respective economic situations: the first, between 1898 and 1914, when companies were affected by the stagnation of the Spanish economy, at least until 1907; the second, between 1914 and 1920, when operating difficulties arose due to the greater relative increase in costs resulting from the Great War; the third, between 1921 and 1930, which was heightened by the problems caused by the weight of debt and financial costs; and finally, between 1931 and the onset of the Civil War, when these already existing difficulties were further compounded by the situation concerning the international economic cycle and the emerging competition.

As already pointed out, Andaluces began to incur losses after 1928, and these were only to increase over the years. The company abandoned operation of its lines in May 1936, when it was taken control of by the State and handed over to another company which had suffered the same fate in 1928, the *Nacional del Oeste de España*. In both instances, the State seized the companies because their concessionaires had ceased to operate the lines. As a result, there was no nationalisation. This was to occur in 1941 for the whole of the normal gauge network and would give rise to the Spanish National Railways Networks (RENFE).

As a result, prior to the Civil War the Spanish railway system was on the brink of collapse. Norte and MZA were running at a loss and investment had once again come to a halt when the Fund suspended support in 1930 and the other two companies had already been seized by the State, who assumed their deficit.

Final Considerations

Railway companies contributed to the process of economic growth in Spain. They helped towards a better distribution of production resources, to a reduction in the price of transport, to the integration of the domestic market, and to the mobility of people as well as their goods and capital. In this undertaking, private capital played a key role, yet so did the State – albeit within its limited scope of action – by sparing no effort, in accordance with the prevailing liberal mentality, when it came to encouraging such investments.

Throughout these almost one hundred years of railways operating in private hands, the sector advanced towards modernisation and convergence. This effort was especially intense in the final two decades of the period considered, and all of the indicators point to this having been the case. The long-term perspective thus acquires particular interest in gauging an effort which, with its ups and down, proved extraordinary: extending and improving the railway system, making unquestionable progress in terms of the volume of goods and passengers carried and, at the same time, including a substantial investment from both public and private initiatives.

Notes

1 For historiographical debates concerning Spanish railways, see Muñoz Rubio 2018.
2 On the role played by the State, (Artola 1978).

References

Anes, R. 1978. Relaciones entre el ferrocarril y la economía española (1865–1935). In *Los ferrocarriles en España 1844–1943*, vol. 2, ed M. Artola, 355–541. Madrid: Banco de España.

Artola, M. 1978. La acción del Estado. In *Los ferrocarriles en España 1844–1943*, vol. 1, ed M. Artola, 339–453. Madrid: Banco de España.

Artola, M. 1978. *Los ferrocarriles en España*. 2 vols. Madrid: Banco de España.

Barquín, R. & P. P. Ortúñez. 2019. "El sector del transporte en la guerra civil española." In *El impacto de la Guerra Civil española en el sector terciario*, ed. M. Fernández-Paradas and C. Larrinaga, 131–152. Granada: Comares.

Broder, A. 2012: *Los ferrocarriles españoles (1845–1913): el gran negocio de los franceses*. Madrid: Fundación de los Ferrocarriles Españoles.

Carreras, A. & X. Tafunell. 2003. *Historia económica de la España contemporánea*. Barcelona: Crítica.

Comín, F., P. Martín, M. Muñoz, & J. Vidal. 1998. *50 años de historia de los ferrocarriles españoles*. Madrid: Editorial Anaya y FFE.

Cuéllar, D. & A. Sánchez. 2008. *150 años de ferrocarril en Andalucía: un balance*. Sevilla: Consejería de Obras Públicas y Transportes de la Junta de Andalucía.

Madrazo, S. 1984. *El sistema de transportes en España, 1750–1850*. Madrid: Colegio de Ingenieros de Caminos, Canales y Puertos-Ediciones Turner.

Maluquer de Motes, J. 2002. Crisis y recuperación económica en la Restauración (1882–1913). In *Historia Económica de España, siglos X-XX*, ed. F. Comín, M. Hernández and E. Llopis, 243–284. Barcelona: Crítica.

Moreno Fernández, J. 1996. *El ancho de la vía en los ferrocarriles españoles: de Espartero a Alfonso XIII*. Madrid: Toral Technical Trade.
Muñoz Rubio, M. 2015. El transporte ferroviario de ganado y el mercado entre 1848 y 1913. *Revista de Historia Agraria* 67: 79–109.
Muñoz Rubio, M. 2018. Los «grandes debates» de la historiografía ferroviaria española y su influencia en la historiografía general y económica. *Revista de la historia de la economía y de la empresa* 12: 89–122.
Muñoz Rubio, M. & P. P. Ortúñez, 2013a. Los transportes y las comunicaciones: La transición de modelos tradicionales a industriales. In *Historia Económica de España*, ed. A. González and J. M. Matés 209–241. Barcelona: Ariel.
Muñoz Rubio, M. & P. P. Ortúñez, 2013b. Los transportes y las comunicaciones en la España de la primera modernidad. In *Historia Económica de España*, ed. A. González and J. M. Matés 551–591. Barcelona: Ariel.
Muñoz, M., J. Sanz & J. Vidal. 1999. *Siglo y medio del ferrocarril en España, 1848–1998. Economía, Industria y Sociedad*. Madrid: FFE.
Ortúñez, P. P. 1999. El proceso de nacionalización de los Ferrocarriles en España. Historia de las grandes compañías ferroviarias, 1913–1943. PhD diss., Univ of Valladolid.
Tedde de Lorca, P. 1978. Las Compañías ferroviarias en España (1855–1935). In *Los ferrocarriles en España 1844–1943*, vol. 2, ed M. Artola, 13–355. Madrid: Banco de España.
Tedde de Lorca, P. 1980. La compañía de los Ferrocarriles Andaluces (1878–1920), una empresa de transportes en la España de la Restauración. *Investigaciones Económicas* 12: 27–76.
Tortella Casares, G. 1973. *Los orígenes del capitalismo en España. Banca, Industria y Ferrocarriles en el siglo XIX*. Madrid: Tecnos.
Vidal Olivares, J. 1999. La estructura de la propiedad, de la organización y la gestión de una gran empresa ferroviaria: la Compañía de los Caminos de Hierro del Norte de España, 1858–1936. *Revista de Historia Económica* 3: 623–662.
Vidal Olivares, J. & P. P. Ortúñez. 2002. The Internationalisation of Ownership of the Spanish Railway Companies, 1858–1936. *Business History* 44: 29–54.

9 The Spanish Travel Agency Business in the Early Years of the Franco Regime

Carlos Larrinaga

Introduction[1]

Currently, there are around 9,000 travel agencies in Spain. This figure is far removed from the maximum number recorded in 2008 when there were more than 13,000 establishments. The severe economic crisis beginning in this year caused this figure to fall to 8,000. The crisis led to the closure of approximately 5,000 offices, including the large networks of the Marsans and Orizonia groups, which went bankrupt in 2010 and 2013 respectively. This reduction in the number of agencies gave rise to a traumatic, yet necessary, restructuring of the sector. In Spain, the sector was too large for the size of the market and compared to other European tourist issuers where there were fewer but larger companies. After 2014, the sector began to experience growth in terms of volume of production and the level of employment. A recovery phase began, and the number of agencies increased to the current amount of 9,000. However, this figure could fall again due to the impact that the COVID-19 pandemic is having on the sector[2].

In addition to the above-mentioned crisis, we should also remember the impact that new technologies have been having on the sector in recent years, particularly e-commerce in the travel industry. The ability to make direct purchases through the websites of airlines or online agencies means that many users opt for this formula and no longer visit traditional travel agencies. On the other hand, there are also users who believe that planning their trips through the Internet requires too much time. For example, 58% of Spanish passengers believe that they invest more time than desired on purchasing a plane ticket online. And 42% feel the same about making a hotel reservation[3]. Factors such as these and the fact that there is still a segment of the population that is unfamiliar with these purchasing techniques explain the existence of a large number of travel agencies in Spain. These agencies have exhibited great resilience in order to survive as a sector. This resilience has characterised the industry throughout its history of over 150 years.

Although this study focuses exclusively on the early years of the Franco regime, travel agencies have existed in Spain since the end of the nineteenth century. In fact, the Compañía Internacional Wagons-Lits opened its first office in Madrid as early as 1880 (Bayón & Fernández Fúster 2005, 31). Thomas

Cook opened its first agency in 1892, also in the Spanish capital (Vallejo & Larrinaga 2020, 9). This was practically half a century after it had organised its first trip between Leicester and Loughborough by train in 1841, transporting a group of people to an anti-alcoholic congress. New travelling possibilities offered by the railways had emerged and Cook knew how to identify them. In fact, it was precisely within this new context of the development of the different modes of transport that the travel agency was born as a new form of business. In this respect, Thomas Cook was a visionary, and he became the world's first travel agent. He sought to organise pleasure trips for large groups of people while also exercising an educational function. His first operation involved transporting 500 people to Loughborough and after just a few years this figure had multiplied. In 1851 he arranged for 150,000 people, all from Yorkshire, to travel to the Great Exhibition in London. Four years later he did the same but this time to the Exhibition in Paris. From then on, his name was associated with international travel. By the time he opened his first office in London in 1865, Cook was a national and international travel entrepreneur. And in 1891, the year when he celebrated his golden wedding anniversary in the Hotel Metropole in London, he had become a global agent (Brendon 1991; Rae 1891).

Thomas Cook had laid the foundations of a business destined for success. The age of industrialisation brought with it the transport revolution and a revolution in travel. This increased mobility led to a transformation in the way people travelled and the sector shifted towards the collective management of travel, thus avoiding the need for each service provider to manage passengers directly. From then on, travelling involved tickets, travel assistance, accommodation, guides, or interpreters once the tourists had arrived in the destination, etc. These functions would become those of a travel agency. This does not mean that all trips, or even most of them, were mediated (Vallejo & Larrinaga 2020, p. 1). Cook laid the foundations of this business model which gradually expanded not only throughout Great Britain (Pimlott 1977 (1947 1ª), Chapter 11) but also across other European countries (Visentin 1995) and the United States (Santis 1978). The first European travel agencies were: Bennett in Norway (1850), Stangen in Germany (1863), Lubin in France (1873), Lissone in the Netherlands (1876), and Massimiliano Chiari in Italy (1878) (Lanquar 1979, p. 5; Visentin 1995, p. 303). Therefore, we should consider these travel broker companies as a fundamental part of the birth of modern tourism, by then understood as an industry and therefore with commercial purposes (Norval 1936).

With respect to Spain, we have already mentioned Cook's first agency in Madrid. From then, the sector developed slowly but gradually gained prominence over the following decades (Vallejo & Larrinaga 2020) In fact, we should look for the origins of travel agencies in the first third of the twentieth century in light of the aforementioned tourism industry. During these years, the first tourism system, with its regional varieties, was taking shape in Spain, incorporating all of the participating agents (Vallejo, 2018). This system included different types of companies and entrepreneurs (hotels, transport, etc.) and, of course, the travel agents. As well as the foreign operators established in Spain, the first Spanish travel agencies were also constituted, such as Viajes Marsansrof (1910) in Barcelona and, a few years later, Eusebio Cafranga in San Sebastián which were among the most important, although there were more. As would be expected, the business was affected somewhat by the Civil War (1936–1939), although it did not disappear. Some agencies, such as Cook and Cafranga, even benefitted thanks to the tourism activities implemented by the Franco authorities in those areas of Spain under their control in the years 1938 and 1939 (Larrinaga 2019).

The Decree of 19 February 1942 Regarding Travel Agencies

Apart from the death toll and the large number of wounded and those who had been displaced or who had fled, the war also had a strong impact on all areas of the economy, including tourism. It is true that before the conflict Spain was not exactly a leading force in tourism. However, the country did have a tourism industry. The International Exhibitions of Barcelona and Seville of 1929 had led to an increase in the number of foreign tourists. Although it only accounted for a small part of GDP, a tourism industry was starting to take shape and in places such as San Sebastián, Santander, Barcelona, Madrid, or Mallorca, it was becoming more prominent. The bombing during the war damaged a good part of this industry and the tourist flows. In this sense, the breakout of the Second World War shortly after the end of the Civil War did not help at all. However, this did not prevent the new authorities of Franco's regime from showing an interest in a sector which, in the medium term, could be an important source of wealth and bring in the sought-after foreign currency (Bolín 1967, p. 333).

Shortly after the end of the conflict, through the law of 8 August 1939, the Central State Administration was reorganised so that the former national ministries became known as Directorate Generals from this date. For the case in hand, the National Tourism Service changed to the Directorate General of Tourism (GDT). The same person remained at the head of this organisation, namely the lawyer and journalist Luis Bolín, who had already held positions of responsibility in tourism at the end of the 1920s. Bolín was a born propagandist and an enthusiast of tourism and believed that Spain could become a leader in tourism, which, in fact, it did. The GDT was created for the purpose of coordinating all the tourist aspects related to the private sector. In fact, through the Franco dictatorship's desire to control the private sector, the GDT carried out intense legislative activity that revealed the clearly interventionist policy of the regime in tourism matters (Correyero 2005, pp. 62–63; Moreno 2007, pp. 152 & 159–160). From the outset, the DGT collaborated in the reconstruction of Spain, stimulating the country's promotion and helping to prepare it to welcome national and foreign tourists. It readily carried out exceptional propaganda work, relying mainly on the private sector, specifically, the Spanish Federation of Trade Unions of Initiatives and Tourism (FESIT in its Spanish acronym) and travel agencies (Correyero & Cal 2008, p. 302).

According to Bolín, it was very important to have the support of travel agencies as they knew the markets and had experience in managing tourism and selling Spain to foreign tourists (Vallejo & Concejal 2018, p. 399). In fact, the new functions of travel agencies in Spain were regulated in the Decree of 19 February 1942 (*Boletín Oficial del Estado* [Official State Gazette], 6-5-1942), which aspired to taking full control of their activity to avoid competition with the state. Tourism as such was the exclusive competence of the state, and, according to Article 2, travel agencies were reserved for the following purposes and business: selling tickets and reserving seats in all kinds of regular transport, booking hotel rooms and services, organising package tours, group tours, excursions, and city visits.

The decree classified the agencies into two groups. Group A would be made up of those agencies which, dedicated to the activities indicated in Article 2, fulfilled the following requirements: 1) they had to be depository entities and be able to issue tickets of the International Union or, failing that, of three European nations; 2) they had to be concessionaires for the sale of combined coupon tickets of the National Network of Spanish Railways; 3) they had to be concessionaires for the sale of tickets of the Spanish Airline Companies; 4) they had to be authorised to sell tickets for the principal Spanish Navigation Companies; and 5) they had to have civil liability insurance arranged to cover the risks of both group and individual travel. Therefore, those agencies that did not comply with these conditions would be included in Group B, acting as intermediaries between the public and the agencies of Group A, only providing the tickets and bonds issued by them.

Once the decree had been issued and published, the applications submitted were studied so that, from the month of December onwards, the classifications or licences granted to group A agencies appeared in the Boletín Oficial del Estado (Official State Gazette). Between 1942 and 1944 the first twelve agencies of group A were authorised, namely: Marsans, Internacional Expreso, Cafranga, Iberia, Wagons-Lits Cook, Bakumar, Hispania, Meliá, Deutsche America Linie, Agencia General de las Compañías Hamburguesas, Sommariva, and Vincit. Of these twelve, four were of foreign origin: Wagons-Lits Cook, Deutsche America Linie, Agencia General de las Compañías Hamburguesas, and Sommariva. Of these, Wagons-Lits Cook and Sommariva had been working in Spain for many years. Furthermore, during the war, the office of Wagons-Lits Cook in San Sebastián had remained open. After the conflict, these agencies sought to position themselves in the Spanish market, so that, once the Second World War was over, they could restore the flow of foreign tourists to Spain. In fact, in 1942, apart from its head office in Madrid, Wagons-Lits Cook had another 12 agencies and 15 sub-agencies distributed throughout Spain, excluding the Balearic and Canary Islands. It was the travel company with the greatest presence in the country. Being one of the first travel agencies to establish itself in Spain at the end of the nineteenth century had enabled it to gain an excellent knowledge of the business and of the country's tourism potential.

In terms of the number of agencies, it was followed by Bakumar, which had its head office in Málaga. By 1943 this company had a further eight agencies. This was followed by Cafranga and Marsans, with seven and five establishments respectively. Of the remaining agencies, the case of Meliá is particularly noteworthy. José Meliá Sinisterra (Valencia, 1911) started his career in the family business, which was a citrus fruit exporter and shipping agency. Then in 1941 he created Meliá y Compañía. The end of the Second World War gave rise to a large number of displacements: the diaspora of deserters, exiles, prisoners, forced labourers, Jews, survivors, fugitive Nazis, people anxious to return to their home countries, and people in search of a new country. Like other agencies in southern Europe, Meliá transported Jews to America and Palestine, which enabled it to gain considerable experience in the organisation of trips, a know-how that would be developed further in his new company, Viajes Meliá, S.A. (1947) (Fernández Fúster 1991, 488; Buades 2004, 94).

At the same time, the first classifications were also being awarded to Group B agencies, that is, to those agencies acting as intermediaries between the main Group A companies and their clients. Taking into account the information in the Boletín Oficial del Estado (Official State Gazette), we can observe a territorial expansion of these agencies and, therefore, an expansion of the business. Moreover, we can see that the first three agencies of Group A (Marsans, Internacional Expreso, and Cafranga) were those with the most intermediaries, enabling them to strengthen their presence in certain areas of the country. Furthermore, the changes occurring between them with respect to the same Group B agency are also interesting, revealing a certain conflict between the large agencies of the sector at a difficult moment in the reconstruction of the tourism business after the Civil War and the Second World War. Indeed, the fact that some of these agencies of Group B ceased trading is clear proof of this.

In addition, the DGT created an Advisory Commission made up of the 12 largest agencies operating in Spain (Group A). This Commission had a merely advisory function and Ricardo Jaspe, representing the DGT itself, occupied the secretariat of an institution known as the Commission of Twelve, which existed until 26 February 1963 (Correyero & Cal, p. 398). The Permanent Commission of Travel Agencies, created on 10 December 1943, was more decisive. This was made up of Group A travel agencies and agents from other sectors interested in resolving certain problems that were affecting the tourism activity in Spain (DGT, RENFE, merchant marine, airlines, or the Sindicato Vertical de Hostelería, to name but a few)[4].

Travel Agencies in Spain After the Second World War

At the end of the Second World War, the government and the different private agents in the tourism sector placed their hopes in the recovery of the flow of foreign visitors to Spain. However, these hopes took some time to be fulfilled. After the surrender of the German authorities in May 1945, Spain became isolated from the world due to its support of the dictatorships of the Axis alliance during the conflict. In fact, Spain was not invited to the San Francisco conference, opening on 25 April of the same year, and was subject to international isolation as imposed by a resolution of the United Nations. The withdrawal of ambassadors and the closure of the French border were direct consequences of this repudiation. This, combined with the destruction of transport infrastructures (roads, bridges, railway lines), buildings (tourist accommodation, for example) and the severe shortages (of food, fuel, etc.) suffered by the country in the years immediately following the end of the Civil War explain the difficult moment experienced by the receptive tourism sector in Spain during these years. In 1945 Spain received 39.2 thousand tourists. This figure more than doubled the following year to 83.6 thousand. From this year the number of inbound tourists increased progressively, and by 1949 the figure had surpassed that of 1930, the highest before the Civil War (Tena 2005, 641). At this point, we should remember that immediately after the Second World War, the political, economic, and social situation of the majority of western European countries did not incite people to take pleasure trips: at least until the reconstruction process began, thanks largely to the Marshall Plan. Only from this moment did the tourist flows begin to recover gradually and the interest in the Mediterranean as a holiday destination began to increase. This would explain the high figure of 1949 and how it evolved in subsequent years.

That said, although it is true that the Mediterranean was becoming a tourist destination before the Second World War (Pemble 1987), it was after the War that this phenomenon spread and eventually consolidated. Improvements were made to the Mediterranean beaches and there was a considerable increase in tourist flow to these destinations. The key to such a flow was the increased economic capacity of European and North American households, which had the money and time needed to participate in tourist activities. There were several factors which contributed to this, namely: the economic prosperity of North America and a large part of Europe, the increase in personal income of increasingly large sectors of the population, the improvement of means of transport (especially aeroplanes), the widespread introduction of paid holidays, and the increase in free time (Pellejero 2005, p. 92).

With respect to the travel agencies, as from the Decree of February 1942, the number of sales points gradually increased. In 1941 there were 49 (Fernández Fúster 1991, p. 481) and by 1951 there were 131 (Serra Williamson 1951, pp. 63–65). This was a considerable increase. A good example is one of the most important Spanish travel agencies of that time, Viajes Cafranga, which, as we have seen, had seven establishments in 1942. In 1945, as well as its head office in San Sebastián, it had eight branches, four offices and two Group B agencies associated to it. After the conflagration, Viajes Cafranga expanded the business considerably, seeking to position itself for when the Second World War ended. In fact, the number of foreign tourists began to recover, although very slowly due to the above-mentioned circumstances. Evidently, this recovery was much slower than the Spanish tourism authorities would have liked. Therefore, the travel agency entrepreneurs placed their hopes in the market of Spanish tourists. They were very few in number, but domestic tourism never disappeared completely. The destinations included San Sebastián, the Catalan coast, or Mallorca. In this respect, we can talk about attempts to promote a domestic tourism linked to the celebration of religious or popular events and trade fairs, such as the Corpus of Toledo, the Pilar festival of Zaragoza, Holy Week in Seville and other Spanish cities, the Fallas of Valencia, or bullfights in different towns. The economic impact was small, but it enabled the promotion of new tourism products, such as honeymoons in Mallorca, only affordable for a privileged minority (Buades 2004, 106).

One of the entrepreneurs who identified Mallorca as a place to promote as a tourist destination early on was José Meliá. However, he was not alone, as Viajes Marsans and Viajes Iberia were also quick to see the possibilities of this destination. In 1947, José Meliá, with a capital of three million pesetas lent to him by his father, constituted Viajes Meliá, S.A. (Galindo 2000, p. 445). The type of company he chose and the large amount of capital invested reveal a determined commitment to travel at time that was not particularly easy. During these years, his business, like the majority of agencies operating in Spain, was focused mainly on the domestic customer. Apart from the sale of tickets or hotel coupons, the activity of Viajes Meliá was focused on cruises to Mallorca, tours, and excursions. The press advertisements between 1947 and 1949 reveal that trips were organised to Avila and the Piedra Monastery, Spanish Morocco, Galicia, or Andalusia, and also to cities such as Valencia, Zaragoza, San Sebastián, or Tarragona. And there were also European destinations such as Andorra, Denmark, Italy, or France[5]. At the end of 1948, Meliá even began to publish a tourism magazine called *España* (*La Prensa* (Granada) 1948 December 06, p. 4.), which addressed topics related to the sector.

In 1949, Viajes Meliá began its international expansion and created Circuitos en Autocar por Europa (Coach Tours around Europe) (Galindo 2000, p. 445). Even in this stage of its internationalisation, branches were opened in Paris, New York, and Mexico in the same year[6]. It was the first time after the Civil War that a Spanish company had expanded overseas (Galindo 2000, p. 445). A good symptom that the business was starting to prosper was the meeting held in Madrid in January 1950 of sixteen branch directors from the different regional capitals in Spain and Mexico, who were even entertained by the American airline Trans World Airlines (TWA) (*Hoja Oficial del Lunes* 1950 January 30, p. 3). Although this may seem like a mere anecdote, it was actually much more than this if we take into account that TWA had been the second airline to fly to Madrid after the World War. In fact, at the beginning of 1946, the state company British Overseas Airways Corporation (BOAC) began operating the first scheduled route to Franco's Spain. Specifically, this was a flight between London and Madrid that initially operated twice a week, but this frequency soon increased to four times a week. TWA meanwhile, began a stopover in Madrid on its New York–Cairo route. Similarly, KLM flew three times a week from Amsterdam to Lisbon, passing through Madrid. Still in 1946, Swissair and AB Aerotransport covered the Geneva-Madrid and the Stockholm-Barcelona routes respectively. Bearing all of this in mind, it is not surprising that in March 1947 Spain was admitted into the first international body, the International Civil Aviation Organization (ICAO) (Buades 2004, p. 102). Moreover, in August 1948, Viajes Marsans was inscribed in the agency registry International Air Transport Association (IATA), which enabled it to directly issue plane tickets of the different airlines belonging to this association. It is worth remembering that until then Marsans only issued purchase orders which the corresponding airline subsequently exchanged for the definitive ticket (Albert Piñole et al. 2005, p. 832).

This lunch with the directors of Viajes Meliá and representatives of TWA should be contextualised within the tourism possibilities that Spain offered in the early 1950s. At that time, Spain's opening up to the rest of the world started to consolidate. In fact, in January 1950, the Director General for Tourism, Luis Bolín began a two-month tour of the United States, Mexico, and Cuba, opening new Spanish Tourism Offices in New York, Chicago, Los Angeles, and San Francisco with the objective of attracting a greater number of North American tourists (Correyero & Cal 2008, p. 429).

Consequently, 1950 can be considered as a year of reference for the definitive opening up of Spain to international tourism. This process had begun a few years earlier when different countries started to lift restrictions and reach trade agreements with Spain, including tourism agreements (Pack 2006, Chapter 2). Moreover, in the United Nations General Assembly of November 1947, the representative from the United States successfully opposed the reaffirmation of the condemnation of the Franco regime and the imposition of new sanctions. There is no doubt that the beginning of the Cold War favoured the interests of the dictator. In fact, Franco attempted to accelerate the forming of ties with Washington by offering logistical advantages and military bases on the Spanish peninsula and islands throughout 1948, although without tangible results (Correyero & Cal, pp. 420–421).

So, it is not surprising that in the aforementioned meeting of the directors of Viajes Meliá, aspects related to the coordination of services and other issues related to national and international tourism were addressed, as the tourism potential of the country was by then very clear. In 1949, Spain received 283.9 thousand tourists. This figure increased to 457.0 thousand visitors in the following year (Tena 2005, p. 641). Therefore, the fact that international markets were interested in Spain from the end of the 1940s seems clear if we take certain factors into account. First, the vice-president of the United Press, Virgil M. Pinkley, also the head of this agency's services in Europe, visited Spain in mid-June 1947. In his statements to the press, Pinkley talked of his highly favourable impressions of Spain. Furthermore, his visit coincided with that of Eva Duarte de Perón, the first lady of the Argentine Republic who put Spain in the spotlight during her stay. Second, at the end of 1947, Stanley Norman Bliss, the director of important North American tourism services, arrived in Spain. Not only did Bliss predict a brilliant future for Spanish tourism, but he even affirmed that many tourists from Europe and America were anxious to visit Spain (Correyero & Cal 2008, pp. 423–426). Third, the agent Eusebio Cafranga travelled to the United States and London at the request of the most important companies of the sector in these countries, interested in resuming the tourism flow with Spain (*La Voz de Galicia*, 1948 November 11, p. 2). Finally, between the 5th and 15th of October 1948, the 2nd International

Hotel Alliance Congress was held in Madrid, bringing together many hotel companies from Europe and the United States (Correyero & Cal 2008, p. 427).

These expectations, and a slow improvement in the standard of living of Spanish citizens, generated new opportunities for the local travel agencies. Hence the increase in the number of travel sales offices that took place from 1951, as previously mentioned. In the specific case of Viajes Meliá, in 1943 it only had the head office in Valencia, but in just seven years it had expanded considerably with 16 agency directors meeting in Madrid in January 1950. Therefore, the company's initial social capital of 3 million pesetas had to be extended to 300 million (Galindo 2000, p. 445). The case of Viajes Iberia was similar. In 1942 its head office was in Palma de Mallorca, but the following years were characterised by a gradual expansion of the firm's activity, with the opening of new offices (San Román 2017, 58).

Moreover, we should not forget that Spanish law stipulated that foreigners had to travel under the care of the officially established travel agencies in Spain, due to the fact that the government wished to conserve the authority of directing these tourists towards the good hotels, comfortable transport, and the approved itineraries. In this way, the risks of unsatisfied tourists and the resulting negative propaganda were reduced as was the possible infiltration of anti-Franco activists. At the same time, these regulations sought to protect the Spanish travel agencies from the competition of the large international firms. There was even a law, passed in 1938, obliging travel agencies to respect the official exchange rates and to inform the authorities of any infractions. Evidently, the Spanish government did not want any surprises and wished to have everything under control. In fact, it was not until December 1948 that a decisive step was taken to promote free travel without the control of Spanish agencies. All visitors would begin to enjoy a special tourism exchange rate of 25 pesetas per dollar and 100 per sterling pound and the condition of a minimum daily amount of money of 200 pesetas per tourist was eliminated in May 1949. Finally, the relaxation of the customs controls in the Pyrenees that year also contributed to the increase in tourists (Pack 2006, pp. 47–49).

The 1950s: New Business Possibilities

In general terms, the 1940s had been weak from a tourism point of view, but things changed significantly in the following years. The number of foreign tourists grew considerably, not yet reaching the boom figures of the 1960s, but definitely leaving behind the meagre numbers of the preceding decade. In 1950, the number of tourists visiting Spain was 457.0 thousand. This increased to 1,560.9 thousand in 1956 and to 4,332.4 thousand in 1960 (Tena 2005, pp. 641–642). This was one year after the approval of the Stabilisation Plan of 1959 which involved not only a greater economic opening up of the regime, but also an accelerated removal of the autarchic policies. In fact, in the light of the recovery of the international tourist flows, many things had begun to change, from both a political and economic perspective.

From the political point of view, we must mention, first, a certain opening of the Franco regime, which reduced the entry requirements of foreigners (Pack 2006, Chapter 2). And, second, the political isolation to which Spain had been subjected at the end of World War II was being lifted. This was further accentuated after the renewal of the government in 1951. In 1950, the UN removed the sanctions that it had imposed on Spain in 1946 and allowed the return of the ambassadors. In addition, between 1949 and 1950, the US government approved the first financial aid items to Spain through three financial entities, namely: the Chase Manhattan Bank, the National City Bank, and the Export-Import Bank. To be more specific, within this opening framework, as we have said before, in January 1950 the Director General of Tourism toured the America for two months to promote tourism in Spain (Correyero & Cal 2008, p. 429). However, this process would culminate with two particularly important events: the signing of the concordat with the Holy See in 1953 and the Madrid Pacts of the same year with the United States, under which four American military bases were to be installed on Spanish soil in exchange for economic and military aid. In 1955, Spain became a full member of the UN and from that year onwards, it was integrated into the various international financial organisations. From an economic point of view, in addition to the propaganda that was carried out from the Directorate General of Tourism, the key to the success of the tourism sector can be seen in prices. The Spanish tourism authorities resorted to the containment of prices to gain competition from other countries. Under a dictatorial regime and with a managed economy, government tourism officials imposed very low prices to make Spain a cheap market (Fernández Fúster 1991, pp. 467–468).

At the same time, in the 1950s, the Spanish economy grew intensely and, as a result, the Spanish population enjoyed a substantial improvement in its level of economic well-being. Private domestic consumption grew by 4.9% per year between 1950 and 1958. This increase was determined by the rise in both nominal and real wages occurring from 1953. One consequence of this wage increase was the growth in the demand for goods and services (Carreras & Tafunell 2003, pp. 317–318). These included tourism services. In other words, apart from the foreign tourists, there was an increasing number of Spaniards partaking in tourism, some of whom opted for mediated trips. Therefore, it is not surprising that the number of travel agencies increased considerably. In 1953 there were 48 travel agencies registered in group A (45 in operation) and 23 in group B (13 in operation), and a much higher number of sales offices. In the same year, there were 329 authorised travel agencies in France (Arrillaga 1955, p. 304).

It is logical that the increase in the number of sales offices implied a greater capitalisation of the existing travel agencies. We have already seen the case of Meliá, although it is not the only one. For Viajes Iberia, the founding capital of 100,000 pesetas had increased to six million, in three capital increases: the first in 1943, the second in 1952, and the last in 1955. The largest of the three increases was carried out in 1955 due to the growth in tourist traffic and in order to transfer and extend the Madrid office. In 1955 the company had eight offices: four in the Balearic Islands and four in Barcelona, Madrid, San Sebastián, and Valencia. Its activity was restricted to selling travel tickets, organising excursions to and around Mallorca, and organising various pilgrimages. However, the Banco of Crédito Balear, the owner of Viajes Iberia, had been trying for years to focus its activity and avoid excessive diversification. At that moment, the travel agency business and even the hotel business did not form part of its plans. The Board of the bank therefore implemented an asset liquidation policy that included the sale of Viajes Iberia. The buyer was Lorenzo Fluxá Figuerola, a local footwear entrepreneur, who, at the beginning of the 1950s, perceived the potential of tourism as the business of the future in the Balearic Island. Turnover was fixed at nine million pesetas, which Fluxá considered excessive. But in the end, he gave in and, in 1956, paid the price. In order to close the purchase, Fluxá went into partnership with a group of businessmen who were mainly from the farming sector. But after a short time, Fluxá bought their shares and became the sole owner of Viajes Iberia.

The start of the business was not easy, because the financial situation of the company was worse than he had imagined. Fluxá tried to sell Viajes Iberia to Viajes Marsans, but the deal did not go ahead. So, if he wanted to relaunch the company, he had to find the right people to help him. In a very short time he added two important names to his business: Gabriel Escarrer Juliá and José Linares Colom. The former was a young entrepreneur who had learned his trade at Wagon-Lits as the manager of the foreign department in Palma. Escarrer was responsible for making hotel bookings for visitors. With his experience, he began his career in the hotel business by buying first the Hotel Altair and then the Residencia Marbella and Hotel El Paso. Escarrer and Fluxá met through a mutual friend, Jerónimo Salleras, who was a manager at the Banco Español de Crédito and also worked as an adviser to Lorenzo Fluxá. The alliance between Escarrer and Fluxá benefitted them both. Escarrer would be responsible for management and strategy in both Viajes Iberia and the hotels, and Fluxá would contribute his business experience and financial support. As travel agents, Fluxá and Escarrer decided to change the focus of Viajes Iberia and concentrate on the inbound tourist business because it offered much greater possibilities than the outbound business. In order to promote this inbound tourist business, Escarrer persuaded Fluxá to hire José Linares Colom, who had worked at Wagon-Lits with him. Linares had extensive experience in the sector, so his input could be highly beneficial for the company. Therefore, Linares began to work in Viajes Iberia as Manager of the Palma branch in May 1961. Also in the same year, the joint hotel activity of Escarrer and Fluxá began when they set up a hotel management company called Financiera Balear in which each had a share of 50 per cent (San Román 2017, pp. 66–69).

The possibilities offered by tourism were continuously growing and Lorenzo Fluxá's interest in both mediated trips and the hotel industry was no exception. There were other travel agents who also began to work in the hotel business, and even before Fluxá. The case of José Meliá, therefore, is paradigmatic. He began his activities in the hotel business with the rental of the Hostal Cardenla in Toledo in 1950. Five years later he opened the Hotel Bahía Palace, his first luxury hotel in Mallorca, the tourist destination that he had been promoting since the end of the 1940s. Known as Hotel Meliá Mallorca, it constituted the first establishment of a hotel chain that over time became the largest in Spain (Galindo 2000, p. 445).

But in spite of the new possibilities offered by tourism to the travel agencies, there were also complaints and even failed operations. With respect to the former, the Spanish travel agencies complained that the British operators hired their services once and then, after acquiring experience, hired these services directly from the hotels that the Spanish agencies had found and selected. In fact, the British tourism companies established direct relationships with Catalan and Mallorcan hotels in as early as 1950. There were even companies that emerged after the war, such as Horizon Holidays and Sky Tours that opted to sign contracts with more modest hotels so as to avoid bureaucracy and bring down the prices. These companies even provided loans to the entrepreneurs who wished to construct hotels in exchange for ensuring the reservation of their rooms for the whole season at fixed prices (Pack 2006, pp. 59–60). With respect to failed operations, it is worth mentioning that of Viajes Cafranga in 1952 with respect to the celebration in Barcelona of the 35th International Eucharist Congress. The Ministry of Information and Tourism had granted the exclusivity of this event to this company. However, the religious and social success of the congress contrasted with a very poor tourism result, giving rise to a significant setback for Viajes Cafranga, which almost led it to bankruptcy (Bayón 2005, p. 337).

However, and to conclude, all of this indicates that the travel agency business, despite the problems that we have mentioned, was a sub-sector of tourism that became consolidated during these decades, particularly in the 1950s, when both domestic and international tourist flows began to increase. This was the case so much so that tourism not only served to compensate the trade deficit, but also began to represent a greater share of Spain's GDP, reaching 1.69% in 1959, the year when the aforementioned Stabilisation Plan was approved. This movement of tourists led to a growing number of visitors opting to use the services of travel agencies, giving rise to the expansion experienced by the sector from the end of the 1940s.

Notes

1 This study forms part of the research project HAR2017-82679-C2-1-P, financed by the Ministry of Science, Innovation and Universities of the Government of Spain and ERDF Funds.
2 www.hosteltur.com/125191_numero-agencias-se-estabiliza-9000-lejos-13000-2008.html (accessed June 12, 2020).
3 www.hosteltur.com/comunidad/nota/021570_los-espanoles-consideran-que-planificar-viajes-por-internet-requiere-demasiado-tiempo.html (accessed June 12, 2020).
4 General Archive of the Administration, Culture (03)049.002TOP.22/44.203-52. 704-box12.423.

5 prensahistorica.mcu.es/es/consulta/resultados_ocr.do (accessed June 17, 2020).
6 dbe.rah.es/biografias/26014/jose-melia-sinisterra (accessed June 18, 2020).

References

Albert Piñole, I., F. Bayón Mariné, & J. Cerra Culebras. 2005. Agencias de viajes. In *50 años del turismo español*, ed. F. Bayón, 815–843. Madrid: Centro de Estudios Ramón Areces.

Arrillaga, J. I. 1955. *Sistema de política turística*. Madrid: Aguilar.

Bayón, F. 2005. Política turística. In *50 años del turismo español*, ed. F. Bayón, 331–380. Madrid: Centro de Estudios Ramón Areces.

Bayón, F. & L. Ferández Fúster. 2005. Los orígenes. In *50 años del turismo español*, ed. F. Bayón, 25–43. Madrid: Centro de Estudios Ramón Areces.

Bolín, L. 1967. *Spain. Los años vitales*. Madrid: Espasa-Calpe.

Brendon, P. 1991. *Thomas Cook. 150 years of popular tourism*. London: Secker & Warburg.

Buades, J. 2004. *On brilla el sol. Turisme a Balears abans del boom*. Eivissa: Res Publica.

Carreras, A. & X. Tafunell. 2003. *Historia económica de la España contemporánea*. Barcelona: Crítica.

Correyero, B. 2005: La Administración turística española entre 1936 y 1951. *Estudios turísticos* 163–164: 55–79.

Correyero, B. & R. Cal. 2008. *Turismo: la mayor propaganda de Estado*. Madrid: Vision Net.

Fernández Fúster, L. 1991. *Historia general del turismo de masas*. Madrid: Alianza.

Galindo, P. 2000. José Meliá Sinisterra (1911–1999). In *Cien empresarios españoles del siglo XX*, ed. E. Torres, 444–450. Madrid: Lid.

Lanquar, R. 1979. *Agences et associations de voyages*. Paris: PUF.

Larrinaga, C. 2019. El empresario Eusebio Cafranga y el negocio de las agencias de viajes en España antes del turismo de masas. In *Empresas y empresarios en España: de mercaderes a industriales* coord. J. M. Matés, 281–301. Madrid: Pirámide.

Moreno, A. 2007. *Historia del turismo en España en el siglo XX*. Madrid: Síntesis.

Norval, A. J. 1936. *The Tourist Industry*. London: Sir Isaac Pitman & Sons.

Pack, S. 2006. *Tourism and Dictatorship*. Gordonsville: Palgrave Macmillan.

Pellejero, C. 2005. Turismo y Economía en la Málaga del siglo XX. *Revista de Historia Industrial* 29: 87–114.

Pemble, J. 1987. *The Mediterranean Passion*. Oxford: Clarendon Press.

Pimlott, J. A. R. 1977, 1947 1a. *The Englishman's Holiday. A social history*. Hassocks: Harvester Press.

Rae, W. F. 1891. *The Business of Travel: Fifty Years' Record of Progress*. London: Thomas Cook & Son.

Santis, H. 1978. The democratization of travel: The travel agent in American history. *The Journal of American Culture* 1(1), 1–17. doi.org/10.1111/j.1542-734X.1978.0101_1.x

Serra Williamson, H. W. 1951. *The Tourist Guide-book of Spain*. Madrid: The Times of Spain.

San Román, E. 2017. *Building Stars*. Madrid: Grupo Iberostar.

Tena, A. 2005. Sector exterior. In *Estadísticas Históricas de España. Siglos XIX y XX* coord. A. Carreras, and X. Tafunell, 773-644. Bilbao: Fundación BBVA.

Vallejo, R. 2018. La formación de un sistema turístico nacional con diferentes desarrollos regionales entre 1900 y 1939. In *Los orígenes del turismo moderno en España. El nacimiento de un país turístico, 1900–1939*, ed. R. Vallejo, and C. Larrinaga, 67–170. Madrid: Sílex.

Vallejo, R. & E. Concejal. 2018. La política y la Administración turística durante la Guerra Civil. In *Los orígenes del turismo moderno en España. El nacimiento de un país turístico, 1900–1939*, ed. R. Vallejo, and C. Larrinaga, 381–420. Madrid: Sílex.

Vallejo, R. & C. Larrinaga. 2020. Travel agencies in Spain during the first third of the 20th century. A tourism business in the making. *Business History* (ed. on line): 1–20. doi.org/10.1080/00076791.2019.1685503.

Visentin, C. 1995. Nuovi viaggi e nuovi viaggiatori: la nascita delle agenzie turistiche in Italia (1878–1914). *Storia in Lombardia* 1–2: 297–311.

10 The International Expansion of the Spanish Insurance Company MAPFRE

Leonardo Caruana de las Cagigas

Introduction

The Spanish insurance company MAPFRE, founded in 1933, developed an expansion strategy from the 1980s onwards. The first step towards internationalisation was taken in the reinsurance sector in the mid-1980s with a view to gaining knowledge about companies that could be subsequently acquired. MAPFRE first broke into the Latin American market and then started operating in the United States, Europe, Turkey, and China. Expansion in the direct insurance market followed, Latin America again being the initial target.

Internationalisation certainly enhanced MAPFRE's reputation. In 25 years, the company became one of the leaders in the Latin American market. In 2015, 70% of its business was conducted abroad. Its success is based on its high levels of efficiency, networking, and cultural ties. In addition, its know-how and its leading position in the car insurance market promoted global expansion in nearly all types of insurance.

The present chapter focuses on MAPFRE's global expansion. The first section describes the strategic planning of the expansion. The next two sections analyse international expansion in the reinsurance market and in the direct insurance market, respectively. The last section presents some concluding remarks.

Planning the International Expansion

The Spanish insurance company MAPFRE, founded in 1933, was initially a mutual company that insured farmers in case of an accident. Thirty years later, it moved to motor insurance. In the late 1960s, MAPFRE considered expanding abroad like other Spanish insurance companies. For example, La Estrella created Goya, a reinsurance firm that operated in Latin America, and La Unión y el Fenix had entered the French market.

This type of expansion is defined as an active internationalisation process. The internationalisation process can be developed in two directions (Martínez Martínez 1987):

1) The entry of foreign companies in the domestic market is known as passive internationalisation. In the early 1980s, foreign companies accounted for

only 5% of the Spanish market as a result of the legal barriers imposed by Franco's dictatorship. Premiums from these foreign companies were distributed into life insurance (26%) and non-life insurance (29%). In other European countries, the distribution of the insurance market was: 13% for life insurance and 17% for non-life insurance in the UK, 12% in both insurance branches in Germany, 13% and 15% respectively in Italy, and finally, 3% and 6% respectively in France. Data provided by Sigma show passive internationalisation in different continents in the 1980s: 5% in the North American market, 40% in Asia. In Europe, the presence of foreign companies was as follows: 11% in Britain, 22% in Federal Germany, 24% in Italy, and 34% in France.

2) The expansion of domestic firms is referred to as active internationalisation. A report published by Sigma reveals the number of companies operating abroad in the 1980s: 608 from the UK, 579 from the United States, 166 from France, 138 from Switzerland, 122 from Federal Germany, 100 from Canada.

The first step towards MAPFRE's foreign expansion was taken in late 1969 by Ignacio Hernando de Larramendi, MAPFRE's CEO, who went to several Latin America countries (Brazil, Argentina, Chile, Peru, Ecuador, Colombia, and Venezuela) in order to explore possibilities of expanding there. At the Board of Directors' meeting held on July 29, 1969, Hernando de Larramendi remarked that one of the objectives of the company in the next decade should be internationalisation, Latin America being the most suitable area for initial expansion (Tortella, Caruana, García 2009). Larramendi chose Latin America on the basis of the cultural ties between Spain and this region (Hernando de Larramendi 2000, pp. 322–323). Nonetheless, expansion plans were abandoned in the 1970s due to the 1973 oil crisis.

In the 1980s, insurance companies expanded. Thus, in 1985, direct insurance premiums in foreign countries managed by Spanish companies were worth 18,268 million pesetas (109.8 million euros), while foreign direct insurance premiums managed in Spain by foreign companies were worth 148,533 million (892.7 million euros). In reinsurance, premiums taken out by foreign clients and managed by Spanish companies were worth 6,000 million pesetas (36 million euros), while premiums managed by foreign companies in Spain were worth 100,000 million (601 million euros). In the case of UK and Switzerland, their companies managed premiums in foreign countries accounting for 65% of the life insurance and 75% of the non-life of their business. The percentages in other European countries were the following: 55% in both branches in Italy; 15% and 27% respectively in France; in Federal Germany, 6% and 18% respectively, clearly outstanding the first 3 countries (Martínez Martínez 1987).

Within this context, in the mid-1980s José Manuel Martínez, CEO of MAPFRE RE and General Manager of Corporation MAPFRE, backed up the company's international expansion. He believed that it was crucial to provide a wide range of quality services to meet clients' demands. There were two strategies to expand abroad: opening offices or acquiring companies. Martinez considered the latter option better. The acquisition of a company involves gaining its clients and insurance experts that help to conduct business in a foreign country. He argued that MAPFRE had more chances to succeed in the Latin American insurance market, which was less competitive, though riskier, since Latin American countries had an unstable exchange rate and fluctuating currencies. In addition, MAPFRE enjoyed a good reputation in Latin America, and Latin American countries were culturally close to Spain.

At the time, MAPFRE also considered expanding in Europe. In a report, Domingo Sugranyes, member of the Board of Directors, highlighted the importance of the European market and suggested expanding direct insurance to Italy, where the number of premiums was three times the number of premiums in the Spanish market. However, at the meeting held on September 12, 1984, the Board of Directors agreed that the company was still too small to enter the European market.

At this point it is convenient to note that it was possible for MAPFRE to expand in two ways. On the one hand, the company could expand in the reinsurance market. On the other hand, it could break into foreign direct insurance markets such as the car insurance market, where MAPFRE's expertise was a competitive advantage.

The management justified expansion in the reinsurance market on several grounds. Firstly, they were certain that the market would grow in the next decades, as it did. Secondly, reinsurance companies all around the world were making losses. Big companies like Lloyd's were going through financial difficulties. Mercantile and General and SAFR were taken over. Despite the fact that MAPFRE was a small company lacking financial ability, the Board of directors thought that the insurance market was in need of more reinsurance companies to solve financial difficulties. This was confirmed by a report from the Insurance Services Office of the United States. Experts claimed that in the late 1980s there was a niche for reinsurance premiums which accounted for roughly 25% of the insurance market. Such demand for reinsurance premiums resulted from the increasing occurrence of natural disasters in the United States and Latin America (Chile, Mexico). This led to an increase in reinsurance premium rates and a reduction in profits in technical results in the long run. On the other hand, costs were cut thanks to improved transport and communication. Therefore, the crisis in the reinsurance market was an opportunity for MAPFRE. The start-up capital was provided by the MAFPRE Group.

MAPFRE's global expansion was mainly achieved through the acquisition of a stake in foreign insurance companies or the acquisition of the whole company, as we shall see in the remaining sections of this chapter. Moreover, both the MAPFRE Foundation and MAPFRE Assistance contributed to the company's expansion. MAPFRE Foundation is a non-profit organisation founded in 1975 with a view towards working on specific areas: road safety and prevention; research into insurance and social protection; research into the history of Spain, Portugal, and other countries linked to Spain; and provision of financial aid to underprivileged people. MAPRE Assistance, founded in 1989, provides assistance on the road and at home as well as travel assistance.

The success of MAPFRE's international expansion in the last 40 years is statistically proven. In 1985, MAPFRE developed 8% of its business abroad. In 2006, half of the business was developed abroad and in 2015, 70%.

International Expansion of MAPFRE REINSURANCE

In its expansion process, MAPFRE followed the steps of big reinsurance companies such as Swiss Re, Munich Re and SAFR (Hernando de Larramendi 2000, p. 323). In the 1970s, there was simply a reinsurance department headed by José Manuel Martínez and Andrés Jiménez. In 1981, MAPFRE took over Nervión, a small reinsurance company owned by the Aurora Group. Nervión was renamed MAPFRE REASEGUROS in 1982. At that moment, the reinsurance business of national companies was run by 11 reinsurance companies and 112 insurance companies. Reinsurance premiums were worth 28,500 million pesetas (171 million euros in 1983). Reinsurance premiums accounted for 7% of direct insurance premiums. The premiums of Munich Re, the world's leader in the reinsurance market, were worth 453,404 million pesetas (2,725 million euros). Spain's market leader was Nacional de Reaseguros, whose premiums were worth 4,687 million pesetas (28.2 million euros). The main problem faced by reinsurance companies was the lack of capital to cover the risk. In fact, the Spanish reinsurance market was dominated by foreign reinsurance companies. The Spanish firms retrocede 74% of the risk insured to foreign companies. This meant that many of these companies were actually mere intermediaries rather than reinsurance companies (Martínez Martínez 1986).

In 1984, MAPFRE REASEGUROS became the market leader in the reinsurance market, with premiums worth 5,605 million pesetas. It was followed by Nacional de Reaseguros with premiums worth 5,274, Albatros, with premiums worth 2,117 million pesetas; CERSA, with premiums worth 1,710 million pesetas, and REUNISA (Reaseguradores Españoles Unidos, S.A), with premiums worth 1,031 million pesetas. REUNISA was a joint venture of Spanish insurance companies that wound up in 1992 (BOE-A-1992–25067).

MAPFRE REASEGUROS's revenues from the Latin American market exceeded those in the Spanish market. The estimated net income was over 700 million pesetas (4.2 million euros). In 1984, MAPFRE opened an office in Mexico and provided a quality service after the earthquake that hit the country in 1985. Damages were worth 650 million pesetas (3.9 million euros). In his memoirs, Larramendi pointed out: "One of the reasons for the initial success of MAPFRE REASEGUROS in Mexico was its prompt action during the earthquake in Mexico in 1985". (Hernando de Larramendi 2000, p. 652).

As MAPFRE REASEGUROS lacked financial ability, it went under the control of MAPFRE Corporation in December 1985. And another reinsurance company was set up December 31, 1986: MAPFRE XL Compañía Internacional de Reaseguros S.A. XL means "excess of loss". In non-proportional insurance the basis of the premium is the claim rather than the risk, so that the premium covers limited risk. Also, in 1986, further offices were opened in seven countries: Brazil, United States, Philippines, Italy, Panama, Portugal, and Tunisia. Two years later, new offices were opened in Venezuela and Luxembourg.

In 1988, the reinsurance business was managed by MAPFRE XL. The company became part of MAPFRE RE, Compañía Internacional de Reaseguros, S.A. MAPFRE RE continued to operate as a captive company for the Group. MAPFRE RE purchased 5% share of Compagnie Internacional D'Assurance et de Reasurance (C.I.A.R.) from Belgium. The next year, 1989, MAPFRE acquired 30% share of *Reaseguradora of Chile*. Founded in 1927, it had over a 50% share of the Chilean market, with a revenue of 65 million dollars in 1987. It was the leader in the reinsurance market of Latin America.

MAPFRE opened another office in Argentina in 1990, and an office in London in 1991. In 1992, MAPFRE bought an 88% stake in *Reaseguradora Hemisphere* in Colombia, with an investment of 550 million pesetas (3.3 million euros). Another office was opened in Peru in 1996. Thus, MAPFRE expanded across the Latin American market, although it could not break into the Brazilian market, where the reinsurance business was controlled by the state. However, an office was opened in Brazil to deal with prevention issues and this office was in charge of the publication of books on technical issues related to the insurance world.

The devastating effects of hurricanes in America posed a big problem. In September 1998, Hurricane Georges struck the Caribbean, and a month later, Hurricane Mitch killed thousands of people. As a result, MAPFRE RE ran technical deficits that year. The company raised reinsurance rates and selected new risks more carefully. Despite its financial difficulties and so many natural disasters, MAPFRE was performing well in the late twentieth century.

In 1999, MAPFRE entered the American reinsurance market through the acquisition of Chatham Re, owned by Shelter Re – a subsidiary of Shelter – and Ecclesiastical, a company related to the Anglican Church. MAPFRE invested 35 million dollars. Chatham Re was renamed MAPFRE Reinsurance Corporation of the United States. Chatham Re had both reinsurance and direct insurance licenses in more than 30 states in the United States. There was an increase of capital of 13,750 million pesetas. MAPFRE invested 10,540 million pesetas (63.3 million euros), while Ecclesiastical and Shelter invested 3,135 million pesetas each.

The company grew significantly under CEO Andrés Jimenez. MAPFRE RE in its revenue increased from 23,583 million pesetas in 1990 (141.7 million euros) to 104,478 million pesetas in 2000 (627.9 million euros). In 2000, MAPFRE's reinsurance business was conducted in Europe (Spain, 32%; other European countries, 21%) and America (Latin America, 34%, United States, 9%) (World MAPFRE 2001, p. 32).

MAPFRE RE was in financial trouble at the turn of the century. The final years of the twentieth century had yielded poor results, and when recovery started, the attack on the World Trade Centre in New York on September 11, 2001 caused about 2982 deaths, and damages amounted to 21,379 million dollars, the third most costly disaster in recent history, after Hurricane

Katrina in 2005 (1,836 deaths and 66,311 million-dollar damages), and Hurricane Andrew in 1992 (22,987 million-dollar damages). In the 1990s there were 100–150 natural disasters and more than 150 man-made disasters. As a result, in 2002 reinsurance companies, including MAPFRE RE, redefined hedges, especially those concerning terrorism. A report published by Swiss Re in Sigma 2/2019 (Sigma 2019) suggested that the number of natural disasters would remain uncertain, while the number of man-made disasters would rise sharply.

A further problem faced by reinsurance firms in the early twenty-first century was competition. For example, the Bermuda market provided more clients because it was tax-free. Within this context, a great number of reinsurance companies were in financial trouble. Enron, whose debt had been endorsed by many insurance companies, went bankrupt; there was a crash in the profits made by firms such as AXA, Zurich, Swiss Re, Munich Re, U.S. State Farm, and General Re.

In 2005 MAPFRE RE broke into the state of New York, the most important financial market of the world, whose strong regulations had not made it possible in the past. MAPFRE RE was authorised in Canada and Australia in 2006 with 7,447 thousand euros in premiums in the first country and 16,417 thousand euros in premiums in the second in the first year.

In January 2007, the Brazilian state-owned reinsurance company IRB Brasil Re stopped cornering the market. The government liberalised 40% of the reinsurance market. Brazil was an important market for MAPFRE (Levy & Chaves Pereira, 2007). Finally, in 2016 MAPFRE RE moved in to the important market of the second or maybe first economy of the world, China. In 2018 MAPFRE RE ranked 19th among the world's reinsurance companies (Best 2019).

Expansion in the Direct Insurance Market

MAPFRE expanded in the direct insurance market through the acquisition of a stake in blue-chip companies in each branch or the acquisition of the whole company. MAPFRE occasionally entered foreign direct insurance markets by opening offices abroad. In Latin America, cultural problems arose. MAPFRE imposed strict control, a single methodology of work, centralisation of information, and internal auditing. It was in the Latin American subsidiaries that many of the young managers who got to the highest positions in the core business areas after 2000 had gained managerial experience. This was the case for Antonio Huertas, MAPFRE's CEO since 2012.

In August 1984 MAPFRE bought a 24% stake in Seguros Caribe from Colombia. The remaining 76% mostly was owned by three families. Founded in 1960, Seguros Caribe was a medium-sized company whose growth rate was well above the average and whose productivity rate was twice the average rate in Colombia. It operated in all branches of general insurance: car insurance (42%), sureties (16%), fire insurance (10%), and life insurance (10%). Again, MAPFRE contributed intangible assets in the form of knowledge, for example technical assistance and staff training (Cardone 1996). In 1988, MAPFRE's stake in Seguros Caribe rose to 40%.

In 1986 MAPFRE bought a 75% share from the Argentinian company Aconcagua, which ranked 35th among Argentina's insurance companies. The business lines were car insurance (28%), transport insurance (25%) and fire insurance (25%). When Aconcagua opened an office in Paraguay in 1988, MAPFRE owned the company. In the same year, in Chile, MAPFRE acquired a 45% stake in Cía. de Seguros Generales Euroamerica and bought a stake in the life insurance company Euroamerica Vida. Both companies grew. In 1991 their premiums were worth 352 million pesetas (8.1 million euros), mostly for motor insurance. Life insurance premiums were worth 728 million pesetas (4.3 million euros).

MAPFRE penetrated the Portuguese market in 1989. They opened an office to provide life insurance. In 1994, the value of its premiums was low (1,357 million pesetas, that is, 8.15 million euros), as compared with MAPFRE's premiums in Spain (48,664 million pesetas, that is, 292.4 million euros). In 1991 an office had been opened to provide non-life insurance. Non-life premiums were worth 6,052 million pesetas (36.37 million euros) in 1995 (Figueiredo Almaca 1999).

In Italy, in 1988 MAPFRE purchased a 6% stake from Universo (251 million pesetas, i.e. 1.5 million euros) and a 5% holding from Varese, (89 million pesetas, 534,900 euros), which were subsidiaries of Reale Mutua. They also bought a 40% stake from Progress, that increase the next year to 58% stake. The revenue of Progress was 1,000 million pesetas (6 million euros). Most of the business was conducted in the motor insurance branch in Sicily. The head office was in Palermo. The problem was that the claims were too high, and so MAPFRE made a loss of 430 million pesetas (2.58 million euros) in 1992 and of 350 million pesetas (2.1 the losses) in 1993. However, the next year losses hit a low of 50 million pesetas (300,506 euros) and the premiums went up to 2,948 million pesetas in 1994. In 1999 negotiations began to sell the company to Middlesea from Malta. In 2004 Middlesea acquired MAPFRE's stake for 7 million euros, while MAPFRE acquired a 15% holding in Middlesea for 10 million euros.

In 1987 MAPFRE invested 1,121 million pesetas (6.7 million euros) to set up MAPFRE Corporation of Florida in San Agustin, founded by Spaniards. The company performed badly because in August 1992 Hurricane Andrew caused 44 deaths and over 30,000 million dollars in damages (of which 15,500 were insured). The company's revenue was 203 million pesetas (1.2 million euros). The cost of Hurricane Andrew for MAPFRE was over 85 million pesetas (510,860 euros). In 1988 MAPFRE bought a 70% stake in the American company Holding Amstar, which provided insurance as well as consultancy, broker, and finance services.

In 1989, MAPFRE acquired a 40% stake in the Mexican insurance firm Tepeyac, whose revenue was around 10,000 million pesetas (60.1 million euros). In the same year MAPFRE acquired the Puerto Rican-American Insurance Company (PRAICO), a subsidiary of Continental, one of the biggest insurance firms in the United States. MAPFRE had had reinsurance contracts with the company since the late 1970s.

The profitability of these businesses varied. In 1991, Aconcagua made 92 million-peseta profits (552,931 euros) and Tepeyac, 624 million-peseta profits (3.75 million euros). By contrast, in Chile, Euroamerica Seguros Generales, focusing on motor insurance, made technical losses as a result of high road accident rates, although they were offset by the positive financial results.

In late 1995, MAPFRE's accumulated international investments were 33,475 million pesetas (201.2 million euros). MAPFRE had been a well-established firm in Brazil since 1992, when it bought shares from Vera Cruz Insurance, Vera Cruz Vida e Previdência. Soon it took control of the Vera Cruz Group. The next year, in 1996, MAPFRE again invested heavily in the Latin American market. Firstly, the company made an investment of 51% share in *El Sol Nacional*, a big Peruvian insurance company in 1997. The investment was of 1,213 million de pesetas (7.3 million euros). In 1999 the company was split in two: MAPFRE Perú Seguros Generales and MAPFRE Perú Vida. Secondly, MAPFRE invested 5,000 million pesetas (30 million euros) to take control of La Seguridad, the leading insurance company in the Venezuelan market with premiums worth 20,000 million pesetas (120.2 million euros). Lastly, MAPFRE took over the Brazilian company Vera Cruz Seguradora and the Chilean company Euroamérica Seguros Generales (Caruana & García 2009).

In early 1997 MAPFRE Vida International was founded. Its mission was to increase MAPFRE's share in the Latin American life insurance market. MAPFRE bought the group Pérez Company in Argentina and La Centro Americana in El Salvador. MAPFRE expanded more slowly in other countries such as Venezuela. The life insurance business is usually less successful in underdeveloped countries. In March 1997, MAPFRE América, a division of MAPFRE Internacional, was created. MAPFRE Internacional operated out of Latin America.

In the same year MAPFRE made further investments in America (12,664 million pesetas, 76.1 million euros). The investment made by American MAPFRE companies accounted for about 2% of total assets. MAPFRE could invest up to 10%, which was the maximum allowed by the Spanish government. In September 1998, it was estimated that the losses of the subsidiaries listed on the American Stock Exchange amounted to 1,400 million pesetas (8.4 million euros). La Seguridad in Venezuela made the biggest loss. MAPFRE sought to make investments in dollars in order to reduce risks. However, MAPFRE made losses due to the high returns on investment in local currency.

As a result of expansion, one third of MAPFRE's direct insurance premiums came from foreign countries. In 2001, non-life premiums taken out in America were worth over 1,500 million euros, distributed across five countries: Mexico (311 million euros), Venezuela (300 million euros), Brazil (285 million euros), Puerto Rico (223 million euros) and Argentina (220 million euros).

The geographical distribution of MAPFRE's workforce in America in 1999 reflects the company's expansion (see Table 10.1).

Table 10.1 Distribution of MAPFRE Employees in America in 1999

	Employees		Employees		Employees
Mexico	1,494	Chile	387	Dominican Republic	15
Brazil	1,137	Peru	264	Ecuador	14
Venezuela	977	United States	153	Costa Rica	11
Argentina	626	El Salvador	111	Guatemala	11
Puerto Rico	515	Paraguay	52	Bolivia	10
Colombia	513	Uruguay	43	Panama	10

Source: author's own elaboration with MAPFRE data. MAPFRE.

Latin America was hit by a new crisis in 2001–2002. In Argentina, the number of non-life premiums halved in 2002. It recovered slowly, and in 2006 it reached the levels of 2001. In Venezuela, the number of premiums declined gradually and also recovered in 2006. In contrast, between 2001 and 2003, the value of premiums rose from 59 million euros to 97 million euros in Chile, from 43 million euros to 58 million euros in Colombia, and from 29 million euros to 46 million euros in Peru. In markets such as El Salvador, Paraguay, and Uruguay, MAPFRE performed less well.

In 2005, MAPFRE's non-life insurance business recovered. Revenue from premiums went up from 1,289 million euros to 1,655 million euros. In 2006, it was over 2,000 million euros. The upward trend continued in 2007, particularly in the Dominican Republic.

In Brazil, growth was linked to the success of motor insurance and life insurance VGBL, with big tax-financial returns. In Mexico the motor insurance business grew. The economic boom led to the purchase of cars and of car insurance and health insurance premiums. In Venezuela, health insurance was one of the core businesses. MAPFRE gained large numbers of clients thanks to group policies taken out by civil servants. Likewise, MAPFRE's health insurance business developed in Puerto Rico through health care plans for pensioners subsidised by the Medicare program. In addition, MAPFRE acquired Baldrich, an insurance agency specialising in motor insurance. Finally, Argentina saw the growth of labour insurance risk and motor insurance.

The life insurance sector also grew. The value of premiums went up steadily: around 200 million euros in 2004, nearly 300 million euros in 2005, over 400 million euros in 2006, and 678 million euros in 2007. The biggest markets were Brazil and, to a much lesser extent, Colombia.

In 2002 BBVA and MAPFRE failed to reach an agreement over the distribution of insurance products in Latin America. What they did try was an agreement that BBVA would distribute MAPFRE's non-life insurance products on an exclusive basis, but this arrangement did not work out (BBVA operated mainly in life insurance). However, BBVA and MAPFRE made co-insurance arrangements in Argentina and Colombia. This co-insurance business was controlled by MAPFRE, which had broader experience in this field. In Latin America, MAPFRE achieved a market share of 9.5% in the non-life insurance market, thus becoming the market leader. It ranked third, only overtaken by Bradesco and AIG in all type of insurance in Latin America in 2007.

MAPFRE Internacional was set up in February 2005 to expand the direct insurance business in the United States, Turkey, Europe (Italy, Germany, Portugal, Turkey), and Indonesia. The US insurance market is the largest market in the world, with a total workforce of 2.5 million. Its premium volume is close to 1.1 trillion dollars, more than a third of world volume. Insurance penetration (percentage of premiums over GDP) accounts for 9.6% (4.4% in life insurance and 5.2% in non-life insurance) in 2007. The US insurance market is heavily regulated, primarily at state level. In fact, each state has its own department and insurance commissioner, although there is some coordination by the National Association of Insurance Commissioners. In 2008, MAPFRE purchased The Commerce Group, with nearly 2 billion euros in consolidated premiums, for over 1,432 million euros. It was MAPFRE's major acquisition. The Commerce Group, founded in 1971 in Webster, Massachusetts, has car insurance as its main business (90% of premiums), and since 1990 it has been one of the largest and one of the most profitable car insurance firms in the state. It operated in 16 further states, and in 2019 it had 2,200 million dollars in assets (ratings.ambest.com/companyprofile).

In 2007, in Turkey MAPFRE signed an agreement to purchase 80% of Genel Sigorta, which ranked 10th in the non-life insurance market, and 6th in the car insurance market, and its life insurance subsidiary Genel Yasam, for 285 million euros. MAPFFE justified entry in Turkey on the grounds that it is a large market (over 70 million inhabitants) with a very low insurance penetration rate (1.6%), which made growth possible.

In Europe, MAPFRE broke into the German market, the 6th largest in the world. German insurance companies employ more than half a million people and with its financial assets it managed 1.6 trillion euros in 2018. In 2014 MAPFRE reached an agreement with the British insurance company Direct Line Group, which had been a telephone insurance division of The Royal Bank of Scotland Group, to acquire its car insurance subsidiaries in Germany and Italy for 550 million euros. The businesses in Italy and Germany contributed 714 million euros in premiums, 1.6 million clients, and 19.5 million-euro profits in 2013. Finally, in 2017 in Indonesia, the fourth most populated country in the world, MAPFRE invested 90 million euros to purchase 31% of ABDA.

MAPFRE'S CEO, Antonio Huertas, postulates a decentralisation policy. Local managers are in charge of the company's offices in foreign countries. And in the last report of MAPFRE 2019, 30% of the premiums was in Spain, Latin America held 29%, 22% was in reinsurance, and other countries held 16% (the last 3% is MAFPRE Assistance, the part of the company that has spread in more countries).

Conclusion

MAPFRE went global in the 1980s. Foreign expansion began with reinsurance, the main area being Latin America, a less competitive, though riskier, market. Cultural ties facilitated the process. Expansion in Latin America took place through acquisition of companies. In 25 years, MAPFRE became the leader in the Latin American non-life insurance market. Expansion continued in the United States, Canada, China, and Australia. In much the same way, expansion in direct insurance started in Latin America and was pursued in the United States, Turkey, Europe (Italy, Germany and Portugal), and Indonesia.

The reasons for MAPFRE's successful expansion process lie in the company's reputation and know-how in all types of insurance, ranging from car insurance to life-insurance. Internationalisation has also allowed MAPFRE to become a global player. It ranked 15th in terms of turnover in 2018 in Europe (Atlas Magazine 2019), with premiums worth 23,043.9 million euros in 2019 and over 28 million clients in the world.

Sources

Interviews: José Manuel Martínez Martínez, Antonio Huertas Mejias, Alberto Manzano Martos, and Andrés Jiménez Herradón.

MAPFRE Archive. Reports of the meetings of the board of directors of the Mutual and of the Corporation.

References

Archive of MAPFRE, Annual reports of MAPFRE (1980–2019).
Atlas Magazine. 2019. *Ranking of European insurers and reinsurers in 2017*. www.atlas-mag.net/en/article/ranking-of-european-insurers-and-reinsurers-in-2017. (accessed April 8, 2020).
Best, A. M. 2019. *Top 50 World's Largest Reinsurance Groups*. www.ambest.com/review/displaychart.aspx?Record_Code=274409. (accessed March 22, 2020).
Boletín Oficial del Estado. 1992, Madrid, Imprenta Nacional. www.boe.es/diario_boe/txt.php?id=BOE-A-1992-25067. (accessed July 2, 2020).
Cardone, C. 1996. *MAPFRE un sistema "asegurado" de éxito*, coord. J.J. Durán Herrera, Multinacionales españolas. Madrid: Pirámide. 1: 209–239.
Caruana de las Cagigas, L. & J. L. García Ruiz. 2009. "La internacionalización del seguro español: el caso de MAPFRE, 1969–2001". *ICE*. 849. Julio-agosto. 143–157.
Figueiredo Almaca, J. A. 1999. *El mercado ibérico de seguros. Retos y estrategias frente a la Unión Europea*. Madrid: MAPFRE.
Hernando de Larramendi, I. 2000. *Así se hizo MAPFRE*. San Sebastián de los Reyes: Actas.
Hernando de Larramendi, I. 1955–1990. *Informes de Ignacio Hernando de Larramendi*. Madrid: Archivo Mapfre.
Holzheu, T. & R. Lechner. 2007. "The Global Reinsurance Market," en J. D. Cummins and B. Venard (eds.) *Handbook of International Insurance. Between Global Dynamics and Local Contingencies*, 877–902. New York: Springer.

Levy, A. & F. Chaves Pereira. 2007. "Recent Developments in the Brazilian Insurance Market", In *Hand Book of International Insurance*, eds. J.D. Cummins and B. Venard, 743–787. New York: Springer.
MAPFRE. 1983. *Cincuenta años. MAPFRE hacia el futuro*. Madrid: MAPFRE.
Martínez Martínez, J. M. 1986. "El reaseguro español: principales problemas". *Hacienda Pública Española*, 98: 255–264.
Martínez Martínez, J. M. 1987. "Internacionalización del seguro y reaseguro. El caso español". *Conferencia en el V Encuentro Inter europeo de Reaseguros*, Madrid: Mapfre Archive. September.
Martínez Martínez, J. M. 2004. "MAPFRE: una experiencia Multinacional". *Trigésima novenas Jornadas de Estudio para Directores del Sector Seguros*, Madrid: Mapfre Archive. March.
Mundo MAPFRE. 2001. "Asamblea y Junta Generales relevo en la presidencia del Sistema Mapfre". *Sistema MAPFRE*. 33.
Sigma. 2019. "Natural catastrophes and man-made disasters in 2018: "secondary" perils on the frontline". *Swiss Re Institute*. 2.
Tortella Casares, G., L. Caruana de las Cagigas, & J. L. García Ruiz. 2009. *De Mutua a Multinacional. MAPFRE 1933–2008*. Madrid: MAPFRE.

11 Spanish Entrepreneurs and the Two Transitions (1975–1986)

Jorge Lafuente del Cano

Introduction

The Transition to democracy has been one of the great issues in the historiography of contemporary Spain. Unlike other events of great relevance, such as the Napoleonic invasion or the Civil War, the relatively pacific change from Franco's dictatorship to a parliamentary democracy was a certain collective success story that has been reflected in the literature of the period (Prego 1996; Tusell & Soto 1996; Powell 2001; Fusi 2018). Nevertheless, works have been appearing recently with a critical viewpoint on the process (Gallego 2008; Guillamet 2016; Molinero & Ysàs 2018). In any case, it is still an open subject with room for new interpretations.

One such interpretation refers to the protagonists of that intense moment of change. The focus has gradually been widened from the political class, both from the Franco regime and those who were in exile or working clandestinely (Powell 1995; Fuentes 2011; Tirado Ruiz 2015), to other actors who also had a notable influence in those decisive years of the country's recent history. Some of these new protagonists are the representatives of the economic sector and, among those, the entrepreneurs. It is not only the analysis of the role of the individual entrepreneurs that is of interest, some of whom had political responsibilities, but also the role of entrepreneurs as a collective through the organisms of representation that gradually became consolidated along with the liberalisation of Spain's public life and those whose aim was to make their voices heard in the most important matters for the country (Cabrera & Del Rey 2011; González Fernández 2012; Lafuente del Cano 2019).

The role entrepreneurs played is also equally important because Spain found itself in a delicate economic situation in the 1970s (Hernández Andreu 2006, p. 786). The effects of the petroleum crisis had a strong impact, similar to that of other European economies. There was a lack of economic measures taken by the last governments of Franco due to the fear of social unrest following the first rise in oil prices in 1973 that lead to the problem becoming pressing two years later, in the middle of the process of institutional change. Thus, following the need to transform the political structures, there came the need to apply measures that would help to overcome an economic situation which, by 1979, had become much more complicated with the second rise in crude oil prices.

This chapter studies the global role of the Spanish entrepreneurs from the Transition to democracy until its definitive completion in 1986. In order to analyse the position of the entrepreneurs we must first define the "two Transitions" that Spain had to face at that time: the domestic and the international Transition. The following section focuses on the domestic Transition and the attempts by the Spanish entrepreneurs to publicly organise to defend their interests on the public stage. Later, we will analyse the entrepreneurial position concerning the international Transition – the return of Spain to the international organisations in which it had not been able to participate because of political questions and in which two institutions stood out above all others in defining the new strategic and economic position of democratic Spain: NATO and the EEC.

Domestic and International Transitions

Following the death of Franco, in November 1975, Spain experienced a double process of change. The domestic Transition supposed the transformation of a regime that died along with its visible head into a democratic system similar to those that were enjoyed by other European countries. The term that could sum up that endeavour was "consensus" (Juliá 2017, p. 510): the renunciation of a program of maximums in order to reach an agreement between the political forces and the social and economic representatives. In spite of a certain initial idealisation of this period, it should be remembered that the solution could have been very different, even radically different to what finally took place. The analysis of the positions of some political forces or of those recalcitrant sectors of the dictatorship (known as the "bunker") reinforces the idea that everything could have turned out differently. Perhaps because of this, the greatest success of the political change was symbolised by the passing of the Constitution of 1978, the first Spanish Magna Carta forged through agreement and renunciation rather than through the imposition of one group over another. Thus the result, with all its ambiguities and problems that gradually appeared over time, has become the constitutional text with the greatest stability in the entire history of Spain. Achieving this objective was the fruit of the interaction between many groups and factions: on the one hand, the government, led since July 1976 by Adolfo Suárez, who would create an electoral coalition: the Central Democratic Union (UCD), which integrated personalities of very different sensibilities but with a common objective – to achieve a reform of the system in order to advance towards full democracy. On the other hand, were the parties that had opposed the Franco regime, from the socialists to the communists, who agreed to participate in the political game: institutions as social representatives (entrepreneurs, trade unions), the Catholic church, and, of course, the Spanish people who had lived through notable social transformations since the 1960s and who were mostly supportive of moderate, yet profound, changes.

Although there were problems, difficulties, and violence, the rapidity with which the change happened was one of the principal characteristics of the domestic Transition. Franco died in November 1975, the first elections were held in June 1977, and the Constitution was ratified by a referendum in December 1978. In just over three years, Spain's political system had been definitively modified.

With the passage of time, another Transition process took on its own prominence (Pereira 2004). The international Transition brought about Spain's entry into those international institutions to which it should have belonged, but which it could not belong during the dictatorship of Franco for political reasons. The dictatorship, which had suffered strict isolation after World War II, from the 1950s onwards during the Cold War, had managed to get a certain international recognition which resulted in bilateral agreements with the USA (1953) and entry to the UN (1955). However, Spain was still vetoed in other prime institutions; in particular NATO and the EEC.

Spain's entry to the Common Market was logical for geographical, cultural, political, and economic reasons. Perhaps because of this, the political and social unanimity, with certain nuances, was the general rule during the process (López Gómez 2016). Spain, which had seen how the members of the EEC had greeted the democratisation of the political system, came up against a more prosaic reality: the assignation of power and interests had already been done in the EEC, and opening the door to a new member was not a simple task. We have to remember that the first expansion that allowed in the UK, Ireland, and Denmark in 1973 was still causing certain upsets within the Community (Gay 2001, p. 137). This meant that the new expansion to the south, for Greece, Portugal and Spain, was probably not going to be as fast as initially foreseen. In fact, it did not happen until 1986.

Entry into NATO, the key western defensive system, was different. The unanimity disappeared and a strong opposition could be seen from some sectors linked to the political and social left (Mateos 2016, pp. 13–14). The question was a subject of discussion even in the governing party, the UCD, in the first years of political change. The entry did not happen until the resignation of Suárez and the start of the mandate of his successor, Leopoldo Calvo-Sotelo. Nevertheless, the process was not definitively closed until 1986 with the referendum called by the socialist government concerning Spain's permanence in the organisation.

The Entrepreneurs and the Domestic Transition

The entrepreneurs began to acquire a relevant role at a time of great uncertainty in both the political and economic situations. Added to the difficulty of an institutional change on the death of the dictator was the complex economic panorama, with the greatest economic stagnation of the previous 25 years. The organisational process of the entrepreneurs at the start of democracy was neither fast nor easy. In this section, we analyse first of all the creation of diverse associations of entrepreneurs that culminated in the formation of a single association that managed to become the voice of Spain's entrepreneurs, and secondly, the steps taken by this association on the road towards the formation of a democratic system in Spain, reflected in the debates that gave rise to the Constitution of 1978. Finally, we examine the position of entrepreneurs, now playing within the democratic game, with respect to the economic policy of the different parties during the centrist presidencies of Adolfo Suárez and Leopoldo Calvo-Sotelo, as well as the first term of office of the socialist Felipe González.

After forty years of dictatorship, with the first steps towards freedom in Spain, there emerged different discourses and values from those that had been heard from the official sources. Among the political proposals that began to appear in the public sphere, there were many that promoted a total removal of Spain's political system, including the economic system. Criticism of capitalism, the free market system, and business began to be heard forcefully from 1976 onwards. In this type of discourse, the entrepreneurial class was identified as being closer to the dictatorial regime than to the new democratic forces. This partly explains why the first collective actions of the entrepreneurs, within their plurality, were of a defensive nature (Flores 2003, p. 504). Their coordination seemed vital in order to try to offer a single voice to modify this negative image of the entrepreneurs, who had not found explicit support from any of the political forces that began to be constituted at the end of the dictatorship.

In July 1976, the king entrusted the presidency of the government to Adolfo Suárez. Despite his provenance as secretary general of the National Movement, the party of Franco, Suárez put all his weight behind carrying out reforms. To do so, he approved a series of legal provisions, starting with the Political Reform Law, which would demolish from the inside the legal apparatus of the dictatorship. He thus opened up the possibility of legalising political parties, trade unions, and entrepreneurial organisations. In this latter aspect, the laws of March 4, 1977 concerning labour relations and that of April 1, 1977 concerning the right to belong to a trade union were particularly important. With the beginning of the process of liberalisation, numerous entrepreneurial associations were founded at both national and regional levels. By June 1977, three of the most important – the Independent Entrepreneurial Group, the Spanish Entrepreneurial Confederation, and the General Confederation of Spanish Entrepreneurs – agreed to initiate a fusion process (Flores 2000, p. 711).

Thus, in June 1977, the same month that the first general elections took place, the association of associations was created. In a short time span, this association would become the consolidated voice of Spain's entrepreneurs: the Spanish Confederation of Entrepreneurial Organisations (CEOE). It is interesting to note the change that its appearance brought about. The attitude of the new organisation would no longer be reactive; on the contrary, it would adopt a high profile in the defence of their cooperative interests and the essential ideas common to them all: in essence, the free market system (Cabrera & Del Rey 2011, pp. 356–357). To do so, numerous acts and meetings demanding entrepreneurial rights were held throughout the national territory. From that time onwards, the CEOE was a consolidated, representative voice in public debates; in fact, its role has been described as taking an active political role, or even of being intrusive (García Crespo 2019a, p. 313). Its voice was heard in the most relevant political and economic affairs at that time: the pacts of the Moncloa, the passing of the Constitution and the initiatives of the governments of the UCD and, later, of the PSOE.

The elections of June 1977 had defined the political and institutional transformation of a Spain that was turning into a parliamentary democracy. In those elections, the UCD achieved a comfortable victory, but did not obtain the absolute majority. In second place, with 47 fewer seats, was the socialist party (PSOE) of Felipe González. The brief legislature that began at that time focused on two points: the drawing up of a Constitution and the search for unity in order to face the economic crisis. President Suárez called all the political forces to a meeting in the Presidential Headquarters, the Moncloa Palace, to try to reach a transversal agreement that would allow the country to face the economic situation with sufficient guarantees – an economic crisis that was characterised by the deceleration in the growth of the GDP and the increase in both inflation and unemployment (Comín & Hernández 2013, p. 307). Involving the opposition forces to the government, he aimed to maintain the collaboration he also needed to draw up the Magna Carta. The pacts of the Moncloa were signed in October 1977. The CEOE warily analysed the pacts, on the one hand because they had not been invited to participate in the discussions, which clashed head on with their policy of consolidating the association as the single voice of the entrepreneurs, and on the other because the agreements seemed to them both insufficient and incoherent for the country's needs, which in their judgment should focus on reaffirming the free market system, freedom to hire and fire, tax reform, and increased productivity of the national economy (Cabrera 2003, p. 55).

Parallel to the economic pact achieved by the parliamentary forces, the process of drawing up the new Constitution also began. The government's aim was for all the parties, but in particular the main opposition party, to actively participate in obtaining a text of minimums that would be agreeable to everyone. The CEOE, through the document entitled "For a Constitution that guarantees social progress and economic liberties", demonstrated their misgivings concerning some concepts contained in certain articles of the constitution, defending the link between democracy and the market economy (Flores 2000, p. 716).

Once the constitutional text had been approved, in March 1979, the second general elections were held, with very similar results to the first. Lacking a profound bond with the UCD, the CEOE tried to influence from outside the economic positions that the government adopted. The relation between the centrist party and the CEOE was difficult; as were the personal relations between the two leaders of the UCD, Adolfo Suárez and his successor Calvo-Sotelo, and the top executive of the entrepreneurs, Carlos Ferrer Salat, a businessman from the chemical and pharmaceutical industry. There was no personal understanding and nor was there any understanding of the concept of economic policy. On several occasions, it was suggested that his own political ambitions lay beneath the criticisms of the leader of the entrepreneurs (Calvo-Sotelo 1990, p. 169).

The CEOE was especially critical of a political centre which they considered to be too close to social democracy in their economic postulations. It should be remembered that the UCD had come about as a coalition of centrist parties and that it only became a political party in and of itself at a later date. The heterogeneity of the preceding parties, their leaders, and their regional organisations meant that their ideology had not been defined in a strict sense and that very different visions coexisted within the organisation. The vertebral axis was the desire to reform the political system without ruptures, and the figure of President Suárez also formed part of that vertebral axis. Reviewing the names of the successive centrist Finance Ministers can give us a good idea of this heterogeneity: Enrique Fuentes Quintana, Fernando Abril Martorell, Leopoldo Calvo-Sotelo, Juan Antonio García Díez. In this state of affairs, the CEOE tried to influence the economic policy of the UCD Executives, hoping for a reconversion to the liberal economic line to face the principal problems that Spain, in their judgment, had to overcome from the start of the democratic process and which were not being resolved adequately: unemployment, debt, trade imbalance, and lack of investment (Flores 2000, p. 712).

For his part, Adolfo Suárez, who always wanted to have a single interlocutor among Spain's entrepreneurs, became ever more critical of them. This President from Ávila was also having to face up to an ever progressive erosion of power. Once he had, in record time, managed to pass the laws that enabled the system change and the approval of the Constitution, he seemed to have trouble finding his way forward. The year 1980 was especially complicated. The economic situation had not substantially improved; terrorism was continuously attacking the State, causing the mistrust of the Armed Forces who were the habitual target of ETA; the PSOE had increased its work of opposition, including a no-confidence motion in the month of May, and the UCD appeared to be ever more internally divided, obtaining poor electoral results in the regional elections of Catalonia and the Basque Country. The entrepreneurs showed a profound lack of confidence in the capacity of the President or the government to redirect a situation that was becoming unsustainable towards the end of the 1980s.

Events gathered speed. In January 1981, Adolfo Suárez resigned. Leopoldo Calvo-Sotelo, the economic vice-President, was elected to succeed him. Calvo-Sotelo was independent; he did not belong to any of the parties that formed part of the UCD and neither had he had a long political career in the Franco era. He was an engineer, had worked for 25 years in the private sector and, with the arrival of democracy, had taken on the roles of Minister of Commerce, of Public Works, and of Relations with the European Communities (Lafuente del Cano & Ortúñez Goicolea 2020a). In spite of his apparent proximity to the entrepreneurs, because of his professional past, the CEOE received the new government with a very hard, critical document in which they asked, once more, for a change in the country's economic direction.

The government of Calvo-Sotelo (1981–1982), which had had to start by dealing with an attempted coup d'état, the now infamous 23-F, in the investiture session itself, maintained a certain distance from the CEOE. Despite the exhibition of social compromise visible in the signing of the National Agreement for Employment (1981), which had the participation of the CEOE and the two principal trade unions, the UGT and the CCOO (Del Campo 1995, p. 90), the CEOE had less and less trust in the future of the UCD. Faced with the weakness of the government and the risk of the opposition gaining power, as already predicted by the polls, the CEOE reinforced their desire to intervene in the country's political reorientation, looking for an agreement between the centre and the right, the so-called "natural majority", that could stand against the left in an election. Throughout 1982, the CEOE tried to promote an alliance between the UCD and the Popular Alliance (AP), led by an ex-minister of Franco, Manuel Fraga. Yet this option was fully opposed by the social democratic wing of the UCD, who aimed to remain in the centre of the political spectrum, without deciding on agreements to either left or right.

Calvo-Sotelo managed to keep some of the promises of his investiture speech, in particular concerning entry to NATO and the law limiting the competences of the autonomous communities (LOAPA). However, he resisted a pact with the right as he considered that it would alienate a part of his electoral support in the centre. The image of the party was, in any case, one of total internal discord that could be seen in their opinion concerning such laws as that of divorce; some UCD members of parliament abandoned the party, moving towards the AP of Fraga, while others moved towards the PSOE. The President of the government decided to go it alone to a new general election, despite entrepreneurial pressure, bringing the election forward to October 1982.

The result was a political turn around: the Socialist Party obtained a decisive electoral victory, Alianza Popular became the principal opposition party and the UCD only obtained a symbolic representation. The CEOE received the electoral victory of Felipe González with certain trepidation, although their public declarations were restrained (González Fernández 2012, p. 49). The naming of moderate leaders for the economic portfolios, Miguel Boyer and Carlos Solchaga, and the first measures that were closer to classic social democracy than to the socialism of Mitterrand brought about closer relations between the socialist government and the entrepreneurs. The expectations of a highly left-biased government meant that the reality was accepted with some relief by the representatives of the entrepreneurs. In 1983, Carlos Ferrer Salat abandoned the presidency of the CEOE and he was replaced by José María Cuevas, who had links to the paper industry. The truce between entrepreneurs and government was maintained throughout the first legislature and only began to deteriorate from 1986, the year of the socialist government's first re-election.

The Entrepreneurs and the International Transition

Entry to the EEC was possibly the central issue of the international Transition. The political impediment to entry during the Franco regime had created an almost unanimous desire in a country that began to identify Europe with modernity and progress (Moreno Juste 2001, p. 169). The end of the dictatorship and the consolidation of the democratic system laid the foundations for Spain's entry, but the negotiation was more difficult and complicated than initially foreseen. Spain officially applied for entry to the Common Market in July 1977 and the negotiations officially began in April 1979 but did not conclude until June 1985.

All the actors who began to emerge during the process of democratisation wished to participate in some way in this historic process; and this included the entrepreneurs. On the other hand, the Spanish government wanted to maintain control throughout the entire negotiations. They aimed to do so from 1978 until 1981 through a specific, newly created organism: the Ministry for Relations with the European Communities and from 1981 until 1985 through the Secretary of State for Relations with the Communities, as part of the Ministry of Foreign Affairs.

In the first phase, the objectives of the Ministry for Relations were to try to start the official negotiations as soon as possible; to coordinate the position on Europe of all the Ministries; and to try to involve the political parties, the economic interlocutors, and society in general in this aspiration (Lafuente del Cano 2017, pp. 60–65). To do so, it was necessary to know their opinions down to the last detail, so the first negotiating team maintained frequent contact with all the country's economic sectors, and, in particular, with the entrepreneurs and their organisations. Between 1978 and 1980, there were a total of 17 official meetings with the entrepreneurs: seven with the CEOE (Spanish Confederation of Entrepreneurial Organisations), five with CEPYME (Spanish Confederation of SMEs), and seven with the Superior Council of the Chambers of Commerce[1]. These meetings allowed the government to be aware of the entrepreneurs' hopes and worries during the initial weeks of the negotiations.

The basic position of the entrepreneurs was as follows: as with a good part of Spanish society, they were in favour of Spain's adhesion to the Common Market and they considered that it would be positive for the country's economy. However, they were particularly cautious about the way to proceed. They feared that a hurried and badly negotiated entry could suppose great sacrifices for the country's economic sectors and its companies. This could be seen in the lack of trust towards the Spanish political class who, since 1979, had suffered a certain deterioration in popularity with the end of the consensus and the start of the party political game so characteristic of a democratic system. The great expectations that had been forged by the vertiginous institutional changes within the country came up against democratic normality. Several problems, especially economic ones, were still unresolved and would remain so for a long time to come. This lack of trust in politicians included the fear that they might sacrifice the country's economy in order to achieve the political success of Spain's adhesion and its consequential electoral gain. This entrepreneurial position could be summed up by a sentence which has often been repeated since then: "Entry yes, but not at any price" (Lafuente del Cano & Ortúñez Goicolea 2020b, p. 137). The President of the CEOE, Carlos Ferrer Salat, acted as the spokesperson of this idea on numerous occasions when speaking with both the negotiators and the media.

These possible sacrifices that the entrepreneurs feared from a hurried agreement could be summed up by a series of points: first, they would be giving up the Preferential Trade Agreement of 1970. This was the framework for relations between Spain and the European Communities until the former's entry to the EEC. It had been signed in 1970 and had several positive consequences for Spain's economy, as the European Communities had underestimated Spain's industrial potential. On several occasions, particularly during the negotiations, some member states of the EEC had suggested that Spain should renegotiate this aspect or even unilaterally renounce it. Secondly, entrepreneurs were afraid of sacrificing the Transition periods that were, in reality, the key to the agreement. This was so because Spain was not negotiating but adhering to the organisation, fully accepting all the EEC's rules. The period of adaptation to this new legislation on the part of the different sectors was thus decisive. Some member countries defended a short Transition period for Spain's industrial sector and a long one for the feared agricultural sector. The entrepreneurs, however, defended more balanced periods. In third place there was VAT, a tax that would be mandatory in Spain once entry to the EEC had been agreed upon. Yet there were many voices in the EEC that asked Spain, as a show of good will and to accelerate the negotiations, to adopt VAT early, despite the misgivings of a good part of the economic sectors towards the proposal.

In any case, Spain's negotiating determination was not sufficient to impress a rapid rhythm to the negotiations. The EEC had to deal with numerous internal conflicts (including the consequences of the British rebate or the impact of the economic crisis) that considerably delayed progress. So, in June 1980, the President of the French Republic, Valery Giscard d´Estaing, delivered a famous speech asking for a pause in the negotiations concerning new membership. In practice, this pause supposed a veto in the Spanish negotiations of some of the most important and most conflictive aspects, such as agriculture (Bassols 1995, p. 237). From this moment on, the successive centrist negotiating teams tried to remove this veto and intensify the negotiations, especially at some particular moments such as the attempted coup d'état of the 23-F or the change in the French presidency after the victory of François Mitterrand. The position of the entrepreneurs did not change, however; they were still cautious about any opportunity to accelerate the process at the cost of renouncing Spain's strong negotiating points.

From December 1982 onwards, a new socialist team headed up the negotiations, with the hope of creating a better relationship with their French counterparts so as to benefit Spain's possibility of entry. The entrepreneurs followed the process with the same desire to influence and to intervene in any eventual deviation from what they considered to be the country's economic interests, in particular in the agricultural aspects that had been at the forefront of the negotiations and of the disagreements between the teams from the EEC and Spain (García Crespo 2019b, p. 264).

The diplomacy finally worked. Once the EEC's internal conflicts had been singularly resolved in the summits of Stuttgart (June 1983) and Fontainebleau (June 1984, when an agreement was reached concerning the UK's economic claim), progress was finally possible in the pending aspects of the negotiation. In June 1985, the definitive agreement was reached and thus Spain became a member with full rights of the EEC starting on January 1, 1986. The entrepreneurs looked at the final agreement with suspicion, since some of their pretensions, such as the Transition periods for certain agricultural products, had not been confirmed. Nevertheless, despite some apprehension regarding the future, they did appreciate the possibilities that such a historically relevant occurrence might bring.

The other decisive element in the international Transition was Spain's adherence to NATO. The differences with the case of the EEC were notable. The consensus that had made the pacts of Moncloa and the drawing up of the Constitution possible was still present, with certain nuances, with respect to Spain's entry to the EEC, but this was not the case with NATO. As the impact on the economic question was much less, the position of the entrepreneurs was not so decided.

The government of the UCD backed Spain's entry to NATO, although they were cautious. In its electoral program of 1977, the party simply mentioned the commitment to the security policy, whereas, in 1979, they explicitly mentioned NATO (Martínez Sánchez 2011, p. 186). Nevertheless, President Suárez did not decide to initiate the entry process, despite pressure from his Minister of Foreign Affairs, Marcelino Oreja. There were numerous reasons that may help us to understand the President's decision, yet it would seem that a fear of an acceleration in the rupture of the internal consensus and possible assistance by the Soviet Union to the terrorists of ETA were both present (Pérez López & Lafuente del Cano 2014, pp. 7–8).

The boost to NATO membership came with the change of presidency. Calvo-Sotelo was well known for his support of NATO membership and he wished to reflect this objective in his investiture speech. The centrist party thus remained united in its support for NATO membership, but it came up against strong opposition in both parliament and in the street. Thus, the question of NATO has been defined as one of the last battles of the left in the Transition (Mateos 2016, p. 13). The PSOE, which expressed an ideological radicality that later contrasted with its moderation in their years in government, proclaimed its well-known slogan "OTAN, de entrada no" (NATO, no entry). All in all, the process continued on its course through parliament and the majority in favour of NATO membership was victorious. Spain's official entry to NATO took place in May 1982.

However, the game was not over, since one of the electoral promises of the PSOE in the campaign of October of that same year was to call a referendum concerning Spain's exit from NATO. Nevertheless, the first years of the socialist government's legislature were a reality check and they turned to pragmatism (Andrade 2007, p. 98). Thus, in the referendum of 1986, the Executive asked people to vote in favour of remaining in NATO. In the heat of the referendum, which ended with the yes vote for remaining in NATO being victorious with 56.85% of the vote, the political and social division around NATO membership was revived.

The voice of the CEOE was not listened to in the same way or with the same intensity as in the other aspect of the international Transition, yet this was in some ways logical because it was seen more as a question of foreign policy or of strategic positioning than as a question of strong economic content as the entry to the EEC had been: the Common Market would affect the economic sectors, the regions, and the companies, so the entrepreneurs wished to firmly show their opinions. In contrast, the CEOE remained neutral concerning the referendum about remaining in NATO, as they considered that the result of the vote would not directly influence the march of Spain's economy. This attitude contrasted with that of Spain's principal banks (known informally as "the club of the seven"), which firmly came out in favour of remaining (*El País*, 06/03/1986). Nevertheless, some authors have questioned the strict neutrality of the entrepreneurs, putting it on par with the strategy of Fraga's party, which supported abstention (Díaz Varela & Guindal 1990, pp. 253–255). In reality, the right was in favour of NATO but considered the referendum to be unnecessary and an exercise of political tightrope walking by the government. Faced with the possibility that an affirmative vote to remain in NATO could be seen as a vote in favour of the government, they decided upon abstention in the campaign.

Besides the official position of their representatives, there is another way to know the thoughts of the entrepreneurs concerning the NATO question. In the light of the polemic surrounding the entry and later permanence in NATO, numerous sociological studies were carried out concerning Spanish society and NATO. These studies showed a majority in favour of NATO, an attitude of "soft NATO support" by the entrepreneurs (Gallego 1986, p. 105). However, there is also evidence of an internal plurality within the collective, as well as the polarisation that was present in Spain around the anti-NATO campaigns. In 1976, 53% of the professional category of managers and entrepreneurs was in favour of NATO; yet two years later, in October 1978, the number in favour had dropped notably as opposed to those who did not answer, while in April 1982, 29% of entrepreneurs were not in favour of NATO as opposed to 23% who were in favour. In any case, in June 1983, the entrepreneurs could be characterised as being a collective where the majority was in favour of NATO (REIS 22, 1985, 187–263). Later on, in 1985, it was calculated that 75% were in favour of remaining in NATO (Pérez Díaz 1985).

Conclusions

Between 1975 and 1986, Spain lived through profound changes in both its political system and its position in the comity of nations. At that moment of democratic consolidation, a new actor began to acquire a singular relevance in public life: the entrepreneurs.

On the one hand, the regime that had been forged in Franco's shadow had become weaker and weaker with the dictator's own decline. Some reformist leaders who had made a career in Franco's regime but who considered that Spain should advance towards democracy, without doubt or hesitation, headed the process of transformation that included parties opposed to the dictatorship, as well as other institutions of public relevance, such as the workers representatives and the entrepreneurs.

On the other hand, the country tried to achieve recognition from an international point of view with the country's entry to NATO and the EEC. NATO membership was complicated and generated strong resistance in both parliament and society, while the Common Market supposed an apparent unanimity in a country that had begun to associate Europe with democracy and modernity.

This entire process of change, which saw many difficulties and much resistance, occurred at a moment of intense economic instability. This was not the only problem. Convinced of the need to derail the process of democratic transformation by force, terrorism exercised constant pressure through violence and death during those years. In 1980 alone, terrorism caused the deaths of over one hundred people.

In this difficult but enthralling framework, the role of the entrepreneurs emerged. As with other sectors, the opening up and political liberalisation of Spain also allowed the entrepreneurs to experience years of great movement and a proliferation of associations. Of these, one institution came to represent an entire collective: the CEOE (Spanish Confederation of Entrepreneurial Organisations). The CEOE not only took on the role representing entrepreneurs in the social dialog, it also wanted to have its own voice in the debates and the political arena. It defended supporting the objectives of its members, while also, publicly and openly, unequivocally supporting the free market system.

This position involved participating in public debates and in the media in order to influence the policies of successive governments. The tension became evident with the centrist governments, which disappointed the entrepreneurs who desired a less Keynesian economic policy than that offered by Adolfo Suárez and his successor in the Moncloa, Leopoldo Calvo-Sotelo. The situation was different with the first government led by Felipe González; with the expectations of policies too far to the left, the moderation of González and the ample support from the electorate in the elections of October 1982 toned down the perspective and the grievances of the CEOE.

The entrepreneurs also took up a particular stance with the international Transition. NATO did not bring great debates, as its economic impact on the country was less. It was a defensive and strategic question in which a good part of the entrepreneurs was in favour of NATO, though the CEOE remained neutral. The Common Market was also a strategic position, but one that had a very strong economic component. Spain had to face reforms to adapt to the European framework and its impact was feared in certain sectors. The Spanish entrepreneurs did not break the consensus in favour of the EEC, predominant in parliament and in society. However, they showed a profound mistrust of the method of entry. They feared that the politicians would sacrifice part of the Spanish economy in order to obtain the political gain from adhesion. They were thus cautious because of the fears that adhesion produced, and they tried to make their voice heard in the negotiating teams. They did not manage to participate directly in the negotiation, which was reserved solely for the government, but they made their presence felt through appeals and constant demands to the Spanish negotiators.

Note

1 Archivo Leopoldo Calvo-Sotelo (ALCS), Relaciones con las CEE, 98, 12.

References

Andrade, J. A. 2007. Del socialismo autogestionario a la OTAN: notas sobre el cambio ideológico del PSOE durante la transición a la democracia. *HAOL* 14: 97–106.
Bassols, R. 1995. *España en Europa*. Madrid: Política International.
Cabrera, M. & F. Del Rey. 2011. *El poder de los empresarios. Política y economía en la España contemporánea (1875–2010)*. Barcelona: RBA.
Cabrera, M. 2003. Empresarios y políticos en la democracia. De la crisis económica a las incertidumbres de la transición. *Economía Industrial* 349–350: 51–62.
Calvo-Sotelo, L. 1990. *Memoria viva de la Transición*. Barcelona: Plaza & Janés/Cambio16.
Centro de Investigaciones Sociológicas. 1983. La opinión pública ante la OTAN. *Revista Española de Investigaciones Sociológicas* 22: 187–262.
Comín, F. & M. Hernández. 2013. Conclusiones. Las crisis económicas en España. In *Crisis económicas en España, 1300–2012: lecciones de la historia,* coord. by F. Comín and M. Hernández, 279–320. Madrid: Alianza.
Del Campo, E. 1995. ¿En el corazón del mercado? Sindicatos y empresarios en la democracia española. *Política y Sociedad* 20: 85–96.
Díaz Varela, M. & M. Guindal. 1990. *A la sombra del poder*. Barcelona: Tibidabo.
Flores, A. 2000. Los empresarios y la transición a la democracia en España. *Estudios Sociológicos* 54: 695–726.
Flores, A. 2003. Los empresarios y la transición a la democracia: Los casos de México y España. *Revista Mexicana de Sociología* 65: 497–522.
Fuentes, J. F. 2011. *Adolfo Suárez. Biografía política*. Barcelona: Planeta.
Fusi, J. P. 2018. La democracia en España: la Transición en perspectiva. In *España constitucional (1978–2018),* ed. B. Pendás, 319–329. Madrid: Centro de Estudios Políticos y Constitucionales.
Gallego, M. D. 1986. Algunas consideraciones sobre el cambio social y el empresariado en España 1960–1980. *Documentación social* 65: 93–114.
García Crespo, G. 2019a. La democracia del libre mercado. La intervención patronal en el sistema político de la Transición. *Historia y Política* 42: 297–330. doi.org/10.18042/hp.42.11.
García Crespo, G. 2019b. *El precio de Europa*. Granada: Comares.
Gallego, F. 2008. *El mito de la Transición. La crisis del franquismo y los orígenes de la democracia (1973–1977)*. Barcelona: Crítica.
Gay, J. C. 2001. El proceso de integración europea: de la pequeña Europa a la Europa de los Quince. In *Historia de la integración europea,* coord. by R. Martín de la Guardia and G. Pérez Sánchez, 123–166. Barcelona: Ariel.
Guillamet, J. 2016. *Las sombras de la Transición*. Valencia: Servei de publicacions.
González Fernández, A. 2012. Los empresarios ante los regímenes democráticos en España: la II República y la Transición. *Pasado y Memoria. Revista de Historia Contemporánea* 6: 33–55.

Juliá, S. 2017. *Transición: Historia de una política española (1937–2017)*. Barcelona: Galaxia Gutenberg.
Hernández Andreu, J. 2006. La transición centrista. In *Historia Económica de España*, coord. by A. González Enciso and J. M. Matés-Barco, 781–794. Madrid: Ariel.
Lafuente del Cano, J. 2017. *Leopoldo Calvo-Sotelo y Europa*. Madrid: Sílex.
Lafuente del Cano, J. 2019. Los empresarios españoles ante el cambio: retos, dificultades y esperanzas. In *Empresas y empresarios en España. De mercaderes a industriales*, coord by. J. M. Matés-Barco, 353–368. Madrid: Pirámide.
Lafuente del Cano, J. & P. P. Ortúñez Goicolea. 2020a. Leopoldo Calvo-Sotelo: ingeniero, empresario y político frente a la integración europea. *Historia y Política* 43: 121–155. doi.org/10.18042/hp.43.05.
Lafuente del Cano, J. & P. P. Ortúñez Goicolea. 2020b. Un objetivo y dos estrategias: el centro, los empresarios y los sindicatos ante Europa (1977–1982). In *La Transición española: una perspectiva internacional*, coord. by P. Pérez López, 125–154. Pamplona: Aranzadi Thomson Reuters.
López Gómez, C. 2016. La sociedad española y la adhesión a la Comunidad Europea (1975–1985): *políticos, asociaciones europeístas, interlocutores sociales*. PhD diss., Universidad Complutense de Madrid.
Martínez Sánchez, J. A. 2011. El referéndum sobre la permanencia de España en la OTAN. *UNISCI* 26: 283–310. dx.doi.org/10.5209/rev_UNIS.2011.v26.37825.
Mateos, A. 2016. La batalla de la OTAN en España. Un tardío ajuste ideológico. *Ayer* 103: 1–13.
Molinero, C. & P. Ysàs. 2018. *La Transición: Historia y Relatos*. Madrid: Siglo XXI.
Moreno Juste, A. 2001. España en el proceso de integración europea. In *Historia de la integración europea*, coord. by R. Martín de la Guardia y G. Pérez Sánchez, 167–214. Madrid: Ariel.
Pereira, J. C. 2004. El factor internacional en la transición española. *Studia historica. Historia contemporánea* 22: 185–224.
Pérez Díaz, V. 1985. Los empresarios y la clase política. *Papeles de economía española* 22: 2–37.
Pérez López, P. & J. Lafuente del Cano. 2014. Leopoldo Calvo-Sotelo y la Transición International: la prioridad europea. *Arbor* 190–769: 1–15. dx.doi.org/10.3989/arbor.2014.769n5008.
Powell, C. 1995. *Un rey para la democracia*. Barcelona: Planeta.
Powell, C. 2001. *España en democracia 1975–2000*. Barcelona: Plaza & Janés.
Prego, V. 1996. *Así se hizo la Transición*. Barcelona: Plaza & Janés.
Tirado Ruiz, J. A. 2015. *Siete caras de la Transición: Arias Navarro, Juan Carlos I, Adolfo Suárez, Manuel Fraga, Torcuato Fernández-Miranda, Santiago Carrillo, Carmen Díez de Rivera*. Madrid: San Pablo.
Tusell, J. & Á. Soto. (eds.). 1996. *Historia de la transición, 1975–1996*. Madrid: Alianza.

12 From the Sector to the Automobile Cluster of *Castilla y León*

Its Study through the History of Lingotes Especiales

Pablo Alonso-Villa and
Pedro Pablo Ortúñez Goicolea

Introduction

Castilla y León is one of the 17 autonomous communities that make up Spain in territorial and administrative terms. It is neither the most populated nor the most developed economically speaking. Nor is it the most industrialised, yet since the mid-twentieth century, it has become one of the leading industrial enclaves in the automobile sector in Spain. Along with Cataluña, it is the region with the largest vehicle production at a national scale. Between them, the two regions account for over 40% of the national total, according to data from the National Association of Automobile and Truck Manufacturers (ANFAC). Exports represent a similar percentage of the total.

This region is home to the production plants of three car manufacturers, *Iveco* – the seventh largest exporting company of automotive equipment in Spain – *Renault Group* – the second, is also the fourth largest in the country as a whole – and *Nissan*. The region boasts a large group of firms who manufacture car parts and equipment. Some of these firms are multinationals who head the national market in these products. Prominent amongst these are, for example, Lingotes Especiales, Grupo Antolín, Gestamp, Benteler, Johnson Controls, Faurecia, Valeo, etc.

For decades, the area has been home to externalities which have had an impact on the competitiveness which the automobile sector has managed to achieve. In the case of certain cities, such as Valladolid, the main nucleus of the sector, these advantages have been present since the first third of the nineteenth century, thanks to the previous existence of a metallurgical industrial district. The creation of the automobile cluster in 2001 was a spontaneous phenomenon, arising from the favourable conditions that already existed in the area. A change has occurred in which the cluster has come to be more important than the automobile sector itself. This is due to the fact that it not only embraces car firms but also a large group of suppliers involved in related sectors, as well as important technological centres and educational institutions.

The following pages examine the most important ideas concerning the theory of industrial location and set out the advantages which, according to authors such as Marshall, Becattini, and Porter, emerge from the concentration of firms. A description is then provided of the development of the automobile sector in Castilla y León and its transformation to the regional cluster. This dynamic is analysed through a study of the business history of one of the leading firms in the cluster: Lingotes Especiales. Also provided is a look at the area's advantages which this company has benefitted from in order to be competitive in international markets.

The Agglomeration of Economic Activities in Economic Theory: A Brief Summary

The location and agglomeration trends of economic activities in an area and the advantages to stem from this concentration have been the subject of analysis in economic science for over a century. The pioneering contribution of Alfred Marshall laid down the foundation of what was to become the general theory concerning industrial districts and clusters. A brief summary of the principal ideas of the authors who have most influenced this theory is provided below.

The earliest references to industrial districts are to be found in the work of Marshall, specifically in his book entitled *Principles of Economics* (1890). According to Loasby (2009), the importance of this concept lies in the fact that it highlights the role of external economies in industrial development processes. The term industrial district introduced by Marshall underpins the fact that firms which are concentrated in a given area and which draw on a single local labour force can achieve advantages in production at a large scale, acting as suppliers to other firms and driving technological innovation, such that the production process is linked to an area's economic and sociocultural resources[1]. Once the industry has set up in the area, it is likely to continue developing thanks to a series of advantages which would stem, amongst other reasons, from the very concentration of firms itself. These advantages or external economies which Marshall reflects in his work are concentrated in three groups.

First, there is the existence of non-codified knowledge to which all the firms and people in the district can gain access. This leads to the creation of a kind of "industrial atmosphere" wherein said knowledge is acquired almost naturally and would gradually be perfected by the member of the district for their mutual benefit.

The second advantage concerns the emergence of a subsidiary industry. The production process within a district is divided into a series of phases or stages which are assumed by the various firms. In addition, suppliers who are specialised in the production of the machinery required to manufacture the product or range of products that are characteristic of the district itself may also appear.

The existence of a specialised labour force constitutes the third advantage, which is external to the firms, but internal to the district. The district's specialisation in one or more products triggers a series of special technical skills amongst the firms' workers. In this way, the advantages for firms in the district when hiring skilled workers who are familiar with the techniques used in that industry would not be found in another isolated firm.

This set of advantages, which Marshall perceived in certain industrial areas of late nineteenth century Britain, have come to be known in economic literature as *Marshallian advantages* in order to distinguish them from another series of valuable factors which emerged in districts and which were subsequently studied by other authors.

The term industrial district was re-established by Becattini in the 1980s. The theory deriving from the works of this as well as other authors, such as Brusco, Bellandi, Sforzi, and Dei Ottati, is known as *neo-Marshallian*. Becattini refers to the district as a socio-territorial entity characterised by the active presence of both a community of people as well as a group of small- and medium-sized companies who cooperate with one another in a historically determined area (Becattini, 1979, 1989, 2002). This notion of district not only embraces the classical advantages or Marshallian externalities, but also adds a further two aspects that were characteristic of the Italian industrial areas he studied: predominance of small- and medium-sized companies and the existence of a cultural, political, and institutional framework specific to that area. This therefore extends the idea of "industrial atmosphere" which is characteristic of Marshall, and districts come to be areas in which the knowledge generated by the agents who operate in them flows (Galletto 2014). Apart from recovering the term district, according to Trullén (2015), the change in the unit of analysis in industrial economy – "from the production sector to the district" takes on enormous relevance within the theory developed by Becattini. In other words, rather than studying the sector in itself, the analysis focuses on the area where production is developed. Amongst the institutions driving the area where the district is located, prominent would be those pointed out by Becattini (1979, 1989) and later by Piore and Sabel (1990): local credit institutions, educational institutions, chambers of commerce or business associations, and local administration.

This phenomenon of agglomeration has been given a number of names: local production or work systems, innovative *milieu*, areas of flexible specialisation, and regional innovation systems. Yet all of them highlight the concentration of firms and the interactions between them. These terms were replaced by one word: cluster, which in the 1990s was coined by Harvard professor Michel Porter (1990, 1991, 1998, 2000). He took the pioneering ideas of Marshall and, based on them, developed a wide-ranging theory on competitiveness in the context of the global economy, yet focusing on a local basis. The international success of sectors and, in sum, of nations, is linked to a high geographical concentration of economic activity. When referring to this concentration, he used the expression cluster or group of firms. He defined the cluster as an agglomeration of firms and institutions that are interconnected in close-knit geographical location (Porter 1998). The economic agents in the cluster engage in complementary actions and compete with one another, but also cooperate.

The cluster's international competitiveness stems from the many advantages generated by the concentration of agents in a given area. First, there is the access to input and specialised workers. Input includes components, machinery, or financial services, which can be obtained at a lower cost. Both advantages refer to the first two Marshallian externalities. The cluster also favours access to information and knowledge. The agents in the cluster accumulate knowledge on the markets and production techniques. The proximity between them also leads to this knowledge circulating within the cluster. A third advantage of international competitiveness is the complementarity of activities; in other words, the possibility that subsidiary industries might emerge, just as Marshall proposed. The cluster also facilitates access to institutions and public goods. The concentration of firms triggers the appearance of an institutional framework which, through public investment in technical education or infrastructures reduces company costs. A fifth factor in the cluster's competitiveness involves competition between the firms it is made up of. The sixth advantage is the fostering of innovation. Rivals who are located close to one another tend to emulate and try to outdo one another, striving to improve in all the stages of production and distribution. Finally, the cluster contributes to the creation of new businesses. There are fewer obstacles to the arrival of new competitors than in isolated locations. A greater degree of externalisation sparks the emergence of new businesses.

The specialised literature seems to agree that the cluster phenomenon is more appropriate for explaining the competitive dynamic of capitalism than the neo-Marshallian vision (Catalan et al. 2011). This might be why interest in clusters is not only confined to the academic world but has found widespread acceptance amongst political decision-makers, from supranational institutions such as the OECD or the European Union, down to national, regional, and even municipal governments. A new form of industrial policy is being sought whose goal is the creation of competitive economies, with the cluster having become a tool to achieve such a goal. As a result, governments have encouraged and supported the development of competitive industrial clusters. The possibility of creating "top down" clusters – and, therefore, seeking to attract companies and economic agents to an area – clearly differs from the spontaneous and natural emergence ("bottom up") of agglomerations of firms and economic agents in a constant process of cooperation and collaboration where, in some cases, the structure of relations dates back decades or even centuries. Such is the case, for example, with the car industry in Castilla y León. We now look at how it has evolved and how a cluster has been created on the basis of already existing competitive advantages and relations between firms in the sector as well as other related firms and local institutions.

From the Sector to the Regional Automobile Cluster

Castilla y León, and in particular Valladolid, which is the principal nucleus of the regional sector, has a long-running tradition of manufacturing cars and car parts. The city's metallurgical industrial district, which began to emerge in the early twentieth century, enabled the development – after the 1950s – of the automobile sector both in the city as well as throughout the region as a whole.

The manufacturing of car parts and components began in the first third of the twentieth century. One of the first companies to manufacture parts for motor vehicles was the Sociedad Española del Carburador IRZ, founded in 1922. In addition to producing carburettors for car engines, its clients included the leading national – Hispano Suiza and Casa Elizalde – as well as international aviation companies, such as the British firm Armstrong Siddeley[2] (Alonso et al. 2019).

The 1940s saw a transformation in the supply provided by firms in the district towards the manufacture of products destined for the transport material sector. However, it was not until Fabricación de Automóviles, S.A. (FASA) was built in the early 1950s that vehicles were manufactured in the region and therefore, that the sector began to develop. This company commenced production of cars under licence from Renault in 1953. They were soon followed by other companies. In 1956, Fabricaciones de Automóviles Diésel, S. A. (FADISA) was set up in Ávila to manufacture vans under licence from Alfa Romeo[3]. One year later, the Sociedad Anónima de Vehículos Automóviles (SAVA) was opened in Valladolid to manufacture three-wheel vehicles with Barreiros engines[4] (Álvarez 2008).

During the 1960s, the industrial policy carried out by the Franco regime helped to boost the automobile sector in Castilla y León. The government promoted the development of the region by declaring Burgos and Valladolid to be "Poles" (Cebrián 2009). Between 1965 and 1970, production in the sector grew at an average rate of 21.6%. It was at this time that mass production started at *FASA*. Its production rose substantially, increasing from 8,400 vehicles in 1960 to almost 170,000 in 1973 (Fernández de Sevilla 2013). The boost given by this company as well as by other manufacturers who had also set up in Spain in the 1950s, SEAT and Citröen, helped to increase the number of firms supplying units and equipment in Castilla y León and nationally. In 1950, there were 429 such firms in Spain, while ten years later the figure had risen to 1,329, (Ortiz-Villajos 2010: 389).

The 1970s saw an upheaval in the history of the automobile, not only in Spain but globally (García-Ruiz 2001). The international automobile sector reached a turning point, which was sparked by the oil shock of 1973. In Spain, the crisis which began that year lasted until the end of the decade (Carreras & Tafunell 2010). In the case of the domestic car industry, internal demand for vehicles fell by 10.4% between 1974 and 1979 (Castaño & Cortés 1980). Faced with this situation, being able to resort to exports, boosted by the preferential agreement which Spain signed in 1970 with the EEC, brought relief to Spanish manufacturers (Fernández de Sevilla 2013).

Despite this downturn, the 1970s heralded a period of consolidation for the sector in Castilla y León. In quantitative terms there was a rise in the level of occupation[5], of the total volume of production – to a greater extent – and, as a result, there were productivity gains. FASA-Renault continued to increase its production thanks to exports to France, spurred by the parent company, Renault, and opened a new factory in Valladolid and another in Palencia, which consolidated the firm's presence in Castilla y León. Two of the most important car component firms, backed by regional capital, consolidated their position in the market. The first of these, Grupo Antolín, set up in Burgos in 1959 and the second, Lingotes Especiales in Valladolid, in 1969 (Alonso & Ortúñez 2020). In addition, the European leader in tires, Michelin, arrived and opened a factory in Aranda de Duero in 1970 and another in Valladolid in 1973.

In the 1980s and 1990s, the sector grew even further following the arrival of major multinational equipment and component firms – Huf, Benteler, Johnson Controls, and Ficosa, amongst others – as well as the creation of firms with national or regional capital – such as Gestamp – who set up in various provinces in Castilla y León. Other manufacturers also arrived, such as Nissan – in 1980 it bought Motor Ibérica S.A and maintained the plant at Ávila – and Iveco, who opened in Valladolid in 1991 after acquiring ENASA.

This proliferation of firms was due to increased internal demand as well as to demand from other neighbouring regions – Basque Country, Navarra, Aragón, Cataluña, and Galicia – where there were vehicle manufacturers. This flow of interregional relations is, amongst others, the reason behind the even geographical distribution of firms around the various provinces of Castilla y León. Together with Valladolid – the leading industrial nucleus where the car industry is present – the main enclaves are Burgos and León. The three of them account for over 70% of all the firms.

For suppliers in Castilla y León, their initial dependence on manufacturers in the region, in particular on FASA-Renault, gradually declined and even began to disappear. In that year, 36% of company sales of equipment and components in Castilla y León were shipped to other regions in Spain and 30% to other countries, mainly in the EU (Camino et al. 2005). In other words, only one third of what regional suppliers were producing was absorbed by the plants which Renault, Nissan, and Iveco had in Castilla y León.

This percentage may well now be even less due to the growing internationalisation of suppliers of equipment and components to the region. This opening up has been based on exports and on direct investment overseas. Prominent examples of this dynamic are Grupo Antolín, Gestamp, and Lingotes Especiales. The equipment and component industry in Castilla y León currently represents 23.4% of the national total, and is second only to Cataluña in regional terms (Datacomex).

Apart from companies' internal factors, this high level of international competitiveness has benefitted from the existence of a series of economic agents present in the region – knowledge centres, specialised service firms, and companies from other related sectors – who maintain a close link – collaboration and cooperation – with the vehicle builders and manufacturers of parts and components, which has favoured the emergence of agglomeration economies and externalities. In 2001, many of these agents decided to group together in the form of a cluster and set up the Castilla y León Automobile Business Forum (Facyl). In this case, unlike what happened in other European regions where automobile clusters have been created "top down"[6], the conditions required for it to emerge were already present in the area, as we have seen, since the mid-twentieth century, such that its creation has been totally spontaneous, or "bottom up".

Facyl has grown since it was set up nearly 20 years ago. It is currently made up of 69 agents or members, approximately half of whom are SMEs, which are classified as follows. A first group comprises the three car manufacturers present in the region: Grupo Renault, Iveco and Nissan. A second group of agents is composed of suppliers of car equipment and components. In this case, a distinction should be drawn between two groups of firms. On the one hand are the subsidiaries of the major international groups of car parts – one key feature is that Facyl includes almost half of those in the world – and on the other are the regional suppliers. Some of these –Lingotes Especiales, Grupo Antolín, or *Gestamp*– have become leading multinational groups. Companies from other related sectors, such as tire manufacturers (Michelin), producers of fibres and fabrics for seats, or metal products, also form part of the cluster. All of them make up the third group of agents in the cluster. The fourth group comprises the knowledge generating units, such as the technological centres (CARTIF and Cidaut), the universities of Valladolid, Burgos, and León, service companies who specialise in engineering and vocational training centres. These technological agents work in the area of ICT. Their potential and knowledge lead them to undertake key projects in conjunction with firms in order to develop products and processes, and to incorporate good practices in management and production. Finally, there are all those local institutions who help to promote the area, such as local credit institutions, chambers of commerce or business associations, economic development agencies, public credit institutions, and local administration.

The turnover of all the agents involved in the cluster – with the exception of the institutions or public entities – exceeded 12,200 million euros last year (21% of regional GDP) and provided direct employment to 25,900 people (2.7% of the working population)[7]. If we compare these figure to those of the regional car industry – 17% of regional GDP and 1.9% of employment – we see how the situation has changed and how it reflects how the cluster is more important than the sector[8]. Until around 2015, the production of the agents in the cluster represented some 80% of that of the sector. Today's data show that the figure now stands at over 100%. In terms of production, overseas companies have a greater weight – it should be remembered that there are three vehicle manufacturers. Nevertheless, those backed by regional capital or, in certain instances, national capital, have a major presence. Grupo Antolín, a family business, is the sixth leading exporting firm of automotive equipment in Spain. Gestamp is present in 20 countries and is the world leader in steel stamping, and Lingotes Especiales, who export over 80% of their production and account for 12% of the European markets in brake discs, are just some examples of the dynamism achieved by regional companies[9].

The possibilities for growth, both in the domestic market and in the overseas market, for firms which belong to the cluster are much greater than for those firms who are outside it. In fact, the most competitive and productive companies are those who belong to Facyl. Prominent in this regard are the three previously mentioned companies plus the factories in the Renault Group in the region who, together with the Nissan plant in Sunderland, have become the most productive and competitive in the whole of the Renault-Nissan Alliance (Alonso & Juste 2018).

There are many externalities derived from the agglomeration of these agents in Castilla y León and they have an impact on firms' competitiveness. These competitive advantages may represent anchoring factors in the area, which is known in the specialised literature as the "territory effect". In the case of Facyl, five advantages are seen to be present in the area.

The first of these is the possibility for cooperation which companies have, particularly SMEs. The option to cooperate may be applied to different scenarios, from fostering commercial and production internationalisation, to joint hiring of services. The strategic lines which Facyl pursues seek to boost this advantage so that a greater number of firms in the cluster may benefit from it. The other externalities present in the territory are linked in one way or another to the idea of cooperation.

Another advantage linked to the cluster is joint participation in R&D projects. The availability of a context of knowledge boosts firms' technological potential and makes them more competitive. In the automobile cluster, many major companies who are able to manage their technological dynamic through their own R&D coexist with an even greater number of SMEs who are not able to economically sustain such departments and who, therefore, need external assistance. For these firms, being able to draw on technological centres and engineering firms is key to undertaking research projects and developing new products and processes. Within the Castilla y León automobile cluster, there are two such centres (Cidaut and CARTIF, who both form part of the European network), as well as six engineering service companies, specialising in providing firms in the cluster with comprehensive solutions.

A third advantage concerns the possibility of subcontracting production tasks which, occasionally or permanently, a firm may decide to outsource. The existence of subsidiary industries is one clearly distinctive feature of clusters. Vehicle manufacturing involves a great number of tasks and procedures and it is necessary to assemble a wide variety of parts and units. Sharing the production of these units provides firms with greater production efficiency. In the case of Castilla y León, there is more outsourcing than in other production activities, added to which it has also grown more quickly (Alonso & Juste 2018). This result confirms the trend pointed out by Myro (2009) for the case of the car industry on a national and international scale. In a context of ever-growing externalisation, company proximity and cooperation is vital vis-à-vis being able to implement a system of lean manufacturing and of supplying just in time (JIT).

The fourth advantage to derive from the cluster is the existence of a specialised labour market. This advantage is undoubtedly the one which the area has been offering the longest. It is linked to the prior existence of a metallurgical based industrial district. Since the late nineteenth century, the area as a whole, and

Valladolid in particular, has had industrial vocational training schools. Over the years, the range of courses offered by these centres has expanded and, since the 1930s, specialised studies in the automotive sector have been available in Valladolid. In the 1950s and 1960s, almost half of all technical engineer graduates from the Valladolid Industrial Engineering Faculty worked in firms involved in the automobile sector (Alonso & Ortúñez 2019). The range of courses gradually spread to the rest of the provinces and 16 vocational training centres in Castilla y León today include courses geared exclusively towards the car industry. The same can be said of the region's universities. Thanks once again to cooperation, there is also the possibility of receiving joint training through the programmes offered by Facyl for life-long learning for workers, middle management, and directors. This stock of knowledge forms part of the traditional and ongoing "industrial automobile atmosphere" present in the region's cities, such as Valladolid.

One final advantage is the presence of institutions or local development agents, as well as business organisations. Castilla y León has an economic development agency, a institute for business competitiveness, and a financial institute. Moreover, and in constant interrelation with the firms in the cluster, there are chambers of commerce and industry in the various provinces in the region. This kind of employers' organisation cooperates with firms and offers a wide variety of specialised guidance services, particularly in the international area with a view to promoting companies' expansion overseas.

The Companies in the Sector: The Case of Lingotes Especiales

1969 witnessed the creation in Valladolid of Lingotes Especiales, one of Spain's leading automotive equipment and component firms. Its industrial and business history may help to understand the changes that have occurred in the sector at a regional scale over the last five decades. Moreover, an analysis of the firm provides an insight into the advantages of the cluster which have helped it, amongst other aspects of an internal nature, to achieve greater competitiveness. The use of these advantages depends on its business strategy and, more specifically, on its management style. Amongst the many companies that make up Facyl, Lingotes Especiales has been chosen as a case study for a number of reasons: a) it is a firm with a long-running tradition in the sector, b) it is backed by regional capital, c) it is one of the leading firms in the cluster thanks to its great competitiveness in international markets, d) it is one of the founding members of Facyl, and e) it currently presides over the cluster's board.

The idea behind Lingotes Especiales came from some young entrepreneurs in the region who set out to cast iron and obtain a range of metal parts for the industry in general. The firm was set up at the time when the national automobile industry was beginning to take off (Alonso & Ortúñez 2020). In this context, the increased number of vehicle manufacturers in Castilla y León, FASA-Renault, and to a lesser degree SAVA, enabled them to have key clients in the region itself who would acquire part of their production. The two car companies soon became regular clients. Since then, many of the parts that Lingotes Especiales has manufactured have gone to car building firms[10]. In the 1970s and 1980s, the firm continued to expand despite the difficulties the car market was going through at a national and international scale. The strategy of commercial diversification it implemented during the early decades of its activity allowed it to overcome these difficulties and in 1990 its annual production exceeded 45,000 tons of metal products, compared to the less than 5,000 it had produced in the early 1970s.

The 1990s heralded a period of consolidation for the company for two reasons. The first was its firm conviction to focus on the overseas market. Its competitive skills in terms of production enabled it to manufacture quality parts at a low price and its commercial strategy in Europe meant that it could easily gain a foothold in that market. The results of its internationalisation strategy are there for all to see. The firm went from exporting less than 2% of its production in 1990, to over 75% in 2000. The second reason underlying its consolidation was the decision to take its production process to the next level and to mechanise the parts it produced, thereby giving them added value. In order to undertake this project, the company decided to cooperate with an Italian firm, Bradi, which up until that point had been mechanising the parts being cast in Valladolid. In 1996, the two companies signed a technical collaboration agreement – a *joint venture* – to carry out the project and created a new company called Braling Conjuntos. The capital for the new firm was split between the two partners and the Castilla y León Industrial Development Society (Sodical)[11]. Four years later, and thanks to the good results obtained, Lingotes Especiales decided to buy out its partner's share and changed the name to Frenos y Conjuntos, S.A. Thanks to the mechanized subsidiary company and to its new product, the mechanized brake disc, exports grew until they reached 80% of total production in 2003. Manufacture of these parts, together with the raw discs, accounts for 12% of the European market.

After 2000, Lingotes Especiales took yet another step forward in its internationalisation and undertook a process which involved investing abroad by setting up production plants. It once again opted for cooperation with a business partner, and various options were weighed. Given the interest of the North-American multinational company Alcoa in knowing the production processes carried out by Lingotes Especiales, that company was chosen. Alcoa, with its automotive sector division, Alcoa Automotive Casting Unit, provided Lingotes Especiales with the chance to access the North-American car market fairly quickly. The agreement between the two firms to manufacture aluminium car parts was signed, and the first phase of the project saw the purchase of a production plant at Leyland, owned by the British company Alloy Technologies Limited (ATL). The first manufacturing tests using technology designed by Lingotes Especiales with the help of Cidaut were conducted at the factory. A second stage involved installing another larger factory in Spain which was for serial production of the aluminium parts. The location chosen to house the new plant was in Castilla y León, close to Valladolid. The two partners concluded that this location was ideal given the advantages the area could offer. Despite the good technical results obtained in the components, these failed to have the anticipated business impact. The agreement began to hang by a thread and eventually Lingotes Especiales decided to abandon the project in late 2004. Although this ambitious adventure ultimately proved unsuccessful, it did provide Lingotes Especiales with valuable experience in techniques for mechanising aluminium parts and components.

The last business project undertaken by Lingotes Especiales overseas was in India. In 2014, the firm signed a joint venture with a car component company in India, Setco Automotive Limited, for the manufacture of mechanised parts. Once again, Lingotes Especiales headed the technical side of the project. The first units were shipped out to clients in Southeast Asia in 2016. Current expectations are to expand the facilities to reach a production capacity of over 50,000 tons per year.

Throughout its 50-year history, Lingotes Especiales has taken advantage of some of the competitive advantages afforded by the area, some of which are now listed. One of the factors, perhaps the most important, which influenced the setting up of the firm and its location in Valladolid was the close proximity of the FASA-Renault and SAVA factories which, in this case and at least at the beginning, served as driving or leading companies, according to the cluster theory. Another reason that explains the firm located in Valladolid was the existence of partners in the city who had a long-running tradition in the metallurgical sector and who were ready to invest. Valladolid's metallurgical tradition, which dates back to the late nineteenth century, enabled it to create a business class that had experience in this type of venture and which had shown its willingness to invest by welcoming the arrival of FASA.

Links with the area and the advantages this entails can also be seen through the use of specialised staff. Lingotes Especiales' first workers in the 1970s included people who had acquired experience in metallurgical activities in local factories. Moreover, throughout its whole life, the firm's staff has included a number of graduates from the University of Valladolid as well as from vocational training centres in the area, and with whom it has set up internship training agreements. This type of cooperation with educational institutions proves beneficial to both parties. It has allowed Lingotes Especiales to choose its workers, taking into account the skills they have demonstrated during their training period. It allows students and future workers, to gain the experience they would not otherwise be able to acquire through their theoretical studies in training centres. Many companies in the cluster – including the Grupo Renault – have benefitted from the existence in the region of the wide range of vocational training courses available.

In the case of Lingotes Especiales the importance of institutions which promote economic and industrial development is also clear. As mentioned, the Castilla y León Industrial Development Society (Sodical) was involved in its mechanising project. This business plan required a substantial financial outlay, 200 million euros, such that the two companies – Lingotes Especiales and its partner Bradi – opted to draw on the financial support provided by Sodical, who provided 20% of the social capital.

Finally, Lingotes Especiales has cooperated with other firms in the cluster and with technological centres. In addition to its participation with other agents at international business fairs or meetings on quality and competitiveness, it has developed the necessary procedures to ensure the correct implementation of the lean manufacturing production system and the JIT supply system, both of which require constant coordination with its clients and with other suppliers. Cooperation also extends to the technological sphere. Lingotes Especiales has maintained close links with the University of Valladolid to engage in joint research into developing new processes and products. It has also fostered the creation of the Cidaut and CARTIF technological centres, with whom it cooperates in R&D issues, even though it has its own department for such purposes. In its alliance with the multinational Alcoa, it was Lingotes Especiales who headed the technical part of the project. Together with Cidaut, it designed the new moulding system to be introduced at the Leyland plant. The advantages afforded by the area meant that Alcoa and Lingotes Especiales decided to house the production factory in Castilla y León, despite the North-American multinational having factories in the neighbouring region of Galicia. Another of the most important technological innovations undertaken by Lingotes Especiales is the European patent obtained in 2016 for the lightweight disc brake, and which meant a 30% reduction in its weight. In this case it also received technical assistance from Cidaut.

Final Notes

Unlike what has happened in other European regions, in Castilla y León there is a clear example of a cluster created spontaneously as a result of the externalities that the area has offered. The favourable conditions for the birth and development of the automobile cluster were present from the mid-twentieth century, with some even dating from the late nineteenth. A relational network has been created that extends between automotive companies and other sectors, technology centres, and institutions, and this is what ultimately drives the competitiveness of the cluster and serves as a territorial anchor for investment. The impact of the agglomeration of these activities in Castilla y León on the competitiveness of automobile companies is clear in the case of Lingotes Especiales. Herein only a sample of the fluid and constant cooperation relationships which this company maintains with the other agents in the cluster has been provided. Future research may provide further insights into the relational structure of this automobile cluster and will shed light on all of the stages this group of agents has gone through. The impact which the cluster has on regional economy competitiveness as a whole is also evident since, according to the cluster theory, the advantages of the production sectors are transferred to the area in which they are located.

Notes

1 Although Marshall mentions the term district, this tends to be referred to as industries specialised in specific locations.
2 Some of the planes which made pioneering flights had IRZ carburettors installed, such as the first flight between London and Cape Town in the early 1920s or the Dornier Wal seaplane or flying boat, known as Plus Ultra, which made the first flight between Spain and America in 1926 (Aérea 1926).
3 In 1965, Motor Ibérica S.A bought FADISA. In 1980, the Japanese firm Nissan purchased Motor Ibérica S.A. and changed the name to Nissan Motor Ibérica S.A. although it maintained its industrial plant in Ávila.
4 In 1968, ENASA, which built Pegaso trucks, bought SAVA. Later, in 1991 Iveco purchased ENASA and since then has been building light trucks at the factory in Valladolid.
5 According to Parejo (2011), 6,295 industrial jobs were created in Valladolid between 1964 and 1974. This represents one of the most remarkable figures among non-metropolitan cities, according to Catalan et al. 2011. Many of these jobs were in the automobile sector.
6 According to Aláez et al. (2010), approximately 70% of the 51 currently in Europe.
7 Direct employment would stand at over 100,000 people, according to the Regional Economy Ministry at the Regional Government of Castilla y León.
8 According to data compiled in the annual Facyl reports and data from the Regional Spanish Accounts of the National Statistics Institute, this is the trend observed since the last decade.
9 Annual report of the Grupo Antolín (2017), ESADE Business School (2018), Gestamp annual report (2017) and annual report of Lingotes Especiales (2017).
10 The company has also often manufactured components for other sectors such as the domestic sector, the electrical and mechanical industry, public works, and railways. The strategy of diversification which the company has pursued has allowed it to overcome the specific and contextual difficulties that the car industry has experienced in Spain and in Europe (Alonso & Ortúñez 2020).
11 Institution of a public nature that promotes, through investment and favourable-term loans, the region's industrial and economic development.

References

Aérea. 1926. *Revista Ilustrada de Aeronáutica* 36: 1–42.
Aláez, R., J. C. Longás, M. Ullibarri, J. Bilbao, V. Camino, & G. Intxauburru. 2010. Los clústers de automoción en la Unión Europea. Incidencia, trayectoria y mejores prácticas. *Economía Industrial* 376: 97–104.
Alonso, P. & J. J. Juste. 2018. El sector de la automoción en Castilla y León. 50 años de crecimiento económico y productividad, 1961–2011. *Revista de Estudios Regionales* 113: 101–136.
Alonso, P., M. Álvarez & P. P. Ortúñez. 2019. Formación y desarrollo de un distrito metalúrgico en Valladolid (c. 1842–1951). *Investigaciones de Historia Económica* 15: 177–189.
Alonso, P. & P. P. Ortúñez. 2019. La formación profesional industrial en Valladolid y su impacto en el desarrollo industrial de la ciudad (c. 1880–1970). *Investigaciones Históricas* 39: 473–516.

Alonso, P. & P. P. Ortúñez. 2020. El proceso de internacionalización en la industria española de equipos y componentes de automoción: Lingotes Especiales, 1968–2018. *Revista de Historia Industrial* 78: 115–154.
Álvarez, M. 2008. *La industria fabril en Castilla y León durante el primer franquismo (1939–1959)*. Valladolid: Universidad de Valladolid.
Becattini, G. 1979. Dal "settore" industriale al "distretto" industriale. Alcune considerazioni sull'unità d'indagine dell'economia industrial. *Rivista di Economia e Politica Industriale* 5: 7–21.
Becattini, G. 1989. Riflessioni sul distretto industriale marshalliano come concetto socio-economico. *Stato e Mercato* 25: 111–128.
Becattini, G. 2002. Del distrito industrial marshalliano a la 'teoría del distrito' contemporánea. Una breve reconstrucción crítica. *Investigaciones Regionales* 1: 9–32.
Camino, V., R. Aláez, C. Álvarez, J. Bilbao, G. Intxauburru, J. C. Longás, A. Pardo, M. Ullibarri, & M. Vega. 2005. *El sector de automoción en Castilla y León. Componentes e industria auxiliar*. Valladolid: CESCYL.
Carreras, A. & X. Tafunell. 2010. *Historia Económica de la España Contemporánea (1789–2009)*. Barcelona: Crítica.
Castaño, C. & G. Cortés. 1980. Evolución del sector del automóvil en España. *Información Comercial Española* 563: 145–157.
Catalan, J., J. A. Miranda, & R. Ramon-Muñoz. 2011. *Distritos industriales y clusters empresariales. Trayectorias históricas de ventaja competitiva en la Europa del Sur*. Madrid: LID Editorial Empresarial.
Cebrián, M. 2009. ¿Industrializar Castilla? El caso del Polo de Desarrollo de Valladolid, 1964–1975. In *Estado y Mercado: los planes de desarrollo durante el franquismo*, ed. J. De la Torre and M. García-Zúñiga, 261–296. Pamplona: Universidad Pública de Navarra.
ESADE Business School. 2018. *Exportación de la mediana y gran empresa en España*. Barcelona: ESADE.
Fernández de Sevilla, T. 2013. El desarrollo de la industria del automóvil en España: el caso de FASA-Renault, 1951–1985. PhD diss. Universidad de Barcelona.
Galletto, V. 2014. Distritos industriales e innovación. PhD diss., Universidad Autónoma de Barcelona.
García-Ruiz, J. L. 2001. La evolución de la industria automovilística española, 1946–1999: una perspectiva comparada. *Revista de Historia Industrial* 19–20: 133–163.
Loasby, B. J. 2009. Industrial Districts in Marshall's economics. In *A Handbook of Industrial Districts*, ed. G. Becattini, M. Bellandi and L. de Propis, 78–89. Cheltenham, UK: Edward Elgar.
Marshall, A. 1890. *Principles of Economics*. Londres: Macmillan.
Myro, R. 2009. *La profunda crisis del sector del automóvil*. Madrid: Colegio de Economistas de Madrid.
Ortiz-Villajos, J. M. 2010. Aproximación a la historia de la industria de equipos y componentes de automoción en España. *Investigaciones de Historia Económica* 16: 135–172.
Parejo, A. 2011. La conformación de distritos industriales en España durante la década del desarrollismo: un enfoque desde la inversión, 1964–1974. In *Distritos industriales y clusters empresariales. Trayectorias históricas de ventaja competitiva en la Europa del Sur*, ed. J. Catalan, J. A. Miranda, y R. Ramon-Muñoz, 175–200. Madrid: LID Editorial Empresarial.
Piore, M. J. & C. Sabel. 1990. *La segunda ruptura industrial*. Madrid: Alianza.

Porter, M. 1990. *The Competitive Advantage of Nations*. New York: The Free Press.

Porter, M. 1998: Clusters and the New Economics of Competition. *Harvard Business Review* November-December: 77–90.

Porter, M. 2000. Locations, Clusters, and Company Strategy. In *The Oxford Handbook of Economic Geography*, ed. G. L. Clark, M. P. Feldman, and M. S. Gertler, 253–274. Oxford: Oxford University Press.

Trullén, J. 2015. Giacomo Becattini and the Marshall's method. *Investigaciones Regionales* 32: 43–60.

Contributors

Pablo Alonso-Villa is an associate lecturer at the University of Valladolid. He holds a degree in Economics, a master's degree in Economics Research and a PhD in Economics from this University. He made a research stay at the Institute of Social Sciences of the University of Lisbon. He has published numerous articles in indexed journals and a book chapter. His research focuses on the industrial history of Castilla y León and especially in the metallurgical sector and its connections with the automobile industry.

Rafael Barquín Gil is an associate lecturer at the Universidad Nacional de Educación a Distancia, Madrid. At present, his main lines of research focus on railroads, integration of cereal market, and processes of literacy in nineteenth-century Spain. Some of his publications are "El consumo urbano en Andalucía Oriental a mediados del siglo XIX" Investigaciones de Historia Económica, 2019; "La influencia del ferrocarril en el desarrollo urbano español (1860–1910)" Revista de Historia Económica / JILAEH, 2012; and "Analysis of Spanish wheat prices (1765–1855)" Histoire et Mesure, 2011. He is editor in chief of Transportes, Servicios and Telecomunicaciones (TST).

Leonardo Caruana de las Cagigas is tenure at the University of Granada (Spain). His research is on insurance and reinsurance history. He has published "From Mutual to Multinational, MAPFRE, 1933–2008" with Gabriel Tortella Casares and José Luis García Ruiz and "The History of Spanish Insurance" with Gabriel Tortella Casares, Alberto Manzano Martos, Jerònia Pons Pons, and José Luis García Ruiz. "About Corporate Forms" was published in Oxford University Press edited by Robin Pearson and Takau Yoneyama. Recently he has published with André Straus (eds.) *Highlights on Reinsurance History*, Peter Lang, Bruxelles, 2017. He has also done research on economic warfare with Hugh Rockoff and published in the *Journal of Economic History* and in the *European Review of Economic History*.

David Carvajal is a graduate in History and in Business Sciences (University of Valladolid, 2007 and 2009). In 2008 he was granted with a National Fellow – University Teachers Training Program (FPU) and in 2013 he finished his PhD dissertation titled "Private Credit and Debt in Castile

1480–1520". He enjoyed two academic international research stays in the University of Cambridge – Queens College (2009 and 2011) and he was awarded with the PhD National Award on Humanities (Real Academia de Doctores de España) and the University of Valladolid PhD Prize. His research lines include premodern Economic History and topics like credit, banking, merchants & trade, networks, and institutions, of which he has published many publications in prestigious editorials and journals. During the last few years he has been a member of several national and international research projects about taxation, finances, and trade. He has also taken part in more than 60 national and international conferences and scientific meetings related with Economic History, Medieval History, and Modern History.

Mariano Castro-Valdivia holds a PhD in Economics at the University of Jaén. He is associate lecturer in the Department of Economics at the University of Jaén and coordinator of several research projects as well as a member of the Jaén Applied Economics Research Group. He is also the secretary of the journal *Water and Landscape*. His research work has focused on the teaching of economics at the Spanish University and on the dissemination of classical economic thought in Spain, of which he has published several works: "La diffussion mondiale de l'oeuvre by Jean-Baptiste Say", "Próceces et impacts sélectifs", "Money and Finance in the Wealth of Nations: Interpretations and Influences", "Giennense participation in economics studies at the beginning of the 20th century in Spain", and "The teaching of Economics in Spain during the first half of the 19th century", among others. He has conducted research stays of more than three months at the Universita degli Studi di Roma «La Sapienza», at the University of Salamanca and at the University of Michel de Montaigne Bordeaux 3. He is a participant and coordinator of several teaching innovation projects at the University of Jaén, with publications such as "Historical research through ICT: a teaching experience".

Mercedes Fernández-Paradas is a doctor and head professor of Contemporary History at the University of Málaga. She specializes in Economic History and public services, especially business history, gas, and electricity. She is the principal researcher of the Research and Innovation Project of Excellence of the Government of Spain "*La industria del gas en España: desarrollo y trayectorias regionales (1842–2008)*". She has carried out several research stays, including at the London School of Economics and Political Science. She has won several awards, including the *Premio Extraordinario de Doctorado en Filosofía y Letras* (Extraordinary Doctorate Award in Philosophy and Arts) for the History Department of the University of Málaga.

Francisco José García Ariza is a doctor at the University of Málaga. He is specialized in Economic History, Business History and Agroindustrial History. He has published several researches on the Sociedad Azucarera Antequera, related to the construction of the sugar factory, its founders, shareholders, sugar production, etc., among them, the chapter published with

Mercedes Fernández-Paradas entitled "La Sociedad Azucarera Antequerana: una respuesta a la crisis finisecular (1890–1906)", en J.M. Matés (coord.), *Empresas y empresarios en España. De mercaderes a industriales*. Madrid, Pirámide, 2019.

Jorge Lafuente del Cano is a lecturer in Economic History at University of Valladolid. He holds a degree in History, a degree in Journalism and a PhD in History. He made a research stay in the University of Oxford and also in the University of Roma-La Sapienza. He is a member of "Studies on Economic History" Research Group and a member of "Studies on Recent History" Research Group as well. Dr. Lafuente has published two books and numerous articles on entrepreneurship, economic history of Spanish Transition to democracy, negotiations for Spain's entry into the European Economic Community, and the figure of former Spanish prime minister, Leopoldo Calvo-Sotelo.

Carlos Larrinaga is an associate lecturer of Economic History at the University of Granada (Andalusia, Spain). His research is in the history of tourism, railways in the 19th century, and the service sector. He is currently leading an interdisciplinary project on the history of tourism in Spain and Italy in the twentieth century, funded by the Spanish Ministry of Science, Innovation and Universities, and the European FEDER funds.

Juan Manuel Matés-Barco is professor of Economic History and Business History at the University of Jaén, bachelor of the University of Zaragoza, and doctor from the University of Granada. He has made stays at the Università degli Studi di Firenze, at the European University Institute (Italy) and at the Université Michel de Montaigne Bordeaux 3. He is a member of the Group of Historical Studies on the Company, a researcher of the Permanent Seminar Water, Territory, and Environment. He is part of the Editorial Board of the journal of *Transport, Services and Telecommunications History*. He is director of the journal *Water and Landscape*, co-edited by the School of Hispanic-American Studies of Seville-CSIC and the University of Jaén. His research is focused on the public water supply service and he has published studies on the economy of contemporary Spain.

Miguel Muñoz Rubio has a Ph.D. in History. He has specialized in railway history, having researched widely on the Spanish railways. He was director of the Railway History Archive and the National Railway Museum and professor of Economic History for ten years at the Madrid Autonomous University. He has published more than fifty books and papers, and was founder and editor of the academic journal "TST" between 2001–2009 and 2013–2015. He also was a member of the High Commission for Administrative Documentation Rating of the Spanish Government, vice chairman of the International Association for Railway History (IRHA), curator of several exhibitions, and secretary of the VIII International Congress of The International Committee for the Conservation of the Industrial Heritage (1992).

188 Contributors

Pedro Pablo Ortúñez Goicolea has a Ph.D. from the University of Valladolid, 1999. He is a senior lecturer in Economic History at the University of Valladolid (Spain). His research interests include the Spanish railway system and the public sector before nationalization of the railway and regulation and business history. He has published his research in books (on editorials of first quartile like Oxford University Press, Ariel, Pirámide, and Comares) and specialized journals (indexed in JCR or Scopus) and has participated in conferences in these fields. He has undertaken research in several stays at the London School of Economics and at the École des Hautes Études en Sciences Sociales (Paris).

María José Vargas-Machuca Salido holds a degree in Economics and Business Administration. She is an associate lecturer of the Department of Economics at the University of Jaén, where she teaches the subjects of Spanish Financial System and World Economy. She belongs to various research groups and teams related to her area of knowledge. Her research has focused on the history of the financial system, especially at the local level. She has published several articles in specialized journals on this topic. Her doctoral thesis deals with "La Caja Rural de Jaén. 60 years at the service of the province of Jaén".

María Vázquez-Fariñas has a PhD in Social and Legal Sciences from the University of Cádiz (Spain). She is a lecturer in History and Economic Institutions Area (Department of Economics) at the University of Jaén (Spain). She has been actively involved as a component of the Esteban Boutelou Historical Studies Research Group, and Lean Management of Production and Hyperconnected Universal Integrated Logistics Research Group, both from the University of Cádiz. She has made a predoctoral research stay at the School of Hispanic American Studies (CSIC, Seville), and in the last months she has been developing a postdoctoral stay at the University of Bordeaux. Her lines of research focus on the Economic and Business History of Cádiz in the nineteenth century, the wine industry of the region, and the development of commerce and the port of Cádiz between the mid-nineteenth and mid-twentieth centuries. Related to these lines of research, she has published several works, such as "The wine business in the city of Cádiz. Lacave and Company business history, 1810–1927", "The wine industry in the nineteenth century in Cadiz. Lacave and Echecopar: winemakers and maritime consignees", "Cadiz: wine city between the mid-nineteenth and mid-twentieth centuries", and "The activity of the port of Cadiz at the beginning of the 20th century", among others.

Index

Note: Page numbers in **bold** denote tables, those in *italics* denote figures.

19th Century: financial services 99, 100–2, 105–6; sugar industry 71–81; water suppliers 82–98; wheat and flour market 41–54; wine businesses 55–70
20th Century: Andalusian financial services 107–12; railways 82–98; travel agency businesses 130–43; two Transitions 156–69; water suppliers 82–98

active internationalisation process 144
administrative concession 82, 92
agents, wine business 55
agglomeration of economic activities 171–3
agricultural freight, Norte 119
Aguas de Alicante 86, **87**
Aguas de Areta 88, **89**; profits 93
Aguas de Barcelona 86, **87**
Aguas de Bufilla 90
Aguas de Ceuta **87**
Aguas de Jerez 86, **87**
Aguas de La Coruña **87**
Aguas del Canto 88, **89**
Aguas de Léon **87**
Aguas de Morón y Carmona 86
Aguas Potables de Barbastro 88, **89**
Aguas Potables de Barcelona 92
Aguas Potables y Mejoras de Valencia 86, **87**
Aguas Subterráneas del Río Llobregat 86, **87**
Aigües de Barcelona 95
Aigües de Catalunya 92
air travel 136–7
Alcazaba-Martínez-Soto company **26**
Alcoa Automotive casting Unit 179
Alicante, water companies 92

Alloy Technologies Limited (ATL) 179
almacenistas, wine business 55
American military bases 139
Andalusia 13–14; education in entrepreneurs 15; water companies 95; *see also* Antequera
Andalusian financial services 99–114; Banks of Issue 103–5; expansion in early 20th Century 107–9; liquidation 111; local banks in early 20th Century 109–12, **110**, **111**; private banks in 19th Century 105–6
ANFAC (National Association of Automobile and Truck Manufacturers) 170
Anglo-Saxon countries 1
ansatiners 14
Antequera 71–3; nineteenth century economic recession 72; service sector 72; textile businesses 72–3; *see also* Sociedad Azucarena Antequerana
Aragon, water companies 95
Arandina de Aguas Potables **87**
Argentina, MAPFRE expansion 148, 150, 152
aristocratic prejudice against work 3
de Arnedo, Pedro 34
associative strategies, Castile history 24
Astudillo *dueña* 22
Asturias, water companies 95
ATL (Alloy Technologies Limited) 179
Austria, water supply companies 83
Austrian school of economics 12
automobile cluster 170–84; 1940s 174; 1950s 174; 1960s 174; 1970s 174–5; agglomeration of economic activities 171–3; consolidation 174–5; cooperation within 177; growth

possibilities 176–7; industrial districts 172; international competetiveness 172–3; multinational companies 175; sector from 173–81; specialist labour force 171–2; subsidiary industry 171; turnover of 176; *see also* Lingotes Especiales

Bailly-Baillère Annual directory 105
Bakumar travel agency 133–4
Balearic islands, water companies 95
Banca Rodriguez-Acosta 105–6
Banco Central: expansion 108; takeovers by 106
Banco de Andalucía 107
Banco de Bilbao 108
Banco de Cádiz 104
Banco de Cartagena 107, 108
Banco de Castilla 107
Banco de España 100
Banco de Jerez 104
Banco de Málaga 102
Banco Español de Crédito 107–8, 109
Banco Hispano Americano 108
Banco Matritense 109
Banco Popular de los Previsores del Provenir 109
Banco Urquijo 108
banking: *Lacave & Echecopar* 59–60; see also financial services
Banking Control Council (Consejo Superior Bancario) 106
Banking Operation Law (1921) 105
Banking Organisation Law (1931) 106–7
Banking Organisation Law (Cambo Law, 1921) 106
Banks of Issue: 19th century 100; Andalusia 103–5
Banks of Issue Law (1856) 100, 104
Barcelona, water supply companies 90, 92
Baroja, Pío 3
Basalla, George 12
Basque Country 18
Belgium, water supply companies 83
Bergamín García, Francisco 74
Bernuy *dueña* 22
Bliss, Stanley Norman 137
BOAC (British Overseas Airways Corporation) 136
Boletín de Comercio: flour trading 45; wheat and flour market 49
Boletín Oficial del Comercio de Santander 47

Boletín Oficial del Estado (Official State Gazette) 133
Bolin, Luis 132–3
Bores Romero, José Maria 76–7
Borrego, Lorenzo 73–4
Botin family 18
Boyer, Miguel 162
Braling Conjuntos 179
Brazil: MAPFRE expansion 152; MAPFRE REINSURANCE 149
British Overseas Airways Corporation (BOAC) 136
brokerage revenues, Reinosa route 47–9
Bucher, Karl 17
Burgos 31, 36
Business History Review 16
business organisations, automobile cluster 178
business studies 17

Cádiz 55; economy in 19th Century 56; export drop 63–4; pre-19th Century 56; water companies merging 92; wine business *see* wine business
Cafranga, Eusebio 132
Cafranga travel agency 134
Calvo-Sotelo, Leopoldo 159, 160, 161–2
Camaras de Compensación (Clearing Houuses) 106
Cambo Law (Banking Organisation Law, 1921) 106
Cambo Law (Spanish Banking Organisation Law) 110
del Campo, Pedro 30
Canal de Isabel II 90
Canal de la Huerta de Alicante 87
canals 15
Canary Islands 32
Cantillon, Richard 10
capital, Castile companies 25
capitalism: Catholic mistrust of 3; nationalist path 42; raising of 14
Cartagena, water companies 88
cartels: legal existence 44; location of 44–5
Casado, H. 33
Casa Elizalde 174
Casco Moreno, Ramón 75
case studies 13–15; entrepreneurship promotion 16–18; entrepreneurship support 15–16; value determination 18–19
Casson, Andrew 12
Castile: wheat and flour prices **49**, 49–50; wheat market in 19th Century 43–7

Castile history 22–40; companies 23–8, 26–7; 15th to 16th Centuries 22–3; foreigners 22–3; geographical area of 28–9; human capital 33–4; local to international commerce 31–3; management changes 33–4; Middle Age to Modern Era 28–37; network creation 34–6; products 28–31; risk management 36–7; services 29–31
Castilla y León 170–84; *see also* automobile cluster
Castilla y León Automobile Business Forum (Facyl) 175–6
Castilla y León Industrial Development Society (Sodical) 179, 180–1
Castro-Mújica company 35
Catálogo de Sociedades de abastecimiento de agua potable 84
Catalonia, water companies 95
Catholic mistrust of capitalism 3
Central State Administration, travel agency businesses 132
CEOE *see* Confederation of Entrepreneurial Organisations (CEOE)
Chandler, Alfred 12–13
Chatham Re 148
Circuitos en Autocar por Europe 136
Citróen 174
City of Las Palmas Water & Power 87
Clark, John Bates 10
collusion hypothesis 41, 44
Colombia, MAPFRE expansion 149
Comisaria de la Banca (Banking Commission) 106
Commercial Code (1829) 47, 60, 100, 101, 105
commercial services, Castile history 31
Compañía Gaditana de Crédito (1861–1867) 102
Compañía Internacional Wagon-Lits 130
company theory 12
concessions, private railways 121
Confederation of Entrepreneurial Organisations (CEOE) 159; NATO refurendum 166; social democracy criticisms 161
Consejo Superior Bancario (Banking Control Council) 106
consulates, Castile history 36
cooperation, Lingotes Especiales 181
Córdoba, water companies 88
La Coruña 90; water companies merging 92
credit companies 99–114; 19th century 100, 102–3; *see also* financial services

Credit Companies Law (1856) 100
Crédito Commercial de Cádiz (1860–1866) 102
Crédito Commercial de Jerez (1862–1866) 103
Crédito Commercial de Sevilla (1862–1868) 103
Crédito Commercial y Agricola de Córdoba (1864–1867) 103
criadera system 56, 61
Cuba, *Lacave & Echecopar* exports 65
Cuevas, José María 162

Daza-Calatayud company 30, 32
Daza-López de Calatayud company 26
Decree Bases for legislating Public Works (1868) 118
demand, water supply companies 93
Denmark, water supply companies 83
d'Estang, Valery Giscard 164
destinations, travel agency businesses 135–6
DGT (Directorate General of Tourism) 132
Díaz-Medina company 26
Directorate General of Tourism (DGT) 132
dissemination of entrepreneurship 9–13
domestic consumption, water supply companies 87
Domestic Transition 157–62; armed forces, mistrust of 161; economic changes 159; economic pact 160; Finance Ministers 161; Socialist Party 162

Echecopar & Company 56
Echecopar, Eduardo 62, 63
Echecopar, Juan-Pablo 63
Echegaray Decree (1874) 100, 104–5
economics 1; 1970s 156–7; agglomeration of 171–3; Austrian school of 12; Keynesian economics 12; natural trajectory of 12; neoclassical economics 10–11, 12; publications in 16
economic theory, perfect competitive markets 41
education, Castillian merchants 33
El Álbum Nacional 61
electricity companies 84
employment, private railways 120
Empresa del camino de Hierro de Jerez al Puerto 58
Empresa Fabril Gaditana 58

Empresa Gaditana del Trocadero 58
Empresas Hidráulicas de Canarias 87
England, Castile merchants 32
Enlightenment Now (Pinker) 52
entry barriers, wheat/flour market 46–7
entry requirement to Spain 139
Escarrer Juliá, Gabriel 140
Esquivel-Sánchez company 26
Europe: MAPFRE expansion 146; MAPFRE Internacional 153
European Union (EU): entry into 162; internal conflicts 164; membership of 158
Explorations in Economic History 16
export numbers, Lingotes Especiales 179
Extremadura, water companies 95

Fabricaciones de Automóviles Diésel, S. A. (FADISA) 174
Fabricaciones de Automóviles S. A. (FASA) 174
Facyl (Castilla y León Automobile Business Forum) 175–6
family: business in 18; Castillian businesses 34–5
FASA (Fabricaciones de Automóviles S. A.) 174
Ferrer Salat, Carlos 160
FESIT (Spanish Federation of Trade Unions and Initiatives and Tourism) 132
Finance Ministers, Domestic Transition 161
financial services 99–114; 19th century 99, 100–2; Andalusia *see* Andalusian financial services; Castile history 31; Castillian businesses 34, 35; company formation 101–2; partnerships 101–2; private banking (1900–1936) 106–7; Spanish Civil War 99
Finland, water supply companies 83
First Industrial Revolution 15; studies on 17
First World War: economic growth 122; water supply companies 94
Fives-Lille, *Sociedad Azucarena Antequerana* factory 77
Flanders, Castile merchants 32
flourcrats 44–5
flour market *see* wheat and flour market
Fluxá Figuerola, Lorenzo 140
Fomento Agricola Castellonense 86
Fontainebleau summit (1984) 164–5

foreign banks, expansion into Andalusia 107
foreign investments, Lingotes Especiales 179–80
foreign (international) markets: automobile cluster 172–3; Castile history 31–3; wheat and flour market 50
foreign operators, travel agency businesses 132
foreign way, railways 115–17
France: Castile merchants 32; water supply companies 83
Franco regime, opposition to 157
Franquelo Díaz, Juan 76
freedom of trade, wheat and flour market 47
freight: MZA 118–19; private railways 118–20
French–Spanish border closure 135
Frías-Medina Huerta company 27
Fuentes Quintana, Enrique 161

García Díez, Juan Antonio 161
García Sarmiento, José 75
gas companies 85
General Confederation of Spanish Entrepreneurs 159
General Law on Railways (1855) 116–17
geographical area, Castile history 28–9
Germany: MAPFRE Internacional 153; water supply companies 83
Gestamp 175, 176
Glorious Revolution (1868) 65
Gómez Tapia, Pedro 30
González, Felipe 160, 162
Gonzalo de Segovia company 32
Granada, banks of 104
Great Britain, water supply companies 83
Greece, water supply companies 83
Grupo Antolín 174, 175, 176
Guerrero de Smirnoff, Diego Vladimir 76

Harvard Business School 16
Hawley, Frederick Barnard 11
Hernando de Larramendi, Ignacio 145
Herreria Barcelonesa 120
Hidraulica Santillana 87
Hispano Suiza 174
History of the Company 9–21; study of 17–18
Holland, water supply companies 83
Horizon Holidays 141

Huertas, Antonio 153
human capital 15; Castile history 33–4

IATA (International Air Transport Association) 137
ICAO (International Civil Aviation Organization) 136–7
ICTI (Information and Communication Technology) 15–16
Imbrechts, José Déez 115
imperfect market competition 41
Independent Entrepreneurial Group 159
India, Lingotes Especiales 180
Indonesia, MAPFRE Internacional 153
industrial districts, automobile cluster 172
industry creation 14
Information and Communication Technology (ICTI) 15–16
information networks, Castillian businesses 35–6
innovation of entrepreneurs 11
institutional framework: automobile cluster 173; railways 116
institutions: automobile cluster 178; Castile history 36–7; risk in water supply companies 93
insurance companies: Castile history 36–7; domestic firm expansion 145–6; foreign companies 144–5; *see also* MAPFRE
intermediaries, wine business 55
internal demand, automobile cluster 175
International Air Transport Association (IATA) 137
International Civil Aviation Organization (ICAO) 136–7
international isolation, travel agencies and 135
international markets *see* foreign (international) markets
International Transition 157–8, 162–6; VAT 164
Inter, Sidney 12
irrigation, water supply companies 87
Italy: MAPFRE expansion 150; water supply companies 83
Iveco 170

Jaspe, Ricardo 134
Jean Bouchard 90
Jerez, water companies merging 92
Jerez de la Frontera 104
Jimenez, Andrés 148
J. P. *Echecopar* 65

Juan Pablo Echecopar & Company 56
Juan Pedro Lacave & Company 56
justice, Castile history 36–7

Keynesian economics 12
Kirzner, Israel 12
KLM 136
Knight, Frank H. 11, 12
knowledge centres, automobile cluster 175

La Aurora (1846) 90
labour movement organisations 14–15
Lacave & Company 66
Lacave & Echecopar 55–70; banking 59–60; businesses, seapration of 65; commercial expansion (1852–1862) 59–63; depression and closure 63–6; diversification strategy 59; domestic market 65; export sales 61–2, **62**; infrastructure expansion 62–3; non-wine businesses 58; origins of 57–9; real estate 60; shipping agents 60
Lacave Mulé, Pedro 63
Lacave, Pedro 57, 58
Lacave Soulé, Pedro-Luis 63
Lacoste Salazar, Ana María 60
La Gaditana 56
La Hondura 86, **87**
La Rioja, water companies 95
late Restoration period, economic policies 42
Latin America: MAPFRE expansion 145; MAPFRE REINSURANCE 147
legal restrictions, wheat and flour market 47
Liberal Revolution 44
Linares, water companies 88
Linares Colom, José 140
Lingotes Especiales 174, 175, 176, 178–81; consolidation 179; export numbers 179
liquidation, Castille companies 25, 28
livestock, railway transport 119
local development agents, automobile cluster 178
London, MAPFRE expansion 148
Lopez, Pedro 106
Los Amigos 56
Luis Petit 90
Luna Rodríguez, Antonio 75–6
Luxembourg, water supply companies 83

Macdermot, Hugo 57
Madrid Pact (1953) 139

Madrid Zaragoza Alicante (MZA) 117; acquisitions 121; financial crisis and 117–18; First World War 122–3; freight 118–19; lack of competition 121
Maeztu, Ramiro 3
Málaga, banks of 104
Mallorca, travel destination as 136
management: Castile history 33–4, 37; Castille companies 25; ownership separation 14
management model, municipial services 82–3
Manzanares, water companies 88
MAPFRE 144–55; direct insurance market 149–53; foreign company acquisition 146–7; geographical distribution 151, **152**; international expansion 144–7; international investments 150–1; life insurance expansion 152
MAPFRE Corporation of Florida 150
MAPFRE Internacional 153
MAPFRE REINSURANCE 147–9; finiancial problems 148–9
MAPFRE XL Compañia Internacional de Reaseguros S.A. 147–8
La Maquinista Terrestre y Marítima 120
marketing, Castile history 29
Marroquín-Sánchez de Toledo company **26**
Marsans travel agency 134
Marshall, Alfred 10, 171
Marshallian advantages 172
Martínez, José Manuel 145–6
Martorelli, Fernando Abril 161
matrimonial ties, wine business 57
Medina-Aranda company **27**
Medina-Calatayud company **26**
Medina-Ram company **26**
Medina-Urueña company **26**, **27**
Meliá, José 134, 136, 140–1
Memorias y Estadísticas Diversas 84
merchant bankers 99–114; 19th century 100; *see also* financial services
merchants: Castile history 23; Castillian businesses 34
metal mining, railway transport 119
Mexico, MAPFRE expansion 150
Mill, John Stuart 10
Ministry for Relations with the European Communities 163
Mitterand, François 164
modernisation, private railways 118–21
monopolies, legal existence 44

Morales Berdoy, Luis 77
Moreno González del Pino, Fernando 74–5
Motril, water companies 88
multinational companies, automobile cluster 175
municipal services, management model 82–3
Murcia, water companies 95
MZA *see* Madrid Zaragoza Alicante (MZA)

National Agreement for Employment (1981) 162
National Association of Automobile and Truck Manufacturers (ANFAC) 170
national banks 99–114; *see also* financial services
nationalist path, capitalism 42
national way, railways 115–17
NATO: adherence to 165–6; entry into 158, 162
natural monopoly 82
natural trajectory of economy 12
Nelson, Richard 12
neoclassical economics 10–11, 12
neo-Marshallian theory 172
Nervión 147
network creation, Castile history 34–6
new customers, water supply companies 93
New World, Castile merchants 32
Nissan 170
non-codified knowledge 171
Norte 117; acquisitions 121; agricultural freight 119; financial crisis and 117–18; freight 123; lack of competition 121

Oeste, lack of competition 121
Official State Gazette (Boletín Official del Estrado) 133
oil shock, automobile industry 174
Omnium Ibérico **87**
Ordóñez y González, Ezequiel 77
Oreja, Marcelino 165
ownership, management separation 14

partnerships, financial services 101–2
passenger numbers, private railways 118
Pereire company 117
perfect competitive markets 41
Pesquera-Silos company **26**, 32

Philippines, *Lacave & Echecopar* exports 65
Pickman & Company 56
Pimentel, Manuel 16
Pinker, Stephen 52
Pinkley, Virgil M. 137
del Plano, Arnao 34
Plazuela-Resxo company **26**
Political Reform Law (1977) 159
political transition 2
Porter, Michel 172
Portillo-Ávila company **27**
Portugal: Castile merchants 32; MAPFRE expansion 150; water supply companies 83
Preferential Trade Agreement (1970) 164
Primo de Rivera dictatorship 42
Principles of Economics (Marshall) 171
private banks, Andalusia in 19th Century 105–6
private railways 115–29; concessions in 1914–1931 123–7; concession system, end of 127; early 20th Century 121–3; financial crisis and 117–18; freight 118–20; growth of 117; modernisation 118–21; protectionism 122; running costs, los; of control 124; share price drop 117–18; State control 124–5; State Railway Fund 126–7; *see also* Madrid Zaragoza Alicante (MZA); Norte
products, Castile history 28–31
profit shares, Castille companies 25, 28
protectionism: private railways 122; wheat/flour market 43
publications in economics 16
public utilities 84–5; analysis of 83; *see also* water supply companies
public works, private railways 120
Puerto Rico: *Lacave & Echecopar* exports 65; MAPFRE expansion 150–1
Pueto de la Cruz 86

Quintana *dueña* 22

railways 15; foreign way 115–17; institutional framework 116; national way 115–17; private *see* private railways; rolling stock manufacture 120
Railway Statute (1926) 126–7
raw materials, Castile history 29
real estate, *Lacave & Echecopar* 60
refundable advance payments, railways 125

Reinosa route 41–54; brokerage revenues 47–9, **48**, **49**; *see also* wheat and flour market
Renault Group 170
RENFE (Spanish National Railways Networks) 127
rentiers 14
research and development (R&D), automobile cluster 177
Reus, water companies 88
Revista de Obras Públicas 84
Revista Seminal 45, 49
risk management, Castile history 36–7
risks 11–12
Rodriguez-Acosta, Banca 104
Rodríguez-Román company **27**
Romero Robledo, Francisco 73
Roquien-Mizariego-Calbet company **27**
Rosenberg, Alexander 12
Rota y Sanlúcar 58
Rothschild company, railways 117
Royal Decree (1835) 47
Royal Order (1844) 115–16
Ruiz, Simón 22
Ruiz-Soto company **26**
Ruiz Zorrila, Manuel 118
Ruy González del Portillo 32

Santa Cruz, Calixto 115
Santander: flour trading cartels 45–6; flour traffic from 50–1, **51**; wheat market in 19th Century 43–7
Santander bank 18
SAVA (Sociedad Anónima de Vehículos Automóviles) 174
Say, Jean-Baptiste 10
Schmoller, Gustav 17
Schumpter, Joseph Alois 11, 12, 16
SEAT 174
Second Industrial Revolution 15–16; Antequerra 72
Second Spanish Republic, economic policies 42
Second World War, economics after 12
de Segovia, Gonzalo 30, 35
Seguros Caribe 149
servants, Castillian businesses 34
service firms, automobile cluster 175
service sector: Antequera 72; Castile history 29–31
Sevilla Water Works 86, 87
Seville 36; banks of 104; water companies merging 92
Shane, Scott 12
sherry 56

Index

shipping agents, *Lacave & Echecopar* 60
Sky Tours 141
slow growth policy, water supply companies 93
small-scale capitalists, what/flour market 46
Smith, Adam 10
sobre cosa señalda 24–5
social democrats, criticisms of 161
Socialist Party, Domestic Transition 162
Sociedad Anónima de Vehículos Automóviles (SAVA) 174
Sociedad Azucarena Antequerana 71–81; company growth 78–9; factory construction 77–8; founders of 73–6; managers 76–7; profits 78–9; sales strategy 78
Sociedad Española del Carburador IRZ 174
Sociedad General Española de Descuentos (Spanish General Discounts Society, 1859–1866) 103
Sodical (Castilla y León Industrial Development Society) 179, 180–1
Solchaga, Carlos 162
solera system 56, 61
Sombart, Werner 17
de Soria, Álvaro 30
South America, *Lacave & Echecopar* exports 65
Spanish Banking Organisation Law (Cambo Law) 110
Spanish Civil War: financial services 99; water supply companies 94–5
Spanish Constitution (1978) 157
Spanish Constitution of Cádiz (1812) 44
Spanish Entrepreneurial Confederation 159
Spanish Federation of Trade Unions and Initiatives and Tourism (FESIT) 132
Spanish General Discounts Society (Sociedad General Española de Descuentos, 1859–1866) 103
Spanish National Railways Networks (RENFE) 127
specialised labour market: automobile cluster 171–2, 177–8; Lingotes Especiales 180
speculation, what/flour market 46
speculators 14
Stabilisation Plan of 1959 138
state concessions 18–19
State Railway Fund 126–7
stock companies 99

Stockholm syndrome 13
Stock Market, foundation (1931) 100
storage, what/flour market 46
Stuttgart summit (1983) 164–5
Suárez, Adolfo 157, 159
subcontracting, automobile cluster 177
Subercase, Juan 115
Subercase Report 115
sugar business 71–81
Suministro de Aguas Potables 87
Sweden, water supply companies 83

Tabacos Ygueravide 58
tariff franchise, private railways 120
tax businesses, Castile history 29
technical obstacles, water supply companies 93
temporal workers, Castillian businesses 34
Tenerife, water companies 86
territorial scope, flour trading 45–6
textile businesses 84–5; Antequera 72; Castile history 30–1
Thomas Cook 130–2
tierras de pan ilevar 50
Tortella, Gabriel 18
tourist numbers 137, 138
town size, water supply companies size and 86
trade fairs, Castile history 31
transection cost theory 12–13
Trans World Airlines (TWA) 136–7
travel agency businesses 130–43; 1950s opportunities 138–41; air travel and 136–7; Decree of 1942 132–4; destinations used 135–6; foreign operators 132; Group A classification 133–4; Group B classification 134; history of 130–1; numbers of 130; post-Second World War 134–8; sales office numbers 139–40; US financial aid 139
Turkey, MAPFRE Internacional 153
TWA (Trans World Airlines) 136–7
two Transitions 156–69

de Unamumo, Miguel 3
uncertainties 11–12
Union Bank of Spain and England 107
unions 14–15
United States of America (USA): MAPFRE expansion 148; MAPFRE Internacional 153; MAPFRE REINSURANCE 149; travel to 137
urban growth, private railways 120

Valencia, water companies 90, 95
Valladolid 170, 173
Vasconi Cano, Luis 74
VAT 164
Verdesoto-Salinas company 31
Viajes Cafranga travel agency 135–6, 141
Viajes Iberia travel agency 138; capitalisation 139–40
Viajes Marsansrof 132
Viajes Meliá travel agency 136, 138
The Visible Hand (Chandler) 12–13
voluntary registration, financial services 110
von Mangoldt, Hans 11
von Thünen, Johann Heinrich 11

wage rises, water supply companies 93
Wagons-Lits Cook 133
water supply companies 82–98; business takeovers 95; domestic consumption 87; early 20th century growth 92, 94–5; First World War 94; historical number variation 83; irrigation 87; large companies 85–8, 87; late 19th century 86–7; merging of 90–2; risk & uncertainty 93–5; size of *vs.* town size 86; small & medium companies 88–93, **89**, **91**; Spanish Civil War 94–5; Western Europe 83–4
Wealth of Nations (Smith) 10
wheat and flour market 41–54; deterioration of goods 50; entry barriers 46–7; foreign market 50; freedom of trade 47; history of 43–4; legal restrictions 47; prices in Castile 49–50; railway transport 119; Santander, from 50–1, **51**; *see also* Reinosa route
Williamson, Oliver 12–13
wine business: business divergence 60–1; export reduction 63–4, **64**; exports 65; Norte 123; price drops 64; production methods 61; *see also* Lacave & Echecopar
wool trade: Castile history 30; railway transport 120
World War I *see* First World War
World War II, economics after 12

Zulueta Samá, Josefa 73